KT-494-259

John Boyle left Scotland at nineteen and has lived most of his adult life abroad. He taught English in Spain and London, managed language schools in Belgium and Holland, then set up a communications consultancy in Brussels. Now a writer and columnist, he still does commercial voiceovers in Brussels, New York and London.

www.booksattransworld.co.uk

Also by John Boyle

GALLOWAY STREET: GROWING UP IRISH IN SCOTLAND

and published by Black Swan

LAFF
A friendship

JOHN BOYLE

BLACK SWAN

LAFF
A BLACK SWAN BOOK: 0 552 77079 5

Originally published in Great Britain by Doubleday,
a division of Transworld Publishers

PRINTING HISTORY
Doubleday edition published 2003
Black Swan edition published 2004

1 3 5 7 9 10 8 6 4 2

Copyright © John Boyle 2003

The author and publishers are grateful to the following for permission to
reproduce copyright material: 'Rip it Up', words and music by John
Marascalco and Robert Blackwell © 1955, Venice Music, Inc., USA,
reproduced by permission of Peter Maurice Music Co. Ltd, London
WC2H 0QY. 'Whole Lotta Shaking Going On', words and music by Curly
Williams and Sonny David © 1955, Marlyn Music Publishing Inc., USA,
reproduced by permission of Peter Maurice Music Co. Ltd, London
WC2N 0QY. 'Corner Seat' by Louis MacNiece published by Faber & Faber,
reproduced by permission of David Higham Associates.

The right of John Boyle to be identified as the author of
this work has been asserted in accordance with sections 77
and 78 of the Copyright Designs and Patents Act 1988.

All the characters in this book are fictitious, and any resemblance
to actual persons, living or dead, is purely coincidental.

Condition of Sale
This book is sold subject to the condition that it shall not, by way
of trade or otherwise, be lent, re-sold, hired out or otherwise
circulated in any form of binding or cover other than that in
which it is published and without a similar condition including
this condition being imposed on the subsequent purchaser.

Set in 11/14.5pt Sabon by
Falcon Oast Graphic Art Ltd.

Black Swan Books are published by Transworld Publishers,
61–63 Uxbridge Road, London W5 5SA,
a division of The Random House Group Ltd,
in Australia by Random House Australia (Pty) Ltd,
20 Alfred Street, Milsons Point, Sydney, NSW 2061, Australia,
in New Zealand by Random House New Zealand Ltd,
18 Poland Road, Glenfield, Auckland 10, New Zealand
and in South Africa by Random House (Pty) Ltd,
Endulini, 5a Jubilee Road, Parktown 2193, South Africa.

Printed and bound in Great Britain by
Cox & Wyman Ltd, Reading, Berkshire.

Papers used by Transworld Publishers are natural, recyclable products
made from wood grown in sustainable forests. The manufacturing processes
conform to the environmental regulations of the country of origin.

For James Lafferty

Suspended in a moving night
The face in the reflected train
Looks at first sight as self-assured
As your own face – But look again:

Windows between you and the world
Keep out the cold, keep out the fright;
Then why does your reflection seem
So lonely in the moving night?

Louis MacNeice, 'Corner Seat'

'Who's to say where truth ends and fiction begins?' I asked myself in the foreword to *Galloway Street*. I did not know then that in *Laff*, which also set out to be a memoir, I would spend so much time floundering in the no-man's-land between the two. It may seem strange that I could recall my childhood more clearly than my adolescent years, but so it proved. As a result, I have come up with an answer to the question – or at least one that works for me: truth ends and fiction begins at the point where memory fails.

Memory can fail us in so many ways. It can let us down altogether – friends or family describe in detail an incident involving us, and we have no recollection of it whatsoever. Or we vividly recall a moment – a face, a voice, a snatch of conversation – which seems to exist in a void: we remember nothing of what went before or came after. For much of the time, writing this book has been the task of filling in the spaces between such moments.

But memory also fails us when the details we remember of a person or an incident seem unequal somehow to the intensity of the impression they left on us. The bare facts, we realize, don't tell the whole story: we need the help of fiction to do justice to the truth.

So how much is true in this story, and how much is fiction? Well, Laff himself is as true as my wayward memory will permit, and so is our friendship. Our family circumstances, Feegie, the Academy, and almost all of the incidents I describe are more or less as they were. With other characters I have used a little licence. Names have been changed for reasons of discretion, and, as if emboldened by these identity makeovers, their owners have emerged in the writing as composites of themselves and others who had to be left out. The alternative would have been a cast of thousands, with new characters wandering onto the stage every five minutes and demanding their share of the spotlight.

I have tried to shine that light on Laff, though he keeps slipping into shadow. Let him glow there, like a will-o'-the-wisp, as he has glowed in my memory for all these years.

September 1958

Another endless afternoon in Feegie. Last days of summer. A few weeks after my seventeenth birthday. I'm sprawled on my bed in the end room at Blackstoun Road, gazing up at the cracks in the ceiling. As if it was a map. As if I might find some clue up there to my future.

If I have any future, stuck here in this dump. Blank as the ceiling, that's how it looks to me. Not like Laff, away sailing the seas. Lucky dog. It makes me jealous, I have to admit it.

There's music coming from somewhere outside. Across the road it sounds like. Somebody's been playing the same old Slim Whitman song, again and again, the whole afternoon. 'China Doll' – Slim yearning for some doll he can call his own.

It must be Big Nessie's house the music's coming from. We still call it that even though they've moved away. We don't know the new people but in this hot weather they've got into the habit of playing their records dead loud with their window wide open. The kind of thing Big Nessie would do, come to think of it. Never gave a tinker's curse. The queen of the lassies, Wullie Logan next door called her, and you could see what he meant. He always reckoned she fancied me and he thought I was mad because I never did anything about it. But what was I supposed to do? What could I say to a lassie like Nessie? The words would stick in my throat. I could never admit that to anybody, naturally. Especially not her. So I would just try and act gallus around her, kid on I couldn't care less. Too late now, anyway. She's long gone. And I've got a girlfriend. Rosemary. Going steady, you could say, more than a year now. Even after that business with Laff ... But I don't think about that. Rosemary's a nice lassie. A Catholic, goes to the convent school. Lives in Ralston, up near the posh houses. My mammy would approve, if she knew. But she won't. Not if I can help it.

Across the road old Slim's still yodelling away about his doll, how blue her eyes are, how true her lips ...

Big Nessie. Her eyes were hazel, in fact. Her lips were beautiful. I draw them sometimes, doodling on bits of paper or just sketching things with my finger in the air the way I do sometimes; it drives my mammy mad. Doting and dreaming about the place, she says. As usual. Ye're like a man in a trance. She's always saying that. I draw them again now like that, with my finger in front of my face. I do the top lip curved like a crossbow, then shade in the lower one, the plump cushion it rests on ...

I'm still looking for clues in the cracks above me. Some days I don't see anything. Other days I see pictures there. Whole landscapes sometimes. The rolling plains and low hills you get in the cowboy pictures. The Badlands. The Black Hills of Dakota. Or the exotic foreign harbours on the postcards Laff sends me. But usually it's faces I see in the cracks. The Fates, old Ichabod would call them. Aye, that's it: the Fates, smiling or scowling at me.

Usually scowling.

Today there's a hand. Misshapen, only three fingers, fat blobby ones, but still a hand. The cracks running across it like the lines on the palm of a hand. Lifeline, heartline, headline – do I know which is which? I hold up my own hand, the left, and angle it slowly, this way and that, trying to mirror the shape on the ceiling, trying to compare the lines.

Where am I going? What's in store for me?

ONE

That first day in 3A at the Academy was nearly as bad as the first time I'd set foot in the place. I couldn't understand it. You'd think after two years I'd have got used to it. So many new things seemed to be happening that year: new teachers, new faces in the classroom, some boys being promoted from 2B to 3A, others being kept back to repeat their third year, and what with one thing and another it felt like that first time all over again. Or maybe it was something else: I'd been scared on my first day at the Academy by the sheer strangeness of it all, not knowing anybody. Now after two years it was more a feeling of hopelessness, the dread of another school year stretching out endlessly in front of me, another year of more of the same, a sense of *what's the use?* Whatever it was, it was as depressing as hell. Here I am, I was thinking, just turned fourteen, you'd think I'd be an old hand at this by now – and I feel like a wee wean just starting out.

It was at the end of that endless day that I met Laff. I suppose I'd half noticed him already in the blur of new faces in 3A, but it was only after school that I really *saw* him for the first time. He was standing by himself at the busstop across the Renfrew Road at the edge of Gallowhill. Where only the Ferguslie bus stopped. And where I was usually the only one waiting – having dawdled along the road to avoid the crush and mayhem of that first bus. I remember feeling a stab of pity for him, he looked such a forlorn figure standing there. It was strange, as if for that moment I had seen myself in him. He was tall, about my own height, with a thick mop of black hair that seemed to surge straight up out of his head. I remembered noticing that earlier, come to think of it, how odd it looked, comical even, like a cartoon haircut. As I came near he slid a sidelong look at me, half startled, half in recognition, then it was back to eyes front, staring into space.

We stood there side by side saying nothing.

When eventually he spoke it sounded wary and defiant at the same time.

D'you live in *Ferguslie*? he said.

This was a risky opener. I might after all have said no, that I got off at some half-respectable destination along the way, like Townhead Terrace or Wellmeadow, but in my relief at finding a fellow outcast I was happy to tell the truth.

Aye, I said. Blackstoun Road. Whit aboot you?

His own relief was so obvious I was practically breathing it in.

Craigmuir Road, he said. Doon the end, but. Near Ferguslie Park Avenue.

Oh, aye? Right.

We waited on in wary silence until the bus came then we shared the front seat on the empty top deck. We both came from Ferguslie Park – *Feegie!* – the worst housing scheme in Paisley, and we were both in the same class at the Academy: that was enough to be going on with. Craigmuir, the street where Laff lived, ran perpendicular to Blackstoun Road and halfway down branched out into a squat cross formed by twin cul de sacs of pebbledash blocks that kind of squared up to each other from opposite sides of the road. This enclave housed what the Council called Problem Families and everybody else called the Undesirables. To live anywhere near that place would make any self-respecting family feel ashamed – the word *Undesirables* hardly ever passed my mother's lips, and then only in a feart whisper, a kind of wonder that such places could exist in the world – but some of the ragged-arsed, snottery weans who did live there wore the stigma like a badge of honour. One of their ringleaders was a frightening wee Toerag called Wee Shuggy. We'd both heard of him – everybody in Feegie had heard of Wee Shuggy. He loved trouble, lived for it. He'd start a fight just for the fun of it. He'd swagger up to his chosen target and say: Ah'm fae the Undesirables! As if to say: Wantae make anythin' of it?

He'd say this with all the pride of a kiltie in the Black Watch or the Highland Light Infantry, which come to think of it is probably where he ended up. If he managed to stay out of Barlinnie.

Most of these characters were barely half our size but they had the unnerving menace of desperadoes who know they have nothing to lose. And though neither of us would have owned up to it, reading between the lines I had sensed that Laff was as uneasy as I was about travelling back and forth on the bus every school day with the likes of these wee hardmen. Wee Shuggy, thank God, was a Proddie and went to a different school, by a different route. But there were plenty more where he came from.

Laff and I were Senior Secondary boys; we had to wear school uniforms. That alone made us stand out, as I knew well by now; in their eyes, we were Snobs.

In our coded exchange at the busstop Laff had been careful to make it clear that though he lived in Craigmuir, it was down at the bottom, what passed for the respectable end. As it turned out he was actually further away from the Undesirables than I was. For all the difference that would make. At the Academy, in Senior Secondary, they looked down on you just for coming from Feegie; I already knew that.

It made allies of us. Our friendship began that day, on that bus. It took us maybe twenty minutes to get to Ferguslie, but it felt like five: we talked all the way. We had so much in common it was uncanny. Laff's first day at the Academy turned out to have been every bit as traumatic as mine. But now, in the comradeship of shared experience, we could look back and laugh about it. What comes back to me across all the years, undiminished, is the intensity of that first meeting, the wonder at discovering a kindred soul, finding my deepdown thoughts and yearnings mirrored in another, like being reunited with a twin brother I never knew I'd lost.

Laff got off the bus one stop before me, in Ferguslie Park Avenue, and for the minute or so the bus took to get to the Blackstoun Road roundabout I sat there in such a trance of joy and relief that I nearly missed my stop. Hope, that had been missing for so long from my landscape, had suddenly reappeared, like a wildflower on waste ground, and somehow the two miserable years I'd just been through didn't matter that much anymore.

*

17

I suppose it must have started long before I ever set eyes on Laff. Somewhere below the surface the soil must have been worked over, made ready, long before the seed landed there, took root and flourished. If I am to understand how it came about, explain to myself after more than forty years why a friendship that lasted barely two of those years should have marked me so profoundly, then I have to go back to those early days after the family had moved from the old tenement, the old life, in Galloway Street . . .

TWO

In the spring of 1953 when I was eleven and a half our family moved to Blackstoun Road in Feegie, though we could never call it that in front of my mother.

God forgive ye, she'd say. That's a horrible name. Can ye not call it by its proper name, Ferguslie Park?

She always called it Ferguslie Park because it had a nice sound to it. Probably hoping that people who didn't know any better might be fooled into thinking it was as leafy and rural a place as it once sounded to her.

Some hope. Everybody in Paisley knew about Feegie.

She'd say: Isn't it only the scruff and the Toerags that live round here, God save the mark, would ever come out with a name like Feegie?

They could come out with a lot worse than that, as I well knew. Some of the boys called it the Jungle; they'd even say it with a kind of perverse pride. *Ah live up the Jungle!* But I could never tell her that for fear it might be the death of her.

My mother hated the nickname Feegie because it sounded just like what it was: the roughest housing scheme in Paisley. She could never get over it that in

Galloway Street we were poor (not like the Cunninghams down in the close who won the thousand pounds in the *News of the World* Prize Crossword and sailed away to Australia) and we were no better off now, yet here in this new place they called us Snobs. I knew from the scruff I met out in the street it was because my mother's Irish accent sounded posh to them and because of her height and the way she carried herself: she put on airs and graces, so they said.

Who does that Missis Boyle think she is? I'd hear them saying. Lady Muck fae Glabber Castle? Then we'd get Wullie Logan's takeoff of her queenly walk: his thumb pushing up the tip of his nose, his pinky cocked like a posh lady sipping tea, the other arm curved like a teapot handle, the fist knuckled on his hip. And I'd have to stand there listening to the jeers, trying to be a sport, act as if I didn't care. (Looking back now from a safe distance, the threat gone, the hurt dulled, I have to admit the boy had talent.)

Of course I could never tell her any of this. She did have a kind of natural dignity and grace about her and she did walk tall with her head high and she longed to believe that Feegie wasn't as bad as it was made out to be. I didn't tell her either how they took the mickey out of my St James's school uniform: the bottlegreen blazer with the grey flannel short trousers and the long grey socks with green and yellow stripes at the top which I used to wear pulled up to the knees. The jeering was hard enough to take without my mother chiming in on the other side. St James's was on the other side of the town: you hardly ever saw any boys round our way wearing school uniform and if they were wearing socks at all they'd have them down around their ankles, which is what I had to do when I was out playing in the street or I'd get no peace from them. *Snob* was what Big Henderson and Wullie Logan who lived in our close called me right from the start; Henderson first – Big Hendry they called him – then Wullie copied him and so did his brothers, and I was feart it might stick and become my nickname forever. Then they found out I was an altarboy and started tormenting me about that as well. They were all Proddies; they didn't know any better. *Holy Boyle*, they'd call me sometimes, and sometimes *St John*, but they could never make up their minds so in the end they just copied Big Hendry – *Bile!* he called me. I wasn't too happy about that, either, to tell you the truth, but at least it didn't make me sound stuckup, or holy.

So much for the new life I was dreaming of the day we left the old tenement in Galloway Street, me with my cricketbat on the back of our furniture lorry, riding shotgun on our covered wagon heading for the Wild Frontier. I knew we'd be passing through Injun country – I just never realized we would end up there.

It seems everybody in Paisley looks down on Feegie, though just down the road from us is the place they put the really rough families, the ones they call the Undesirables, and even the folk in Feegie look down on them. The trouble in this place is, you can't keep yourself to yourself even if you want to. In Galloway Street our backdoor was scruffy enough, with its brokendown washhouse and coalbunkers, but at least it was separated from everybody else's by high dykes, and it was a great place to play. In Blackstoun Road our backdoor has long ago disappeared. There's supposed to be fences separating us from the closes on either side, and from the back greens of the houses on the far side, in Candren Road, a cul de sac they call the Keyhole, but the fences were flattened long ago. So when you look out our windows at the back all you see is our back green with the four iron poles for the washing lines then this huge expanse of field with nothing in it but long grass and weeds. The first day we got here we were showing wee Bernard, my baby brother, all the space we had, and we tried to put him down in the long grass. But when he saw it all waving and rippling in the wind he thought it was alive, a dragon or something, and he burst out greetin', he was that feart. We laughed at him at first, but then we worked it out: he'd only ever been in the old tenements, he'd never seen a field of long grass before in his life, so how was he to know?

The worst part of all this is that our close is on a straight line between Craigmuir Road and the Keyhole, and it turns out there's one of these street bookies living in the Keyhole, so all the scruff from the Undesirables that want to put a bet on come tramping through our close to save themselves the trouble of walking the long way round the road. The neighbours in our close must have got used to this shortcut because they never do anything about it, but it drives my mammy mad. Whenever she hears somebody walking through the close and out the backdoor she rushes out and latches the door behind them. This is not a right of way, she shouts after them. It's a private close! Right of way. Private close. In Feegie! They probably think she's talking a foreign language. Anyway, it doesn't make a blind bit of difference. Some of them have even got the brass neck to come back the same way and then it's much worse because they have to force the door open from the outside and you can hear it smashing back against the close wall. It makes a helluva racket, with the echo in the close and everything. Whenever I hear that noise I pray my mammy will just let it go this time, let them get on with it, please, anything for a quiet life. But no, she always rushes out to the close and starts telling them what for and of course they shout back at her. I'm always feart that one of them might hit her, because there's some real hard cases in the Undesirables, and then I'd have to go out there and probably get duffed up. But that never happens, thank God. Maybe it's because she's a woman. Sometimes I think that in some funny way they're a bit scared of her, this tall, respectable-looking woman who keeps coming out and facing them, rough as they are, drunk as they are half the time, and she won't back down, won't give up.

What with one thing and another my mammy has a hard time of it in Feegie. Not long after we move to Blackstoun Road I start to see a look on her face I've only seen once or twice before and hoped never to see again. It's the way she'll stand at the kitchen window keeking out through the net curtain, or in the end room keeking out the back window: the same feart, clenched way she used to look out at the Orange Walk back in Galloway Street. Except here there's no parade to watch, there's nothing but the scruffy weans running wild in Blackstoun Road or in the wasteland out the back: the Wild Frontier between us and the Keyhole. She'll just stand there shaking her head and muttering away to herself.

God forgive me, I used to think Galloway Street was bad but this place is beyond the beyonts. It's beyond the beyonts altogether.

It's all right for you, I used to think, watching her. You don't have to go out and play in it.

But seeing her like that makes it all the harder to bear;

to tell you the truth, it frightens the life out of me. Her face is that white and her jaw that tight you'd think she's suffering from shock, and watching her sometimes I wonder will she ever get over it.

By the time we'd made it into our first summer in Feegie I could hardly wait to get away. I was even looking forward to going to my new school, St Mirin's Academy. The Academy. I liked the name, the sound of it. Like the College, or the University. Better than St James's, anyway.

And I was to be in Senior Secondary. Very grownup by the sound of it. I'd get my long trousers at last. I'd be one of the big boys.

You'd think I'd have known better. You'd think I'd have realized by then I was as bad as my mother with her *Ferguslie Park*, judging a place by the sound of its name.

I went up to look at the school one day near the end of the summer holidays. I'd turned twelve by then and knew I'd be going there soon. I was very nervous about it and thought it might help if I could see it beforehand. So one Sunday I asked one of the older altarboys at St Fergus's, Big John McPaul, where the Academy was and how to get there.

Ye walk up the Renfrew Road, he told me, till ye come to these big red sandstone bildins . . . and for a moment there he sent my hopes soaring, picturing myself in some posh manor house set in spacious grounds maybe, like Greyfriars College in the Billy Bunter stories. And he must have seen that in my face because he just shook his head and laughed, but a good laugh, not a sneer. Naw, he said. Ye keep goin', *past* the red bildins, till ye come to a big *grey* bildin. *That's* the Academy. The Academy's the worst, he said, grinning at me (that perverse pride again). Ye cannae miss it.

I knew what he meant the day I walked past it and got my first sight of the grim, grey pebbledash building down off the Renfrew Road, the hard lines of its squared-off H-shape and the tall narrow windows that stared blankly back at me across a vast stretch of deserted tarmac behind high iron railings. To tell you the truth, it gave me the creeps just to look at it. It looked more like a prison than a school. Like the way you might imagine Barlinnie. Or Alcatraz.

But it was even worse on that first day, the playground packed and heaving with big boys in long trousers shouting and running mad all over the place. At St James's I'd been one of the biggest boys. But not here. And to make things worse I was still in short trousers. The St Mirin's uniform was navyblue so my mother had bought me a blazer from somewhere, secondhand as usual, a bit too big as usual (Ye'll grow into it, she said, as usual) and with a big rip on the sleeve that she'd had to patch and darn.

Arra isn't it on the inside, she said when I complained. Who'll ever see it?

But she wouldn't buy the badge for the blazer: we can't afford it, she said. Even worse, she drew the line at buying me long trousers, because I still had my short ones from St James's and they were grey, the right colour for the Academy. I was mortified but she wouldn't budge.

Ah'm twelve, I protested. How can Ah wear short trousers?

Ah, you'll wear them and be glad of it. Isn't there good wear in them yet?

So all the boys here looked and acted older than me, and the worst of it was there were no familiar faces. I couldn't even see Foley and McColl, the only other boys from St James's who had made it into Senior Secondary.

I went looking for them in the playground at the first break.

Jeez, John, how'd ye make A? McColl said.

I'd done quite well at the Qualifying Exam, so I'd been put in 1A. They were in 1C.

The way they stood there and looked at me you'd think they envied me. But I was the one who envied *them*. And not just because they both had long flannels on and new blazers. It was because they were together. To me they felt different already; separate. I knew I was on my own.

I don't remember much about the classes: strange names being called out; a blur of unfamiliar faces. One thing I liked: the black cloaks – gowns, they called them – the teachers wore, the way they swished and billowed as they walked by. It gave them a look of masters in an English public school, or so I liked to think: I was still clinging to the wreckage of my Greyfriars fantasy. No mortarboards, though; that was a bit of a letdown. Probably too sissy for a West of Scotland man. Our class teacher turned out to be a grim wee man with a deathshead face that would put the fear of God into you. Wee Jazza, they called him, and the way they said it, even the big boys, you could tell they were a bit feart of him as well. I don't know how I got through that day, especially the mayhem in the playground. At first I stuck close to an older boy I recognized from St James's, Francis McQuaid. I'd never liked McQuaid much (used to despise him a bit, in fact): he was tall and stooped and wore thick specs that gave him a swotty, glaikit look. But he seemed to know his way around this frightening new place and all through that first morning break in the playground I stuck by his side, practically hanging on to his jacket, like a drowning man clinging to driftwood. I couldn't help myself, but later I felt ashamed. There would be a longer break at dinner-time and I knew I'd have to make it on my own.

The sheer bedlam in that yard made me keep thinking of the time I nearly drowned in Paisley Baths and the way I'd learned to hide after that, when we went back there on school trips from St James's, clinging to the sides of the pool in case somebody pushed me under. On that first day at the Academy and for days after it I hung back in the shelter of the school building, keeping well away from the riotous games that were going on, all at the same time it seemed, with boys rushing about, sliding, tackling, swearing. You hardly ever saw anybody in that play-ground just walking, or even talking in an ordinary voice: it was all charging about and shouting. In a way it was worse than the Baths, like being adrift in a rough sea with big waves rearing and crashing and threatening to swamp you any minute. There weren't even any lassies about the place to calm things down, because St Mirin's was Boys Only.

That's whit's great aboot the Academy, the big boys kept saying. Nae lassies tae spoil yer fun!

At least that's what they said, and you had to say the same even if you thought different. If you said anything else they'd call you a sissy. Or worse. You'd never hear the last of it, anyway.

About the only consolation I had was that I wasn't the only one skulking by the wall. I soon realized there were other boys doing the same, Firstyears like me, some of them in short trousers, trying like me to look casual, not that interested, not bothered at all. Like the Mississippi gambler you see in cowboy pictures, dead gallus in his frockcoat and bootstring tie, standing at the saloon bar with a wee cynical smile on his face and watching the cowpokes and ranchers at their poker game. He doesn't say anything, he doesn't need to, the smile says it for him. Hey, it says, I'm standin' here because this is where I wanna be, out on the edge, watchin'. I'll join in when I feel like it, OK? When I'm good and ready.

The cowpokes whooped and stomped and hollered and we stood there on the sidelines, the Mississippi gamblers, watching the stampede.

I don't know if we fooled anybody, but at least it got us through the break.

THREE

The Academy was the only secondary school for Catholic boys in the Paisley area, so the boys came from all over: some from the few tenements that were still left standing in the town, many more from the new housing schemes in the surrounding areas: Gallowhill, Glenburn, Hunterhill. Even in Senior Secondary, most of the boys came from families as poor and working-class as mine was, but at least they had one thing going for them: they didn't live in Ferguslie. *Feegie!* Any hopes I'd had that its reputation might not have reached this far, or at least be blurred by distance, were soon shattered. Even on that first day, when we were still circling around each other with the wary politeness of strangers, I could sense the scorn – or worse, the pity – as soon as they heard the name. I knew I'd have to brace myself for worse to come. One or two of the boys in 1A even lived in private houses – *bungalows!* – in outlying villages like Houston or Bridge o' Weir. To me, this was luxury beyond imagining.

Later I got talking to one of them, Cantwell, a big boy with fair wavy hair who lived in Houston. He looked very elegant: his blazer was brand new, made of some rich-looking material – It's barathea, he told me, though that left me none the wiser – and it actually fitted him, and he wore long trousers in a charcoal grey that was darker and smoother than most. I made some remark to him about this and he said: Och, that's ma daft mother. Pressed them the wrong way. Stupid woman. Look!

And he showed me how she had ironed his trousers to sharp creases, but down the side seams, not down the front.

I was shocked and impressed that a boy of our age could dare to call his mother daft like that, but I didn't say. I was worried in case he'd thought I was taking the mickey.

Ah never even noticed the creases, I said. Honest. Ah just thought they looked smart.

What aboot yer blazer, he asked. How come ye're no wearin' the badge?

Oh, eh, ma mamm— ma mother couldnae get it in the shop. Sold oot.

Too bad, he said. Nifty blazer, that. But ye should try and get the long flannels as well, big guy like you. An' the badge. The badge sets it aff. Ye know?

Anybody that knows this much about clothes, I was thinking, must have *seen* my blazer isn't new. He might even have noticed my patched sleeve. He seemed nice enough, though; I felt I could talk to him.

It's no' new, mind, I explained. It belonged to . . . ma big cousin. Ma mam – mother had to fix it up a bit for me. There was a big tear in the sleeve, here.

He looked at it, fingering the stitching like an expert, and nodded.

Hey, that's a grand job she's done there.

Going back in I felt better. I'd made a friend, somebody I could talk to!

Later in the afternoon we were sitting between periods waiting for the teacher and I saw Cantwell chatting to some other boys. I got my courage up and walked over to join them, doing my best to act casual, one of the gang.

He looked up as if he was surprised to see me.

Oho, he said. Here's Boyle, whose maw's a dab hand at the sewin'!

Does she take in washin'? another boy said.

They all burst out laughing and thank God the teacher chose that moment to walk in because the way Cantwell had said it, it was obvious he'd told them the whole story. I just shrugged and walked back to my seat quite the thing, as if nothing had happened, but to tell you the truth if there'd been any way I could've kept on going, I'd have done it.

Just keep going, out the door, out the window even. Anything. Just get away from there.

Schoolwork was hard going. The worst thing was realizing that I wasn't top boy anymore, the way I'd been, more or less, in my last years at St James's. But here it was a different story. I was in 1A, a class of about twenty-five boys, and I wasn't even sure if I was in the top half. All these boys had been top, or near enough, in their primary schools; I was in a different league now. Was I going to end up being one of the dunces? It was a frightening thought. I had to learn new subjects like French, Latin, Science, Mathematics. Mathematics was the worst. Even Arithmetic had always been a nightmare for me at St James's. But Arithmetic turned out to be just the introduction – and an easy one at that, according to our

31

teacher, Big Paddy, a grimfaced man with a massive bald head – to a whole family, as he called it, the family of Mathematics. *Mathematics*. Just the sound of it scared the life out of me. And then Big Paddy introduced the rest of this grim family and I heard *their* names: Algebra, Geometry, Trigonometry, Logarithms. To me, they sounded like diseases.

French was a new subject and that was hard as well, but at least it was language, like English. It was just different words, words you could hear and learn and make sense of, so you could talk to French people and understand them. I liked the idea of these people in another country, not that far from ours, dressed much the same, probably talking about the same daft things, but somehow different, more exotic, because they'd be speaking this foreign language.

Our French teacher was Big Wullie, a nice man who could be quite funny, though not always in the way he meant.

Remember, boys, if you want to speak French properly, you've got to make the face – *ze fess* – he told us at the first lesson. Then he'd purse his lips and droop his eyes the way you'd think he was getting ready to kiss somebody. The first time he did this he did it for a laugh, but what he never seemed to realize was that his face *always* went that shape when he spoke French and you felt like bursting out laughing. You had to watch yourself though: some days he'd take it all right but other times he'd be in a bad mood and go into a huff like a big wean. That only made it all the funnier but then we'd have to sit there with straight faces trying hard not to look at each other in case somebody set us off. Sometimes I felt a bit sorry for Big Wullie: he was only trying to be pally, even if it didn't always work. I think he liked me too, because one day the class joker Joe Duffy talked back to him in a funny French accent, taking the mickey, and he had the whole class in stitches, including me. And Big Wullie gave me this sad look, like a man betrayed, and said, '*Et tu, Brute?*' At the time we were doing *Julius Caesar* for English and I knew that was what Caesar said when his best pal Brutus stabbed him and I felt ashamed.

The playground wasn't much fun either. Most days I'd join in at football and play at right back. That was my favourite position because you could hide there – at least nobody expected you to score goals. That must be the worst responsibility anybody could have. There was the goal in front of you, and you had to get the ball into that wee space, you had to shoot hard and straight. If you missed an easy chance, a sitter, everybody saw it – that was the worst. At right back, all you had to do was kick the ball away, anywhere as long as it was up the field, away from your own goal. I was big for my age and learning how to use my weight – I could stop a tricky winger running rings around me by just blundering into him: if you made it look like an accident you could get away with it. I wasn't bad, but I wasn't good, either. There were boys in that playground who had such natural skill and style you'd bet on them playing for Celtic one day. Or St Mirren at least, the Paisley team. The best I could hope for was to get through the game without making a clown of myself, miskicking a clearance, say, or kicking it in a panic to somebody on the other team and then seeing him score an easy goal with all his teammates cheering and my own howling abuse.

Aw for CHRISTsake, Boyle! Whose side are ye OAN?

*

As a break from the football a gang of us used to gather near the steps and talk about the pictures we'd seen at the weekend at the La Scala or the Regal. Our ringleader was a square-built boy with fair curly hair, Wee Davie. He was wee all right, but he made up for it with sheer energy. He was a good laugh, I have to admit. It was never enough for him just to tell you the story of a picture he'd seen: he'd act out all the parts as well. The gangster pictures were his favourites. He could copy the American accents better than any of us. He could do Humphrey Bogart and George Raft and a terrific Edward G. Robinson. Jimmy Cagney was his favourite: *Yooo dirty rat!* he kept saying. He had us all at it, acting out scenes from pictures we'd seen, or making up wee sketches from others we hadn't, but we always had to go along with Wee Davie's idea of the story. He seemed to have seen every gangster picture that ever came out of Hollywood, so his favourite sketches were about cops 'n' robbers and they always turned out the same way no matter what part he was playing. When he was the cop, which he usually was, he'd have great fun pushing and slapping us hoodlums around (they were supposed to be pretend slaps but he put plenty of zing into them), locking us in handcuffs and then strongarming us into the cells.

Get in there, ya lousy bum, he'd say as he bundled you in, one fist clenched tight on the back of your collar, the knuckle of the other one used as a gun barrel and jabbing painfully into your backbone.

Jest you wait there till we're ready for ya, palooka! he'd say, and give you a shove in the chest that was supposed to be just in fun, just kidding, but sometimes caught you off balance and sent you flying.

After a while I got fed up and complained. I wanted to be the cop next time.

Sure, Wee Davie said, cheerfully. Ah'll be a hoodlum.

And I thought, Great. Now at least it'll be my turn to slap *him* around and frogmarch *him* into the courtroom. And I did that all right with the other boys: they only pretended to resist. But as soon as I tried it on Wee Davie he broke out of my grip, whipped round, grabbed me by the tie and slammed me up against the wall.

Get yer crummy hands offa me, ya lousy cop!

Hey, ye're supposed tae be in handcuffs!

All the better to strangle ya wit, ya crummy cop! he said, jamming his wrist against my windpipe. Within seconds I was blue in the face and gasping for breath.

Wee Davie. He was good-natured enough and he could be very funny but he was one of life's born tough guys and he had a real chip on his shoulder about his size. I became one of his favourite targets, probably because I was the tallest. Many years later I saw another tough little guy, Joe Pesci, doing his scary hardcase act in *Goodfellas*, and I felt an uneasy echo of Wee Davie and our playacting sessions at the Academy. I suppose by today's standards he'd be called a bully, but there was no malice in him – he just got carried away with his roleplay. And with all his funny voices and antics and the faces he'd pull, you had to forgive him. But after a while I decided I'd had enough of this playacting. It was getting a bit too rough for my liking and I went back to playing football, where there was less chance of injury.

Another boy I had mixed feelings about was Cantwell, who had so embarrassed me on that first day. Away from his clique of jeerers in the classroom he acted friendly enough towards me, but he had this sneaky trick of coming up to you in the playground and putting his arm round your shoulders, dead pally, chatting away quite the thing just to put you off the scent, then hooking you into a vicious headlock. He'd hold your head imprisoned in the crook of his arm and twist and squeeze until you had to beg for mercy. I saw him once getting into a fight in the playground with this big hardman from Junior Secondary, Big Crimmond. To look at the two of them you wouldn't have given Cantwell a chance; with his wavy hair, elegant blazer and flannels, he looked like a pushover. But he won the fight quite easily by getting Big Crimmond in his headlock and squeezing till he howled for mercy. Maybe I shouldn't have been surprised, remembering all the practice he'd got on the likes of me.

I gave him a shock one day, though. To tell you the truth, I shocked myself. I'd been reading something in a comic about self-defence, with little drawings to show different parries and throws, and there was one about how to break out of a headlock. It looked easy, too good to be true in fact, so I talked my wee brother into helping me to practise it at home. It seemed to work all right, though I knew Cantwell would be a helluva lot tougher to handle than Frankie, and anyway I would probably never have the guts to try it. But this day he had me trapped in another excruciating headlock and though I'd called out several times, *Ah gie in!* he wouldn't let go. It was torture. In desperation I tried the move I'd practised with Frankie, my left palm spread over his face, pulling his head back, hard; and my right forearm hooked behind his knees to sweep his legs up from under him. I couldn't believe how easy it was. One minute I was bent double, helpless, begging for mercy, the next I had swept Cantwell off his feet and was holding his body across my chest, high above the ground, like a circus strongman with barbells. A sense of total power rushed to my head; my blood was pounding. In that moment I knew I could easily smash him to the ground, and he knew it too.

OK, OK, he said, in this tight, strangled voice I'd never heard before. OK! Ye can let me doon noo!

I swung his legs back down.

He stood there, getting his breath back, rearranging his blazer, smoothing his hair down.

Serves ye right, I said. Ye asked for it.

I didn't know what else to say. I was elated and a bit scared.

He looked at me reproachfully.

Tut tut, Boyle, he said. Nae need tae get carried away, ye know.

He shook his head as if he was feeling sorry for me or something, and started to walk away. Then stopped and turned round.

And don't look at me in that tone o' voice, either, he said, wagging a finger at me. Like Big Paddy giving me a telling off. He grinned and strolled away, looking as casual and elegant as ever. It was as if my wee triumph had never happened.

That's the trouble with Cantwell and his kind. Just for once you think you've taught them a lesson, and they still come out of it with style.

FOUR

During our first few years in Feegie I was glad of any
excuse to stay in the house: it was the only way I could get
a break from the grimness and the vague air of menace
that lurked out in the street. At that age, I still looked forward to the visits we'd get from our Irish friends and
relatives. Barney Molloy and his missus, neighbours from
the old days in Galloway Street, would take the bus out to
see us now and again. Uncle John, my old man's brother,
and his adopted mother, Auntie Bradley, already lived in
Feegie. And soon new relatives and family friends started
turning up. A Mrs Hanley who lived a few streets away
turned out to be a second cousin of my mother's from
Achill and she and her husband Joe came round to see us
so often that we were soon calling them Auntie Beattie
and Uncle Joe. My mother treated all these visitors as if
they were family.

Aren't they Irish, God help us? she'd say. No more than
ourselves?

I already knew from the old days in the tenements that
the Irish love a good story, especially about ghosts or
fairies or banshees, and I heard plenty of them around the

fireside in the new house in Blackstoun Road. Old Jimmy Bradley had been the champ when it came to stories about the banshee (until the day the banshee came for him, too) but Uncle Joe was every bit as good in his own way. Later in life I was instinctively drawn to the company of raconteurs, and I'm sure that had its roots in those evenings I spent listening to these yarnspinners.

We'd sit round the fireside in the livingroom – a rare treat, since my mother always kept that room empty and no fire in the grate. Years later when I left for London, and for a long time after that, I carried a cosy image in my mind (like a dog-eared snapshot you'd carry in your wallet): all of us crowded around listening to ghost stories, the firelight flickering on our faces. It was a scene worthy of a Christmas card, which is probably where my erratic memory pinched the idea. The truth was that outside the shifting loop of light the room was freezing cold; you couldn't get near the heat for the grownups gathered round the fire, their eyes moist with the steam off their tea or their toddy, swapping reminiscences about the Oul' Country, while an audience of hobgoblins heckled and hissed among the coals. At evening Mass years later, during a Mission in St Fergus's, I heard a sermon by one of those firebrand priests that the Church always seemed to parachute in for these occasions. This one specialized in graphic Doomsday predictions and was spelling out for us, with relish, his personal vision of Hell: it featured cackling demons, horned and hooved, wardancing on fiery slopes, and with a sudden shiver of *déjà vu* I was back in that crowded livingroom, watching the grownups hunched in silhouette around the fireplace, whispering, and beyond them the red coals tumbling and flaring.

I always liked it when Uncle Joe came round. He was a

big broad-faced countryman with a violent head of ginger hair, and tales to tell that could chill the heat out of the fire. He didn't have much of a repertoire, so he was inclined to repeat himself – not that we minded, since the stories were different every time he told them. Even their names – 'The Man who Met the Divil', or 'The Woman Cursed by the Fairies' – could put the fear of God into me. My favourite was 'The Great White Ship of Achill Sound', which he told us at least once a year and that at Christmas or thereabouts.

Did I ever tell ye now, he'd begin, without a hint of irony (irony was a foreign language to Uncle Joe), about the great white ship I saw one day in Achill Sound?

Nobody ever dreamed of stopping him and back would go the massive head, the huge red builder's hands clasped across the waistcoat, the watery blue eyes gazing back into a distant childhood.

I was playing one day on the bridge at Achill Sound. I would have been no more than a gorsoon at the time, about nine or ten years old, and I was looking out to the sea, when suddenly I saw a great white ship making in towards the sound. Well, I declare to God, it was the loveliest sight you ever saw, this marvellous ship all white and gleaming and the grand sunny day that was in it. And there were fine, elegant people standing on the deck looking up towards the bridge. And there was meself, on the bridge, waving . . . until, all of a sudden like, I began to get the feeling that there was something odd about it – all those people just standing there and not a wave out of them and not a word did they speak. Just stood there, looking up at me, as the ship began to pass under the bridge . . . And then, well, you know how you are when you're a child, I ran to the other side to watch it come out.

At this point, with instinctive dramatic timing, he would pause and look around at his entranced audience.

Well, I declare to God, Mick, upon me solemn oath – and here a huge shovel of a hand would fly out and slap my old man violently on the knee, a habit of Joe's that he knew and dreaded, but never quite managed to forestall – that ship never appeared at the other side, nor was she, nor any of the poor souls that were on her, ever heard of agin from that day to this!

Nobody ever challenged this unlikely tale. Not me, certainly, because as a boy I believed every word of it and the day when I first felt the shadow of doubt about it and others of its kind I look back on as a very bleak day indeed. Like the day you learn, as a child, that there is no Santa Claus. Or the day, years later, when the Hound of Hell you've fled down the labyrinthine ways finally has you cornered and the message in the black void of its eyes is the one you knew and dreaded all along: there is no God, either. But back then my faith in Joe's stories, like my Catholic faith, was absolute. Even my mother, an Achill woman herself and by force of circumstance the only realist in the family, would restrict herself to a sigh or a smile or a shake of the head.

Ah, he's an awful man altogether, that Joe, always yarning out of him.

This of course after Joe had gone – nobody would have dreamed of suggesting to his face that his stories were anything but Gospel truth.

Long years after I left Scotland I stood for the first time on that very bridge at Achill Sound and I could see at a glance that you would be hard pressed to get a rowing boat under there, let alone a great ship, white or otherwise. I felt no resentment, only a sense of wonder at the leap of the imagination that had given this humble stone crossing the elevation and span of the Golden Gate Bridge.

What I enjoyed most about those evenings, cocooned there together against the harshness of the world, was the sight of a natural raconteur making the most of his moment. When Uncle Joe took the floor, he held it. Nobody dared interrupt his flow; it would have been a kind of sacrilege. On the other hand, interjections along the lines of *Holy Mother o' God!* or *The Lord bless us and save us!* were allowed and even encouraged, the way the sermons of a Southern Baptist preacher in full flow are lent rhythm and force by the responses of his enraptured congregation. It was my first inkling of the power of poetic licence: the unwritten code that protects the raconteur. As if the borrowed mantle of the Muse some-how takes on the powers of a suit of armour.

In my early days in London, I was entertained for a whole evening in a pub by another red-haired Irishman, a bearded, wild-eyed satyr from Cork City, with the most incredible tales of his exploits in bedsitterland. The more we drank, the more his exaggerations mounted in out-rageousness and the more his sing-song accent spiralled upwards with them, till at one point the mad storyteller himself seemed to be levitating before my eyes. But his final anecdote was a fantasy too far. It seemed he'd come home drunk one night – *destroyed with the drink!* – only to find that he'd locked himself out of the house, having left his keys in his room upstairs. He'd rung every bell on the door but got no response: either there was nobody home, or nobody was going to open the door to a drunken Irishman at that time of night.

At this point, he said – and his instinct for dramatic

timing brought to mind my Uncle Joe's – I must have passed out. The next thing I remember is waking up the following morning, freezing cold, lying on my own bed, still in my clothes from the night before. My keys were still on the inside of the door where I'd left them. The window behind me was wide open, my fingernails were all torn and bleeding – and I swear to God, my room was on the fourth floor!

The suggestion that, blind drunk as he was, he had somehow metamorphosed into the Human Fly and shinned up the façade of a four-storey building at dead of night without benefit of rope or crampon was too much even for me to take. I was shaking my head and on the point of telling him exactly what I thought of his story, when I found that I couldn't do it. The expression of scorn and disbelief that had started to form on my face was easing, of its own accord, into one of wonder and admiration.

By Christ, I heard myself say. That is uncanny.

He was lying of course; he had to be. Yet he had given himself so totally to his fantasy that I felt I could not challenge his story without in some way damaging him. In different company he would have been dismissed as a bullshitter, and he undoubtedly was, but we had reached that stage you sometimes reach with strangers in bars, where you bask in the glow of mutual bonhomie, in sympathy with each other's woes, in perfect tune with each other's dreams: we had become, for that instant, soul mates and I thought, Who am I to judge him? Aren't we all lost souls at times, trying to improve on our humdrum reality with a little harmless embellishment?

Maybe it was just old-fashioned politeness that saved me from the sacrilege of doubting his story, but in my heart I don't believe that. I like to think that the ghosts of Uncle Joe and the wonderstruck boy who had sat at his feet flew back in the nick of time, like Batman and Robin, to save a fellow wanderer in those enchanted realms where fantasy is the breath of life itself.

September 1958

The sounds of Slim Whitman are drowned out by a
sudden commotion in the street. Then it's in the close,
right outside our door. It's a woman greetin', but with a
sound I've never heard before: a low continuous moaning,
as if she's chanting or keening. She's hammering at the
door, not using the knocker, not ringing the bell.
Hammering with the flat of her hand, it sounds like, the
heel of it. Like she's pounding to be set free or something
– to be let out, not let in. The door panel shudders, the
hollow boom sounds and echoes up the stone stairwell.
The moaning's getting louder now, more insistent.

I lie there on the bed, listening to all this racket. It's just
annoying at first, then I start to get a bit feart. It's giving
me the creeps, to tell you the truth. But I don't do anything. This is grownup business. Must be. Nothing to do
with me.

I hear my mammy's hurried footsteps, her old slippers
scuffing along the lino in the lobby.

Oh, Jesus, Mary and Joseph, what in the name of God
has happened now?

FIVE

I came to look back on those early years in Feegie, those first years at the Academy before Laff appeared in my life, as my Dark Ages – years that memory seems to have blurred, for reasons I can only guess at. I peer back through the murk and grope for clues, fragments of meaning, as if I am the the only customer at a fairground sideshow – *Memory Lane!* – watching the seedy Memory Man crank his magic lantern to project on an improvised screen a series of watery slides, like underlit scenes in a film, or like the shifting shapes and faces I used to imagine on my own bedroom ceiling, in my own theatre of dreams. I sit in the dark and strain to see what's happening on a screen that is barely less dark. The actors move like ghosts in patchy gloom, their faces blurred or in shadow, their words unclear. And with the bizarre logic of dreams, one of the few faces that comes easily into focus is Laff's, as if he was always there, a leitmotif, though recall and reason (and a hurried glance at the script) assure me that he had not yet made his entrance. I strain to distinguish other faces and voices in scenes that have the ghostly transparency of the slow dissolve, the shifting substance of half-remembered dreams, and yet hint as dreams do at hidden meanings, treasure as yet untrove that once exposed to the light may sparkle and jingle and make everything clear.

Every so often a scene swims slowly into focus, like a Polaroid developing.

If there's one good thing about living in Feegie it's that we've got plenty of room in the new house and the lavvy (with a sink! and a bath!) is inside, so we don't have to go running down to a cold, damp landing the way we used to in Galloway Street. I even have a room to myself now, the end room, so I can lie in bed reading and turn the light off whenever I like and not have to worry anymore about Frankie and wee Vincent girning and twisting in the bed beside me. But on Friday and Saturday nights I always turn it off early, because I'm desperate to get to sleep before my old man comes in from the pub.

I lie there in the dark praying for sleep, or at least that he'll come in early this once and not be drunk. Sometimes I'll hear my mammy opening the front door and going out into the close and I know she'll be standing out there looking up the road to see is he coming. She does that even though I know she hates it. What'll the neighbours think?

Then she comes back in, sighing and moaning under her breath.

What a man, he's a disgrace, so he is . . . Out drinking in the pubs and wouldn't even come home from his work first for a wash and a bit o' dinner. What kind of a man is he at all that would carry on like that?

She shuts the door but leaves the snib off. Then stops outside my door and whispers through it.

John, are ye sleepin'?

Naw, no' yet.

Ah well, just go to sleep now, son, she says in a hope-less, doomy voice, and I'll hear her clicking off the lightswitch and her slippers skliffing away along the lobby.

Sometimes I don't even answer her in case she starts moaning to me about him and I won't know what to say. So I pretend to be asleep already, practising for when he comes in . . .

The door to the big bedroom closes and the house goes dead quiet and now I know. I know he'll be coming home drunk because these are the signs.

I lie there dreading the sound of his footsteps in the close: they're the giveaway. If they skliff and stumble he's drunk for sure and I'll hear his keys stabbing and scrabbling at the lock and him muttering: Arra Jesus, Mary and Joseph, or: The curse o' Christ on ye! And then the front door lurches open and I curl myself tight into a ball with my head under the blankets and my heart thumping and me whispering to myself: Please God don't let him come in here, let him go past my door this time without coming in. Please.

But he nearly always comes in anyway and I can feel him standing there and hear his breathing wheezy in his clogged-up, broken nose.

Are ye shleepin', son? he whispers and though I keep my eyes tight shut and kid on I'm fast asleep and breath-ing steady, in and out, I feel his weight sinking down heavy on the bed and making the mattress dip and I have to cling on tight not to slide down the slippy sheet. And then he peels back the covers slowly, so as not to wake me, and puts his hand on my head.

Ah God above, wee John's shleepin', I hear him sighing, and he's stroking my hair. Wheesht, wheesht now.

And I'm lying there praying, Please, please God make him go away, and trying to keep my breathing even, in and out, in and out, the way he'll think I'm sleeping. The worst bit is when he starts greetin' and leans over to kiss my cheek even though I've got my face turned in to the pillow so all he can reach is my ear. I'm near smothered in the smell of stale beer and cigarettes and my hair's all wet with his tears and slavers and I'm pleading: Please God please make him go away, please, and my heart's dying in me because he's my daddy and I'm ashamed of him and I don't want to be.

Mother Machree, he says. The besht wee boy in the worl', thash what ye are. Ye are indeed, I declare to God. The besht in the worl'.

And he sits there hunched on the edge of my bed greetin', grieving for God knows what, and I just keep on breathing, in and out, in and out, and the house all round us is that quiet and echoey it feels to me as if the whole world's asleep and we're the only ones left awake in it.

Scenes like this soon took on all the familiarity, though none of the comfort, of routine. I look back on them now and I wonder about the boy I was then: why these pathetic scenes should have caused him such pain. My older self can get quite impatient with him, even indignant: *What was his problem? Didn't he know when he was well off?* All I can be sure of is that the boy felt desperately alone, at school and at home. Since he didn't have any friends worthy of the name, he must himself be unworthy, incapable of something other boys seemed to do naturally, without effort. My best guess is that at some deepdown level he had sensed the need for a companion, a guide and protector, and what was unbearable to him was how far his father fell short on all those counts. He longed for a hero – a Galahad, a Lionheart! – and all he had was this simple, flawed, loving man who drank too much.

The day after the old man comes in drunk, and sometimes for days after that, the whole house is eerie with my mammy's silence. She hates the Drink, or the Booze, or the Loony Juice as she calls it and she especially hates any sign or breath of it on the old man. And when he comes home scattered drunk, as she says, and puts us all to shame in front of the neighbours, as if the Irish hadn't a bad enough name already, God help us, then the Silence is her revenge.

She won't speak to the old man at all, only goes around with her mouth set in a thin line and her face white with anger. She won't even talk to us except when she has to, and then in a tight angry whisper as if we're partly to blame for the disgrace he's brought down on us. When we try to talk normally among ourselves we can't do it; it's as if all the life is being drained out of our voices by this cold, grey cloud that has come down over the house, so we end up whispering as well.

The old man mooches about the place doing daft wee jobs he never usually does, sweeping the floor or cleaning the windows or dusting and polishing the sideboard or even blackleading the fireplace, and we know he's Doing his Penance. It's like having to say decades of the Rosary in Church after a hard confession. Doing Good Works. Making Retribution. We try to keep out of his way because it's painful to watch but if he happens to come across any of us he'll raise his downcast eyes and say Mornin'! in a tone that tries to be cheery but comes out sounding hollow and false; you can tell his heart's not in it. So he ends up padding and dodging about the house not saying a word, with his head down and his eyes lowered as if he's in chapel or something, and trying to keep out of my mammy's way, which God knows ought to be easy enough because she won't go anywhere near him if she can help it. But her Silence goes seeping out through the whole house like a damp fog or the thick, sick smell of gas and he can't get away from that and neither can we.

SIX

When we'd lived in Galloway Street, which God knows was scruffy enough, we'd always thanked our lucky stars that at least we weren't living across the road, in Brown's Place. We learned early on that no matter how badly off you feel there's always someone or someplace that's worse. But at the time, the wrench of leaving the old life for a new place called Ferguslie Park was made easier by the hope that at last we'd be clear of Brown's Place, and headed for the Promised Land. Some hope. Some promised land. Ferguslie Park soon revealed its true nature – *Feegie! The Jungle!* – this purgatory on earth where we now had to serve our sentence and do penance for our foolish aspirations. One of the first shocks was to realize that Brown's Place had moved with us, at least in spirit. It was flourishing just down the road from us in the Undesirables. Worse, it was actually living next door, with the McNairs, and up on the top landing with the Hendersons and the Bairds.

Slowly, reluctantly – I had little choice – I got to know the McNairs through Wullie Logan, their third son. His odd surname was a puzzle to me and, as it turned out, a clue to the kind of family they were.

After about a year in Feegie Big Hendry and the rest of the pack had grudgingly accepted me as a permanent feature on their landscape. I started joining in the games they played out on the road: football, usually, or Barley-Doh – where one boy was Het and the rest of us had to charge past him without being tackled and caught. If we'd used a ball I suppose it would have been a street version of rugby league, minus the rules. Fortunately I was a good runner and big enough to take punishment, because Big Hendry made it obvious he'd be doing me no favours. He was not that much bigger than me, but he was scary to look at: he got his hair cut at home by his father, cropped almost to the scalp, leaving only a thick tuft at the forehead. It looked quite funny, to be honest, a brutish version of Tin Tin the Boy Detective, but nobody laughed at Big Hendry. I made sure I never provoked him, just nursed my bruises as the price of admission. After a while I got quite pally (any port in a storm) with Wullie Logan. He turned out to be a gentle soul who had little in common with the rest of the pack, including his three brothers – not even, as you could tell from their various surnames, a father.

We've a' got the same maw, though, he told me defiantly one day in our close. I must have looked unconvinced because he felt obliged to add: Aye, a durty maw, eh? with a grin that tried to be knowing but failed the exam. He had round, red cheeks and a natural innocence that shone through his habitual pose as a tough guy. I'm sure it was this doomed bravado of his that drew me to him.

Mrs McNair's eldest son Chic, two or three years older than us and a born hardcase – he had that unmistakable *don't tangle wi' me* look about him – was a Robertson.

Then came Jake McNair, then Wullie Logan, and then another McNair: Andy, the youngest. Mr Logan, Wullie's father, must have been a brief fling which the stoical Mr McNair (the only one of this trinity of boyfriends who'd bothered to marry her) had presumably forgiven, and his wayward wife long forgotten. She'd given Wullie only sketchy descriptions of his fly-by-night father, descriptions that varied wildly according to her mood. She'd told him once that the man was a travelling actor, and Wullie clung to this dubious claim like a prized marble or a bully chestnut, a lucky charm he would brandish as if for protection whenever Big Hendry or one of his cronies called him, with clunking emphasis, *Ya wee bastart!*

Ah'm no'! Ah'm no'! Ma auld' man wis an *actor*! he would protest with pathetic pride, as if this artistic connection somehow cancelled out the stigma, then he'd bear the jeers this provoked with his trademark cocky despair. Looking back, I recall his real gift for mimicry, vocal and physical (what became of all that, Wullie? What became of *you*?) and realize with a pang of guilt that this myth of his long-gone father might well have been true, though for some reason – his early impersonations of my mother still rankled – I could never see that at the time, and was not above joining in the jeers.

As for Mr McNair, Wullie's old man by default, I can still picture him: leaning out of their groundfloor window, elbows grooving the sill, skippit bunnet everpresent on his head, an ashladen Woodbine drooping from his lips. *Ma man suffers terrible wi' his back* was the wellworn catchphrase of his wife, whose big, blurred face and body showed no visible trace of the temptress who had once ensnared Robertson and Logan. Whatever the reason, he never seemed to work and made only rare appearances in the outside world, usually on his way to Ibrox whenever Rangers had a home game. Not one of nature's extroverts, he wore his Rangers scarf tucked discreetly inside his jacket, quite conceivably out of consideration for his Catholic neighbours – he was a gentle soul. He was even a discreet drunk, the kind of wee man you'll see sometimes in the West of Scotland staggering along the pavement with his dignity oddly intact, pursuing a zigzag course determined by some private compass in his bunnet, like a homing pigeon buffeted by sidewinds. Amazingly, my mother approved of him. Ah yes, he might be a *Rangers supporter* (this in her fearful whisper) but if he is itself he doesn't shout it from the rooftops like some of them, and if he does take a drink now and again, God help him, you'll never see him making a show of himself like some people I could mention! (Meaning my old man of course – he would pretend not to hear but invariably gave the game away, tossing his head back in a silent *Tut!* and rustling his *Daily Record*.)

When in later life I first came across Andy Capp, I knew beyond any doubt that his prototype could only have been Mr McNair, and I resented the way they'd replaced his homespun Glasgow gutturals with some quaint North of England dialect.

Loud, unruly and unpredictable as they were, the McNairs were more interesting to me – probably because they were more threatening – than my own family. By now I had three younger brothers and two sisters, but to me at that age they were mere distractions, noisy irritants on the outer edge of my experience. *Leave me alone! Can't you see I've got problems of my own?* was the warning signal my moody silences were intended to send out to the world. I was tiptoeing fearfully into my teens –

though I'd have died rather than admit to the fear – and the last thing I needed was any extra burden. My mother had granted me certain privileges: my own room to retreat to, and almost exclusive use of the livingroom for my 'homework'. She must have sensed that the best way to deal with a teenage boy packed with hormones and confusions was to leave him to himself.

The top landing had the Bairds, a family of females. The mother was an arthritic and asthmatic woman we hardly ever saw: she had such a hard time of it heaving herself noisily up and down three flights of stairs that she was virtually a recluse up there. I don't recall a Mr Baird, but he must have existed at some time because there were two daughters that I knew about: Maggie, a quiet, glamorous-looking girl who was already working at Coats's mill and reminded me a bit of her namesake in *The Broons*, and Senga, her younger sister, a fat girl about a year older than me. Senga had stringy fair hair cut in a rough fringe over a broad, flushed face. She also had huge breasts for a girl of her age, but far from trying to hide these blatant symbols of her sexuality, she actually flaunted them in tight blouses and T-shirts. There were times I hardly dared to look in her direction for fear of being caught staring at her chest. I never liked meeting her eyes anyway: they were a hard, pale blue with a challenging look about them; they seemed able to see right through me. She had a sneaky trick of glancing downward, half demure, half admiring, at her swollen chest, then flicking her eyes back up to trap anyone else who might be looking. She caught me out quite a few times and far from being annoyed would fix me with a look of scornful triumph.

Got ye. Heh heh.

*

A few of us are standing talking in the close one day: Big Hendry and Wullie and Senga and me, and Big Hendry's telling one of his dirty jokes. Normally I'd join in laughing just to keep in with them, show I'm a man of the world, but this time I can't. I'm feart my mother might hear us (I know she listens at the door sometimes) and I'm mortified that he's talking about such things in front of a lassie, even if it's only Senga Baird. Not that Senga's likely to be shocked, as I've good reason to know. I can feel the blood rising in my face and I'm thinking I better go in the house for my own peace of mind, when I feel her eyes on me.

Big innocent Boyle, eh? she says, sneering at me. Big hypocrite, mair like it.

She's got no idea how close she is to the truth. Not long before that, I'd been lying in the end room one evening. It was just getting dark outside. I'd been reading and must have fallen asleep. And I was just getting up to take my clothes off and get into bed when I heard a scuffling and whispering outside my window. I was a bit feart at first: it sounded like somebody trying to climb up to the window to look in. Then I recognized Big Hendry's voice, urgent and pleading, and Senga Baird's, moaning as if in pain. What in the name of God, I wondered, are they doing? Still feart but excited now I rolled slowly off the bed and tiptoed to the window, being careful to stay behind the curtain. I couldn't see anything but I could hear every word.

Take them aff, Big Hendry was saying hoarsely. C'moan! I'll help ye!

Naw, naw, Senga said. Ye kin jist shove them doon a bit
. . . Aye, like that.

She was moaning again.

Oh aye, like that . . . like that . . . that's nice.

More hoarse breathing and moaning and pleading. I
couldn't believe this was going on just outside my
window. I was terrified somebody might come into my
room and find me standing there in the dark. But I stayed
where I was. I couldn't help it. I was rooted there, straining to hear.

Let me pit it in!

Naw, no' here. Ah cannae! Jist yer haun . . . That's
good, intit? D'ye no' like that?

No' as much as you, ya hoor ye . . . Here, haud this!
Grab it in yer haun! Gaun!

Hmm . . . 'Sthat nice? 'Sthat better?

Aw cummoan, Senga! Fuck sake! Let me stick it up ye!

Naw, we cannae . . . no' this time . . . no' here . . . but
Ah'll rub it for ye . . . C'mere . . . c'mere . . . c'mere . . .

What shocked me most was that 'no' this time, no'
here'. It could only mean that somewhere else, somewhere
a bit more private, she'd have let him put it in her, no
bother. Maybe she already had! I could hardly believe a
fifteen year old lassie would do that, a mortal sin, that
easily. Even a Proddie, even Senga Baird. It was disgust-
ing, and unbearably exciting. My wullie was already hard.
I grabbed it through my trousers, squeezing it in my fist,
desperate for relief. The moaning and whispering and
breathing outside was getting faster and louder now, more
urgent: I could hear these frantic rubbing noises, like
somebody's back scraping against the pebbledash under
the window and all the time these fast, lapping sounds
like the noise slippy mud makes under your shoes when

you run through it. What were they doing? I was going mad with frustration and lust. My wullie was that hard, tethered there in my trousers, it felt like a bow bent back to its limit: I was feart it might snap any minute under the strain. I started rubbing it savagely through the cloth; even hurting myself brought some kind of relief. I was dying to take it out but didn't dare. The bedroom door might open any minute.

It didn't last much longer. Big Hendry suddenly let out a deep, shuddering groan as if he'd been punched in the stomach or something, but it couldn't be that because Senga let out this wee, dirty giggle – she was actually laughing! I could hardly believe it – then all the noises stopped except for the breathing. They stood there whispering a bit longer, then I heard more noises: clothes being straightened, a skirt rustling, fabric sliding on skin, elastic snapping. Then the furtive, shooshing sounds as they came sneaking in the backdoor and Senga's steps going up the stairs. Just hers: Big Hendry must be waiting out in the close, not wanting to go up at the same time, give the game away. I tiptoed back to my bed and fell across it face down, shaking, still desperately clutching the bulge in my trousers, not wanting to let go of the pictures flaring in my mind. Somehow I knew I'd be remembering them later, again and again. I had no idea how often.

And now, only a few weeks later, here's the same Senga Baird standing staring at me, her pale, shrewd eyes staring right through me. And what that look says is: Ye cannae kid me, Catholic or no, altarboy or no, Ah know what ye're thinking. Ye're nuthin' special. Ye're nae better than the rest of us.

The thought of this depresses the hell out of me, because I feel it's true, and I'm shamed by it. I'm terrified she might guess somehow that I heard them that evening, was spying on them. Pathetic, she'd think: watching, listening – too holy and too feart to do anything himself. From that day on I feel guilty and on edge any time I'm near her. Nobody else can make me feel so ill at ease, so repelled and aroused at the same time. Or at least that's what I think, until the day I meet Big Marian.

I was coming out into the close one day and had turned to shut our door when I found I was breathing in an over-powering aroma of scent. I heard high heels clacking gingerly down the stairs just behind me and turned to look. On about the fifth step up I saw, coming down towards me, a woman's sturdy but shapely legs in black fishnet stockings, balanced on heels impossibly high; then a short, tight black skirt with a shiny patentleather belt, cinched tight, and above it a plump roll of bare flesh beneath an open-knit crochet sweater, through which I could have sworn I saw big, heavy breasts with – *but how could it be? Surely she must be wearing a brassiere?* – one stray brown nipple poking through the mesh. I jerked my eyes guiltily away and up and found I was staring into hers.

They were big and dark and lined with black, the eye-lids heavy with mascara, and the mocking expression in them said, as clearly as if she had spoken: *Seen enough, have ye, son?* I saw a cloud of frizzed black hair framing a face coarsely handsome in thick make-up, a wide voracious mouth gleaming with lipstick and twisted in a smile. Despite her colouring there was a clear resemblance to Senga Baird in the puffy, sullen face and with a jolt I realized that this must be the mysterious oldest sister, or half-sister, the notorious Big Marian who worked down in

London and sent money up regularly to her mother. The whisper in the close – Big Hendry the source, Wullie the breathless messenger – was that she was a *prostitute*: a notion so shocking, so exciting, so downright *dirty* that I'd never quite been able to believe it. But on the evidence that now stood before me (she had stopped for some reason on the bottom step) I realized with horror that it could well be true.

I was still staring up at her, as helpless to look away as I would have been if the banshee itself had appeared in front of me. God only knows what I must have looked like to her. She just stood there, not moving, staring back at me, scarlet lips still twisted in that sarcastic smile. At last I realized why: I was standing directly in her way. Mortified, my face burning, I stepped back, catching my heel and tripping on the McNairs' worn and stringy door-mat, so that my back slammed against the close wall and knocked the breath out of me.

You should get *danger* money, son, she said, with cruel emphasis, stepping down, and her derisive cackle echoed her sister's. She swung her big breasts past me, sending my senses reeling in the musk that wafted up from them, and clack-clack-clacked out through the close. For an instant she paused in the closemouth and her big, sinful silhouette stood clearly outlined in the oblong of daylight, her wild hair haloed in the glare. Then she was gone, though the clack-clack-clack of her high heels along the pavement echoed in the close for a long time. I stood there, embarrassed, scared and oddly exultant, my nostrils and throat still clogged with her scent and that vivid image still flaring in my brain, like some satanic parody of the apparition of Our Lady at Fatima.

At the bottom of Blackstoun Road, barely fifty yards from our close, was the burn, then a field, and then Menzies General Store and Licensed Grocers, an isolated, detached building which at that time we considered the last outpost of civilization, standing as it did at the outer limit of Paisley and District. Beyond it ran a raised railway line, like a boundary fence between us and Inkerman: mile after mile of flat farmland, open countryside, which we thought of then as some kind of moonscape, beyond the pale, of no real interest to us.

One hot day in the long summer holiday a gang of us are down by the burn, some of the boys and two of the lassies, Big Nessie and Maggie Baird. Wullie Logan's there, and Big Hendry, and some younger boys. We're playing games along the banks, trying different ways of getting across the burn, using boulders or bricks as stepping stones, picking up old warped planks or boughs fallen from the trees and throwing them across as bridges, daring each other to walk them without falling off. There's not much water in the burn, not more than a trickle in some of the narrower places, you can hardly see it among the long grass and the weeds, but if you fall in you'll land in mud in some places up to your ankles. But none of that matters as much as falling in in the first place: that's the last thing you want to do.

Big Hendry's worked out a scoring system to decide the winner.

We'll hiv a winner o' the boays, he says, and a winner o' the lassies. The lassies arenae as good as the boays, so it widnae be fair.

I wonder about this because I can see already Big Nessie's as good as any of us, not scared to walk the branches, no matter how bendy or springy, or take on the biggest jumps. I think Big Hendry's just feart he might get beat by a lassie. Then he says the best of the boys gets to wrestle the best of the lassies afterwards, to see who's the winner of everything, and the two next best get to wrestle for second place. I sneak a look at Big Nessie, standing there breathing hard after a jump, her eyes laughing, ready for anything the way she always is and I think, She's beautiful. And that's when I figure it out: Big Hendry's expecting to win and he just fancies the idea of getting his hands on Big Nessie, because it's obvious she's going to be best lassie. Just thinking about it sickens me and so I make up my mind: I'm going to try my hardest to beat him.

It doesn't work. Somewhere near the end I lose my balance on a wobbly branch and fall in the burn, mud up to my ankles. It's my only mistake – I manage the last jump no bother – but Big Hendry doesn't make any, so he's the winner. I'm only second. Then a funny thing happens. The lassies come after us, doing the same jumps and walking the plank and everything and Big Nessie's beating Maggie Baird quite easily. But when she's crossing the branch I fell off she suddenly stops in the middle and turns back to look at us and especially at me it seems and spreads her arms out wide like an actress or a dancer expecting applause. As if to say: Look how easy it is when you know how. It makes me feel rotten to think Big Nessie would show me up like that but then she tries to do a curtsey or something on the branch and slips and falls in. And though I should be pleased, thinking, Serves ye right, that's whit ye deserve, I'm actually feart she might have hurt herself. But no, she's all right, she just laughs.

That's whit Ah get for showin' aff, she says, and trudges

back up the bank.

She's lost points but all she's got to do now is the last jump and she'll still beat Maggie Baird. And I've seen her jump it twice already, dead easy, when we were only playing about, before we started counting in earnest. Maggie goes first, and she just makes it, just clears the muddy bit on the far bank. Now it's Nessie's turn again, and again she starts acting the fool, showing off, taking that long a run-up you'd think she's going for the world record. And then after all that buildup she hesitates at the takeoff and does this daft wee jump that's not like her at all, the kind of jump you'd expect from some wee lassie that's scared of getting her nice frock dirty. But not Big Nessie. Not the Queen o' the Lassies. For the second time in a row she lands in the burn, up to her ankles in mud. And again she just laughs.

Well, ye know whit they say, she says, wading up the bank. Pride comes afore a fall.

We can hardly believe it, especially Maggie Baird because now she's the winner. Big Hendry doesn't look too pleased but rules are rules and anyway Maggie's a nice-looking lassie. So the two of them start circling each other, Big Hendry doing his gorilla act with his arms swinging low and his fingers trailing in the grass.

Me Tarzan, you Jane, he keeps grunting, till Maggie starts laughing. Then he rushes her and they start rolling around in the grass.

It's actually good fun watching them, especially because it's Maggie he's rolling about with and not Nessie. Then Nessie is standing in front of me, her eyes laughing as usual.

Well, Mr Second? she says to me. Are we no' supposed to wrestle as well?

I've been trying to act as if I forgot but to tell you the truth I've been thinking about nothing else. And now she's looking that pleased with herself I get a mad notion that she might have lost to Maggie Baird on purpose, so she wouldn't have to wrestle Big Hendry. Did she do it so she could wrestle me instead? It's such an exciting thought I hardly dare to think it. What if I'm wrong and she was to find out? Anyway, now we've got this wrestling match. I'm that excited about actually touching her I'm dying of nerves, so I kid on I'm trying to get out of it.

Och, naw, I say. We don't need to wrestle. You can be second, I don't care.

She stops laughing and gives me a hard look. As if to say: Ye better not start backing out now, pal. Then she's laughing again, and stalking around me.

Oho, she says. Feart, is that it? Feart ye're gonnae get beat by a lassie?

She moves in on me and grabs my wrists and that's it, we've started.

How can I describe the feeling of wrestling with Nessie that day? The first thing I notice is how strong she is. The only way I can get my wrists free of her grip is to force my arms round her, low down on her hips, bending her arms back behind her. Of course this brings her chest hard against mine, and our faces so close we're breathing the same air. I've never been this near to her before. I've never been this close to any lassie before, except at parties, playing Postman's Knock or Stations. But this is different, this is something else altogether. I can see her teeth glistening, see the spittle on her red tongue, flecking her lower lip. We're that embarrassed we start giggling and yet all the time I'm thinking how beautiful she is and how easy it would be, how delicious, to kiss that laughing mouth.

And I get the feeling, in fact I'm nearly positive, that she wouldn't mind, wouldn't mind at all, but I know it's impossible and so I don't and the moment is gone. At the same time I can still feel the heat of her straining against me, the swell of her young breasts against my hammering chest. We sway there together, not giggling anymore, too breathless for that, locked in silent struggle in this embrace I don't want to end, and I'm fighting to keep my balance not just because of her weight pushing and pulling against me, and she is unbelievably strong, but because the sensation is making me so dizzy I'm losing my head completely.

At last I wrench one wrist free of her grip and the force of it carries me sideways and down and I grab at her arm to steady myself and down she comes with me. And now we're locked together and rolling in the long grass and the weeds, fern and dock leaf, dandelion and buttercup, and nettles or thistles because something definitely stings the back of my neck but it doesn't matter, doesn't matter at all, and all these smells and sensations keep blending and stirring in my head, and then she's on top of me, the warm weight of her sturdy bum on my belly, her limber thighs straddling my chest, her face laughing down at me and I'm breathing her tang of earth and moss and sweat, near fainting with the intensity of it and thinking, This is what it must feel like to be drunk.

I think I might even have passed out, but only for a moment, because the next thing I remember is opening my eyes to find Nessie still kneeling astride me, still pinning my wrists, peering down into my face, half worried, half wary. I took a deep breath, then thrust up with all my strength, bucking her off me and reversing our positions, though I had a feeling she complied in that, too, her resistance just enough to be plausible. And that complicity was still between us as I gazed down at her in my turn, my hands on the pale undersides of her tanned arms, pinning them above her head, and we held it there a good while longer, Nessie squirming and straining under me, but never enough to dislodge me, both of us knowing we liked each other, that this game gave us a freedom to touch that was rare indeed. Until at last – I felt I couldn't hold it any longer without giving the game away – I gallantly (and truthfully) declared it a draw and got up off her. We stood apart and stared at each other, smiling, heaving, gasping for breath, the sensations still intense, but the bond broken, the intimacy already receding.

We never got that close again, though we'd often be playing in the same game out in the road, Kick the Can or Barley-Doh, and she still had that way of looking at me that was flattering and unsettling, friendly and challenging at the same time. I'm sure she knew I fancied her, and she didn't mind, quite liked it even, and she was probably puzzled that I never said anything or made any move towards her. I know it puzzled Wullie Logan: in his quiet way he had picked up the signals, and told me about it, though I only scoffed at him. The truth was that I was scared of Nessie: she was only a few months older but she seemed so much more than that, so much more like a woman than a girl, and I had no idea how to handle her, no idea at all, even in my fantasies, which in Nessie's case were always romantic and tentative. It's obvious to me now that I was in love with Nessie, but at the time I could never have admitted that, even to myself.

By the time I did acquire the beginnings of confidence, or at least the outward show of it, I'd thought up other barriers. Insane though this now seems to me, as I got older I began to worry that Nessie, a Proddie and a Feegie girl, might somehow not be the kind of girl I should think of in that way. These teenage fears and follies got the reward they deserved. One day I realized I hadn't seen her out in the street for a while and it was Wullie who told me, with a sly shrug – *whit dae ye expect?* – that she and her family had left Feegie, moved to another scheme on the other side of the town: Hunterhill, they called it. She might as well have moved to Australia. And that was that. Nessie had gone out of my life and I'd never said anything, never declared myself.

SEVEN

Such was our life in Feegie in the early years. Maybe it wasn't as bad as I've remembered it – maybe it was worse. As the eldest son, I was closest to my mother and my perception of the place was coloured by hers. A dignified countrywoman from a remote island off the west coast of Ireland, she never got over the shock of finding herself and her family condemned to live in such a place.

Apart from the usual Catholic–Protestant divide and all the wariness that came with that, and the odd shouted insult from street corners provoked by the sight of my school uniform, there was no real hostility towards us. But the very atmosphere was threatening. She never expressed it openly, yet I knew my mother's greatest fear: that the crude behaviour and language, the neglect and vandalism we saw all around us might one day become the norm for us as well; we would grow to accept it, 'go native', be dragged down by our surroundings.

But we were not the only innocent souls in this purgatory. There were decent people living in Ferguslie, though it took us some time to realize that. The evidence had been there all along, in little pockets of respectability that survived here and there like wildflowers on barren rock.

In the better streets you could pass a whole series of neat houses and gardens and see only rare lapses into neglect. Even in Craigmuir Road you could be hurrying nervously past the Undesirables with its dismal vistas of wrecked fences and overrun gardens, usually with façades to match, the windowpanes cracked or broken, the curtains no more than sagging rags, and suddenly you'd come across an intact fence, its upright palings bolstered from behind by a sturdy, square-trimmed privet hedge, protecting a garden with borders and flowerbeds, all overlooked by clean windows with neat curtains and – the ultimate status symbol in those days, in that place – the linen blind in the top window, with the fringed tassel at its hem. We came to realize that there were gardens like this all over Feegie, many of them better than our own, outdoing even my old man's aspiring lupins or – his pride and joy – his impossible, nodding sunflowers. I always wondered about the kind of people who lived there. Why did they bother? Where did they get the – what? The courage? The pretension? – to maintain their tiny oasis of respectability in this wasteland? Most of my pals would openly scoff at these houses as evidence of misplaced snobbery, absurd delusions of grandeur, and I was too craven to argue. But in my heart I was always moved by them, inspired even; they were proof that the human spirit could rise above its environment. To me – and certainly to my mother, who never passed such places without an approving glance and a heartfelt sigh of recognition and relief – they sent out a silent message of sympathy and solidarity.

Don't despair, it said. You are not alone.

*

70

The year after we come to Feegie, a new family moves into the close next to ours. The McArdles, they're called. The older boy looks about my height and age and though I don't recognize his face I can see from his blazer and badge that he goes to the Academy as well. I don't know why, but this gives me a wee surge of hope.

A gang of us will be out playing football in the fading light and McArdle will appear, walking along the pavement towards the burn at the end of the road, trying not to look at us, acting as if he's dead interested in the windows and gardens on that side, or just staring straight ahead. There's nowhere to go. The expression on his broad, pasty face looks superior and feart at the same time, and I think, He's just like me when I first came here. Maybe that's what gave me hope that first time – this new boy could be company for me. A pal, even.

So this day I deliberately kick a pass wide to the wing and the ball bounces handily off the fence in front of McArdle. He traps it – not bad, a bit flash, even – and sidefoots it back. Thanks, mate! I shout to him, laying it on a bit, and get on with the game. So when he passes by the next night it's easy enough to start talking to him, draw him into the game, help him to feel one of the crowd. It gives me a bit of a boost, I can tell you: here's me, the outsider, who used to feel like an outcast, and suddenly I'm transformed into the insider, the go-between who can offer him membership of the tribe.

McArdle's dead shy and quiet at first; he keeps himself to himself. Then after a few weeks he seems to relax and starts joining in at the football nearly all the time; he's pretty good, too, which is a big relief to me – his sponsor, in a way. But then suddenly, overnight it seems, he starts talking in this loud, showoffy voice – bummin' his load,

71

Wullie Logan calls it – and acting the cock of the walk. He's got this loud, braying voice and a vicious tongue when he turns on you. Ye hivtae watch that McArdle, Wullie warns me, and he's right enough. Wullie's not the cleverest card in the pack but he turns out to be a better judge than me. For some reason I can't understand I become McArdle's main target. Snob! he starts calling me at first, because when I thought we were still pals I was daft enough to tell him what Big Hendry and Co used to call me. Then he comes up with a new name for me: Flirter! They all laugh when he says that, even Wullie – he's probably just relieved it's not him. I'm sure they've got no idea what he means. Neither do I, to be honest, though I brood about it for long enough. Flirter? It's true I've been trying to keep in with some of the gang because I'm feart McArdle's turning them against me. Is that what he means? He's older than the rest of us and he tries to impress us, coming out with all these big words. He soon finds out I'm harder to confuse than the others but he's that crafty he keeps coming up with bigger and harder words. I get the feeling he's looking them up in the dictionary every night just so he can make a fool of me the next day. We'll be playing football and I'll try something tricky like a backheel and that'll be it – that's enough to set him off.

See that? he blares. See that Boyle? He disnae even know the rudiments o' fitba' and he tries a' this fancy stuff. Disnae even know the rubrics o' the game and look at him!

Rudiments. Rubrics. He must have been on the R's last night. I'm dying to say that to him, sneer back at him the way he sneers at me, but I just can't do it – it feels like I've been punched in the stomach. I've only got a rough idea what the words mean; not enough to challenge him, never mind respond. But I can't admit that, naturally. The problem is, I feel I *should* know them, and McArdle senses that, he knows exactly what he's doing. He won't leave me alone: anything that goes wrong is my fault and he makes damn sure everybody knows it. The worst of it is, I can't defend myself. When he says these things to me it's as if I've been struck dumb. Even if I think of something to say back the words won't come out: they're trapped in my throat, choking me. After weeks of this all I can think about is how much I hate McArdle. I lie in bed at night praying something will happen to him, he might die in his sleep, even, so I can get up the next day and never have to suffer his sneery voice again. I know it's a mortal sin and I feel dead guilty about it, but night after night I lie there in the dark and pray:

May God forgive me, but I hope he dies.

That he may die roarin'! – as an Irishman I met in later life would have said, cheerfully, without a hint of remorse – *And that the eyes may be poppin' in his head when he goes!* But he was Irish from Ireland, the real McCoy, not the secondhand version like me: he had not been born on alien soil and strained (the very word) as we had through the experience of immigration, that ordeal which gives us our edgier, chip-on-the-shoulder nature, the burden of Catholic guilt without the buoyancy of native irreverence to lighten it, and underneath it all that vague, unfocused yearning, the sense of something precious lost (but what? what?) that must somehow be replaced.

Maybe the sense of loss I felt in those Dark Ages was no more than a sense of solitude. It seems strange to talk of feeling alone in a family of six children but I did. Above all I felt different. I felt different from my younger siblings: I might go through the motions of acting the responsible older brother, but most of the time I wanted as little as possible to do with them. I felt different from my parents: by going to a school where I was learning things like Latin and French I'd moved so far beyond the scope of their experience that I'd become a mystery to them. Yet I was enough of my mother's son to pray that I was different from the scruff we saw all around us (when Big Hendry called me a snob, I now realize, he wasn't far wrong). At times I wallowed in this sense of difference and the loneliness that came with it. I would wrap myself in it like protective armour and moon about like the misunderstood hero (the Dark Knight!) in a tragedy written by me, for me, performed to an audience of one. To paraphrase an advertising slogan at the time (for deodorant soap), I was not 'nice to be near'. Other times I longed to break out of it, to try to be like the rest, one of the gang, but I could never get it right: I'd end up saying something daft that only widened the gulf between us. There I was, surrounded by family and neighbours, kids of my own age, and I had nobody I could talk to, nowhere to go.

This was the boy who met James Lafferty at the Feegie busstop that day.

September 1958

The woman outside is Mrs McArdle from the next close. I know her voice as soon as my mammy opens the door. She's trying to say something but she's greetin' that hard she's practically choking. I can hardly make out what she's saying at first – something about the Manchester Ship Canal, it sounds like – then I hear what it is and I wish to God I hadn't.

What she's saying is so impossible, I know at once it must be true.

My mammy shushes her and lets her in and shuts the door, quickly. Worried I can hear them, probably. Worried about the neighbours, as well, even at a time like this. She takes her along to the kitchen. Shuts that door, too. Something she never does.

Muffled sobs and sighs. Mutterings of consolation. Rattle of cups and saucers.

I don't react. I just lie there and let the terrible truth of it seep into my system. Like at the dentist's when they give you the anaesthetic. First the jolt of the jag, then the slow numbing.

The Manchester Ship Canal . . .

In the cracks on the ceiling I see a dockside skyline at night: jagged, crisscrossed with black cranes and girders. Like prison bars, shutting out the sky.

EIGHT

In the packed bus on the morning run in from Feegie, in the thick fug of underage smoking on the upper deck, Laff and I were for a long time the only two wearing school uniform. (McArdle had always sat downstairs, for reasons he kept to himself – and I never asked, glad of any excuse to avoid him.) The Toerags, as we privately called the worst of the wee hardmen from Junior Secondary who were all around us, had a 'uniform' of their own: skimpy T-shirts, hand-me-down khaki tunics which their demobbed dads had never got round to handing back to the Army, and sandshoes, however wet or freezing the weather. In our blazers and school ties we two stood out, easy targets. But we were big, there were two of us, we could pretend to hold ourselves aloof from the shouting, the swearing, the occasional aimed taunt. We could have bought peace at a price by sitting downstairs, away from the war zone, but that would have been a shaming admission of defeat. Downstairs was for women and weans (and McArdle; even after forty years I can't resist a dig at him, nor a jolt of joy at the realization – it's just come to me – that he was probably too scared to sit upstairs). Eventually we worked out a compromise: if we took the bus from Feegie only as far as Paisley Cross, we could leave the mayhem behind us and make a tactical switch to the Renfrew bus, where we'd find a lot more school uniforms to blend in with. In the mock public school accents we put on sometimes for our own private amusement – Laff turned out to be as big a fan of Bunter and Greyfriars College as I was, and an avid listener to *The Goon Show* and *Hancock's Half Hour* – we could kid ourselves, and we did, that we were only looking for more congenial company.

Least a chap can expect, eh, what?

I should jolly well think so!

But the truth of it was, any excuse to get off that bus was good enough for us.

Meanwhile at the Academy the attacks on the other flank, the occasional digs and cracks about Feegie, mostly from a small clique of professional jeerers in the class, were at least more subtle in tone; at times they almost qualified as wit. They were boys whose most likely re-action to just about anything anybody else said or did was a sneer – as far as we could see the single characteristic they had in common. Cantwell was prominent among them, of course, with his posh clothes and supercilious manner. Another ringleader, Big Don they called him, actually lived in Feegie, up at the Red Road end, but his manner betrayed no sense of shame on that score, as if membership of this clique had granted him some kind of immunity. They acted like a secret society, greeting each other in the corridors and the playground with one fist raised, palm-side out. The Don Gang, they called them-selves. Privately, Laff and I called them the Ministry of Sneer, and tried to keep out of their way.

In any case the insults and innuendoes were much easier to shrug off (Laff's instinctive reaction) or shoot down (mine – my experience with McArdle had taught me to sharpen my own tongue) now that there were two of us.

James Lafferty was his full name. Like most of us at the Academy he was a son of Irish immigrants in the West of Scotland. In the average class, more than half the names in the register would be Irish, followed by a few token Scots, an Italian or two, a solitary Pole.

Laff was tall by local standards, nearly six feet by the time he was fifteen, with a curiously pale, elongated face and chin. It was the kind of face that would have been considered handsome by the time the Swinging Sixties came along, in all their glorious technicolor, but in the austere, monochrome climate of the mid-Fifties it just looked odd, as a Cavalier might have looked among Roundheads. That fierce mop of thick black hair surged up from his head. Cropped as it regularly was in the severe short back and sides of the time it gave him a look that was almost comical. We were always kidding him about this, calling him Uncas, the Last of the Mohicans, urging him at least to let it grow out a bit at the sides, even it up a bit. But nothing doing. Orders from his old man, he hinted, not wanting to talk about it. And that was that. I soon learned that when Laff didn't want to talk about something, especially his family, he withdrew to some secret place inside himself where nobody could reach him.

For all his height and athletic-looking build, Laff turned out to be unbelievably awkward. In the schoolyard, play-ing football, he was a joke. *A Laff*, as some of the would-be wits in the class liked to put it. *If ye want a laugh, gie it tae Laff!* they would chant at his more spectacular failures. Few sports are so ruthless at showing up any lack of natural talent, and Laff ran with a shambling, halting gait that was almost painful to watch. When the ball came to him – by chance usually, since after a while nobody on his side would take the risk of actually passing it to him – he was just as likely to trip over it as kick it. So when the two captains were picking sides in the yard he was nearly always the forlorn last. I was never that far ahead of him, mind you, hobbled as I still was by the fear of making a fool of myself, but alongside Laff even I must have looked like a natural. He played football, in the harsh judgement of our schoolmates, *like a big lassie*. But he still insisted on joining in, refused to give up, would stand stoically in line until one or other of the captains had to pick him by default – and I knew from my days at St James's how terrible that felt. I was embarrassed for him at first, then embarrassed *by* him, resentful even as I was defending him. Didn't he realize he was letting me down, making me a target for the jeerers as well? Didn't he think I had troubles enough of my own? I never mentioned these treacherous thoughts to Laff, of course, but for a time I was seriously tempted to distance myself from him, try to pretend we weren't that pally, not really, it was just that we lived near each other. But I soon got over that and to this day I thank my lucky stars that I did. I drew the line at joining in the mockery – which I'd have had to do to have any credibility with the jeerers – but there was more to it than that. Somehow I had sensed that Laff was worth defending.

As it turned out, I was not the only one. He was mocked mercilessly for a while for his antics at football, yet he had a kind of dogged dignity about him that could disarm all but the most chronic jeerers. In Wee Pete's PT class, it was the same story. Stripped down to his gym-pants, Laff displayed an astonishing combination of superb natural physique and a lack of physical co-ordination so total that he was virtually disabled by it. In our unlovely assembly of skinny bodies, watered-milk skin and plooky backs, not to mention the dismal array of ill-fitting gympants, Laff stood out like an advertisement for the Charles Atlas bodybuilding course popular at that time, though he swore he'd never had any help from that source. And you had to believe him: his build looked much more natural, more linear, with none of the chunkiness of bodybuilders; more like one of those Greek or Roman statues we'd see pictures of in History and Art lessons. The trouble was, he only looked good standing still. As soon as he started to move it was as if the statue was miraculously coming to life, yet somehow retained the mass and solidity of marble. He would have a go at all the exercises that Wee Pete put us through, blushing visibly down through his neck and shoulders – the kind of blush I'd only seen once before – whenever his big, perfect, awkward body let him down and he had to suffer our laughter or, worse, our embarrassed silence. And then he would try it again. When he managed a simple exercise like vaulting the buck – usually scraping awkwardly over on the third or fourth attempt – there was something almost miraculous about it. Even Wee Pete, notorious for his sarcastic tongue, would look on without comment, occasionally shaking his head in wonder. We were watching the triumph of strength and will over a body that had not yet fathomed how to function. It was as if it was shackled, somehow, though we couldn't see the shackles. What we were witnessing was a kind of heroism, though I don't know if we recognized that at the time. All I know is, the taunts died on our lips.

One of the great things about having a mate is it makes things a lot easier.

In Feegie you never know where to look when you're walking along on your own and you meet another boy coming the other way. It's always dead awkward. It's OK if you *know* him – you might stop and talk, or just give him a nod or a wave and keep going. But if you don't know him it's a different story. It seems to me that every boy in Feegie tries to act tough, especially in front of strangers. And if you want them to leave you in peace, you have to do the same. So you try to get that look on your face, too; you try to walk the way that says: *Better no' tangle wi' me, pal!* At the same time you don't want to act *too* gallus because the other guy might think you're challenging him, or taking the mickey. And then you're in trouble, because he can't just walk by and let you get away with that.

I always thought I was the only one that worried about these things but when I start talking to Laff about it I'm relieved to hear he's just the same.

Ye never know where tae look, dae ye? he says. Ah mean, if ye look at the other guy and he catches ye lookin', he might say: Hey, who d'ye think ye're lookin' at, pal? And that's you in trouble.

Aye, Ah know, I say. Because then ye have to keep starin'. Because if ye look away, he might think ye're feart and pick on ye just the same. So ye're in trouble anyway.

Right enough, says Laff. So whit are ye supposed tae dae?

Ah just try tae look casual, I tell him. Ye know, wi' ma

hands in ma poackets, whistlin' and staring into space –
but even then Ah'm worried what the guy's thinkin' when
he walks past. Or Ah'll kid on Ah'm dead interested in
somethin' else, somebody's gairden, maybe, or a bus goin'
past. But ye've got tae get the timin' right, ye don't want
tae start too soon, because ye have tae be still looking at
whatever it is when the guy goes past. And that's you
stuck sometimes, starin' at some daft lamppost or fence
for ages 'n' ages. The guy probly thinks ye're a nutter.

Aye. Or else he might figure out why ye're tryin' so hard
not tae look at him, Laff says. And that's you – ye've had
it. Listen, he says. One time this big hardman is walking
towards me, right? So Ah'm like you – Ah'm kiddin' on
Ah'm dead interested in these wee Toerags playin' in the
street. An' guess what?

I hunch my shoulders and shake my head.

The big hardman walks right past, nae bother. But then
the wee Toerags start shoutin' at me: Hey you, big yin!
Who d'ye think ye're lookin' at? D'ye want tae take ma
fotie, or whit?

You can't win, any way you play it. We have to laugh,
because it's actually quite funny when you think about it,
though there's definitely nothing funny about it at the
time. We decide maybe the best thing to do is just cross
the road and avoid the problem altogether. Though even
then you have to do it dead casual, and make sure you do
it far enough in advance because you don't want the other
guy to *know* you're crossing the road to avoid him. And
then you might meet somebody else on the other side. You
could end up crossing the road back and forth two or
three times, people turning round to look at you as if
you're a loony . . .

That's the great thing about having a mate. There's two

of you, so you haven't got that problem. You don't have to worry about where to look, or crossing the road to avoid people. You can just keep talking away to each other till the other guy's gone past. No bother at all.

Another thing we talk about a lot is smoking. All the wee hardmen on the top deck of the Feegie bus smoke and we sometimes wonder if maybe we'd stick out less if we smoked as well. In fact, nearly all the boys around us in Blackstoun Road and Craigmuir smoke. They're not supposed to, so they only do it out the backdoor or in the closes when there's no grownups about to see them. Except Wee Shuggy, of course. He's from the Undesirables. He doesn't care, he'll smoke anywhere. He's always got fags in his pocket and sometimes you'll see him walking up Craigmuir with a wee dowt stuck behind his ear, like an old man. Big Hendry in our close does the same. Wullie Logan gets the odd dowt off his big brother Chic, but he always smokes it in the close as soon as he gets the chance.

One day Wullie lets me take a drag just to see what it's like and his mammy calls him in the house so I'm left with the dowt. I hide it in my blazer pocket and Laff and I have a wee puff at it the next day on the bus coming home, when we get the empty front seat on the top deck.

D'ye think maybe we should start smokin'? I say to him.

He's trying to blow a smoke-ring, but it must be harder than it looks in the pictures.

Whit d'ye reckon?

Might as well, he says. Gi'e it a try.

All the cowboys and the gangsters in the Hollywood pictures smoke and it makes them look dead tough. So we figure maybe it could do the same for us when we're walking through the scheme. Especially when you're walking on your own. You could walk about with a dowt behind your ear, dead hard, like Wee Shuggy or Big Hendry, and not give a damn. That would give the Toerags something to think about. If they saw you strutting about with a fag end dangling from the side of your mouth, dead casual, like Humphrey Bogart or Jimmy Cagney, maybe they'd get the message: *Don't tangle with me, punk.*

So after we've had a few more puffs at other people's dowts, we make up our minds. We're going to buy a packet of five Woodbine and smoke the lot and see what happens.

By the time we've finished, I say to Laff, we'll know if we're smokers or no'.

Right, he says. Ye're on.

So we scrape up the money for five Woodbine and buy the thin, bendy paper pack along with a box of Swan Vestas the Smoker's Match in a newsagents up near the Cross. We walk all the way home from school that day, the back way, along St James's Street, past the County Buildings and on down towards the gasworks, and all the time we're walking, we're puffing away at these fags. (That's after we get them lit. It's a blowy day and we've used up nearly half the box of Swan Vestas before we get used to it.) First we try blowing smoke-rings but we can't get the hang of it at all. We have to settle for sending out wee puffs, one after the other, like Indian smoke signals. Then we try to work out the best way to hold the fag between our fingers, so it looks like we're used to it, but that's no good either. In fact Laff looks that funny doing it, with his fingers stuck up in a V-sign, I burst out laughing.

Laff, I say to him, and I'm near choking because I forgot about the fag in my mouth. For the love a God cut it out. Ye look like a big lassie.

Whit d'ye mean? he splutters back at me. He's near choking as well. Hiv ye seen yerself? Ye're like some posh aul' woman drinkin' tea wi' her finger stuck oot.

We decide maybe we better just concentrate on the actual smoking. So we practise keeping the fags in our mouths and talking at the same time, out the side, like Humphrey Bogart and George Raft.

Who d'ya tink killed Mister Big?

Hank the Hitman. He sure bumped him off good.

But it's dead hard: the fag keeps falling out as soon as you move your lips. And even when it stays in, the smoke gets up your nose and makes your eyes water.

Ah don't know how they dae it, Laff says. Honest tae God.

Anyway, we keep at it. It's a good long walk and when we finish the first two Woodbine we light up two more under the railway bridge in Underwood Road. This time I remember to do what my old man does, because I've watched him hundreds of times. I turn my back to the wind and make a wee cup of my hands and light my fag. Then I light Laff's, and I only use two matches! I give the last match a shake and flick it away between finger and thumb, dead gallus. I must say it looks great looping away through the air, like a wee firework, the tip of it still brightred in the dark under the bridge and the wee wisp of smoke trailing behind it, and for that moment, watching it, I begin to feel like a real smoker. And here's the funny thing. No sooner has that thought entered my head than I start to get a queasy feeling in the pit of my stomach. Not long after that I realize my head doesn't feel too good either.

I take a quick look at Laff, but he seems fine. He's walking along quite the thing, puffing away.

This is great, intit? I say to him.

Oh aye, he says. This is the life, eh?

At least that's what he says. He doesn't sound all that sure of himself, though. And is it my imagination, or has his face gone even paler than usual? Anyway, that's the last thing we say to each other for a while: the conversation kind of dries up after that. I'm doing a lot less puffing now, and a lot more of holding the fag down by my side, between my fingers (and so is Laff, I notice). In fact I'm not really puffing at all, to be honest, just cupping my hand in front of my mouth and trying to sook big breaths of fresh air in between my teeth instead. It makes a funny hissing sound and at first I'm worried I'll give the game away and Laff's bound to notice I'm not doing it right. Then I stop caring, because I'm beginning to think this could be a matter of life or death and anyway there's a lot of hissing coming from Laff as well if I'm not mistaken. All I can think about now is what excuse I can invent to tell Laff so we don't have to light up that last fag, because I've got a feeling, in fact I know as sure as I've ever known anything in my life, that if we do it'll be the death of me. At the very least I'll vomit on the pavement in front of Laff, and how will I ever live that down? But as it turns out I don't have to worry, because the two of us are as sick as dogs before we even make it to the gasworks.

And that's that. We don't talk much about it afterwards – we're both a bit embarrassed, to tell you the truth   but somehow it's understood between us: it might be tough living in Feegie and having to deal with the likes of Wee Shuggy and Big Hendry and all the Toerags on the bus, but if it comes down to it we'd rather do that any day than be forced to smoke another fag.

NINE

In the early days of 3A Laff and I were hanging around in the schoolyard one morning break with time on our hands. We'd been joking and teasing each other, with a bit of pushing and shouldering that gradually turned into a boxing match. It was all in fun, of course: Laff was one of the least aggressive people I've ever known. Early in our friendship we'd been walking down the Renfrew Road when I rashly spat into the wind, which blew my spittle onto his trousers. He was furious, and with any other boy I'd have expected some form of instant retaliation: a punch, a slap, or at the very least a return of the compliment. Reacting on instinct, Laff made a few half-hearted attempts to rub his trouserleg against mine to get rid of the mess by transferring it, then when that didn't work – I tried to dodge, of course, and for a few moments we were half hopping, half prancing in tandem down the road like some novelty dance team – he just shrugged, blotted it with his hanky as best he could, and forgot about it.

But on this day he looked so funny when he took up his stance for sparring, his back straight and his guard so oddly stiff and formal, I swear he was the spit of John L. Sullivan in his oldfashioned longjohns. I mocked him for it and soon we were both mimicking the comically erect stance of the oldtime prizefighters, fists held high, and exchanging insults in fake posh accents.

Insult me, would you, sirrah? Egad, put up your dukes!

Egad, sir, I shall knock your bloody block orf!

And away we went, skipping and circling, backs ramrod straight as required by the caricature and aiming mighty haymakers at each other, taking good care to miss, or at least hit nothing more painful than a shoulder, or an upper arm.

Stand still, damn you, and fight like a man!

Call me a coward, would you, blackguard? Egad, you'll pay for that!

Then we noticed that another boy from 3A, McNocher, was standing nearby and looking on with some interest. He was a dour, moody boy who'd kept himself to himself so far, and he lived in Renfrew, so we didn't know him very well. But we had an audience now and I for one began to play up to it. We were still shouting daft insults at each other in posh voices, but it was becoming more like an exhibition sparring match now; we were taking it more seriously, or at least I was. I was showing off, to be honest, and after a while I landed a right quite hard in Laff's midriff, accidentally on purpose, hard enough to skin my knuckles on his belt buckle. He winced and backed off, still in character and protesting vigorously.

Low blow, sirrah! Foul play, I say. I appeal to the judges.

Left alone in our imaginary ring, I started skipping around in triumph, clasping my hands above my head, shadowboxing, throwing fast, flashy lefts and rights at an imaginary opponent's head.

The great John L. Sullivan triumphs again! Is there no man who can stand against him? Is there not a man in the house that will take up the challenge?

Laff was now sitting on the wall rubbing his midriff, so most of this was aimed at McNocher. He didn't say anything but put up his guard and started circling around me. It was a while before I noticed that there was nothing funny about the way he was squaring up to me, and he was not smiling. I was too busy playing the clown, feinting and weaving and carrying on with the banter.

Aha, a challenger! An unknown pretender steps up from the crowd! To do battle with the mighty John L.! Little does he know what lies in store . . . !

But this McNocher character didn't seem to be in any mood for play. His face was flushed and serious and set like stone, and I saw now that his stance was worryingly businesslike, with his right forearm angled to cover his upper chest and mouth and his knuckled left fist probing my guard, which was becoming more tense and defensive by the minute. He wasn't tall, not really, just above medium height, but his arms seemed disproportionately long and looping and after I'd taken a couple of bruising punches on the forearms, I began to realize that my challenger was taking this very seriously.

Hey, I said, dropping the public school accent. Go easy, eh?

It didn't make any difference. All he did was shake his head dismissively and keep coming after me. His eyes were fixed intently on mine over the top of his guard and I was staring into them, trying to make sense of their expression, when his knotted fist whistled past my right ear, so close that I felt the wind of it. I knew at once that if the punch had landed he'd have flattened me. This was beginning to feel ominously like a real fight.

Hey, take it easy! I protested again, cutting the play-acting altogether. We're only fightin' in fun, ye know. It's no' in earnest!

Still he said nothing. I was beginning to get worried. As far as this McNocher was concerned, it seemed, as long as you had your guard up the fight was still on. And to him a fight was definitely a fight. In the next few seconds I took a punishing left to the bicep on my right arm which nearly paralysed it, and I just managed to jerk my face out of range of a short, vicious uppercut.

I backed off, breathing heavily, and threw up my hands.

Hey, hey, hey, what's the game? I said, trying to laugh and not quite succeeding. We were only actin' the clown, ye know.

To my intense relief he straightened up. He still wasn't smiling, though.

Oh aye? he said. It looked kinda serious to me.

I began to suspect that maybe this had something to do with the punch to Laff's midriff. I knew McNocher had seen it, and I felt vaguely ashamed, as if I'd been caught out doing something underhand.

Laff got to his feet and stepped forward, smiling his shy smile, his hands spread wide.

Och, naw, he said. That wis jist in fun.

Sure it was, I said. But it came out sounding lame and half-hearted. We were jist – fightin' in fun.

McNocher looked at me. Then, to my great relief, he grinned, an incongruously cheeky grin, like a wee boy bent on mischief.

Fightin's fightin', he said. Nothin' funny aboot it.

Oh aye? Nothing funny about it the way *you* do it, I

was thinking, but said nothing. I was too relieved that this stonefaced avenger no longer had me in his sights, stalking me round the ring.

You *like* fightin', do ye? I asked him, warily.

No' really, he said. It's jist – it's no' somethin' ye play at.

You're McNocher, aren't ye? Laff said, and now I remembered how this boy had reacted when Wee Jazza had called out his name in History on our first day in 3A. *McNocher*, the teacher had pronounced it, with the soft Scottish 'ch' as in 'loch'.

Naw, sir. It's McNocker. Wi' a hard 'c'.

McNocker? said Wee Jazza, with deliberate comic emphasis. Surely not?

We all laughed, but McNocher didn't. He flushed crimson, but not with embarrassment.

Aye, McNocker, he said, with equal emphasis, dead serious. It's *our name* . . . sir. That's how we pronounce it.

His tone bordered on what they called in the Army at the time 'dumb insolence'. Wee Jazza gave him a hard look but, to our amazement, he let it go.

McNocher with a hard 'c' now turned to Laff.

Aye, he said. That's me.

He looked at us both and shrugged. Ma mates call me Nocky, he said.

The words were friendly enough but his tone was oddly defiant, like a challenge. Take it or leave it, it seemed to say. Be with me or be against me.

Laff and I exchanged glances, and I could see he was as puzzled and wary as I was. We didn't know how to take this McNocher character. But we couldn't just laugh it off, either. He took himself too seriously for that. We stood there in silence for a while, in an awkward three-way standoff.

At last Laff grinned.

Nocky, eh? Sounds like a name aff *The Goon Show*.

Nocky looked at him sharply for a second.

Aye, maybe, he said. Then the cheeky grin was back. But a jolly sight better than Neddy Seegoon, don't you think?

It was a good imitation of Harry Secombe's funny voice; we had to laugh. We were all still doing Goon voices when the school bell rang and the three of us walked back together across the yard.

Another dull day in Geography with Big Chic O'Donnel, or When I Was in the Army as we call him because he's always going on about his Army days.

This day he's reading aloud to us from the textbook, some boring stuff about escarpments, and by the sound of him he's as bored as we are. Even his old Army stories would be better than this. It's a dreich, grey West of Scotland day, nothing to look at beyond the misted windows, and not much happening inside either, just Big Chic's voice droning on endlessly. It's getting that bad I'm actually starting to look forward to the wee noises he makes when he turns the page with wetted finger and thumb and smoothes it down – rasp, flap, slide – then the quick indrawn breath before the relentless drone starts up again. I'm just thinking how pathetic this is, and rehearsing how I'm going to tell Laff about it afterwards, for a laugh, when suddenly the drone stops.

Big Chic's looking up at us, his head cocked.

Who was that?

We all look at one another.

Come on, own up, he says. Who's the funnyman?

Nobody says anything. Nobody heard anything. What the hell's he talking about?

Big Chic goes and lays the book facedown slowly on his desk, reverentially almost. Father O'Donnel, up there at the altar, enjoying his moment. Then he turns to face us, hands clasped behind his back and under his gown. Now he's Sergeant-Major O'Donnel, reviewing his troops.

So nobody heard anything but me, is that it?

Silence. We stare back at him. We don't know what to say.

All right, he says, we'll soon get to the bottom of this. Hands up all those boys who heard something.

A few half-hearted hands go up. Cantwell, Carroll, Donnelly.

Aha, we're getting somewhere. Keep your hands up, boys, so everybody can see you. Right, Cantwell, Big Chic says, who was it?

Cantwell is embarrassed to be asked first, you can see it.

Well, sir, I thought I heard something, but I'm not sure what it was.

You thought. You're not sure. Carroll, what about you?

I just heard a wee noise, sir.

Who was it, Carroll?

I don't know, sir. I mean, I don't think it was anybody speakin', it was just . . .

You don't think, Carroll, that's your trouble. So. Are ye all going to sit there and tell me nobody knows who it was?

The boys with their hands up shake their heads. Wee Davie Muir speaks up from the back.

Please, sir, maybe it wasn't anybody. It was just a noise. Maybe—

Did you hear it, Muir?

I heard something, sir. But it was like a squeak, or . . .

You heard something. Why wasn't your hand up?

But, sir, I—

I'll deal with you later, Muir. Put your hands down, the rest of you. This is sickening. Sickening. Here we have a class of supposedly Catholic boys, in the A stream too, prepared to tell lies to protect one of their own. You boys are supposed to be the cream, the future of the Catholic community in Paisley and District, God help us all. You're supposed to be shining examples to the heathen, not liars and connivers. Well, I won't let you get away with it. I'll teach you how to behave. We're going to find the culprit if it takes us all day.

He turns and points to the crucifix. It's high up on the wall above the blackboard, the way it is in every class-room in the Academy.

See that crucifix up there? Christ Our Lord is watching your every move. Christ who died in agony on the Cross so that boys like you could grow up decent Christians. Our Lord has no time for liars and connivers and by God neither have I. So I'm going to ask every boy in this class – each one of you in turn – to come up here and swear before the holy crucifix that you heard nothing. If you heard something, then you will swear before the crucifix that you don't know who it was. Nobody leaves this room till we get the truth. And woe betide any boy who lies in the face of Christ.

We're all looking around at each other. We can't believe he means it. It's daft but it's scary as well. Swearing before the crucifix is no joke. I don't think I heard anything, but can I swear to that? I try to catch Laff's eye in the next row but he's just sitting there pale in the face, staring at Big Chic. Then I notice that some of the boys who had their hands up are sneaking sidelong looks at him. Surely they don't think he had anything to do with it?

Big Chic does what he says. He goes through the whole register and makes every boy go up to the front of the class and swear before the crucifix that he heard nothing, or if he heard something he doesn't know who it was. The register starts Andrews, Boyle, Bradley, Callaghan, Cantwell, Cowan, so I'm one of the first to go up. And even though I'm innocent I'm actually shaking as I stand up there and swear my oath because by now I'm not so sure. Maybe I did hear something. Since I don't even know what the noise was, what if it was me that made it and I didn't realize? What will happen to me now if I tell lies in the face of Christ? When I sit back down my hands are sweaty and my knees are still shaking and I feel like you do after a hard confession, feart and dead relieved at the same time. And that's how it goes, right through the whole class, down to Whelan at the end. When Laff goes up his face is pale but his voice is steady; he swears he never heard a thing. But after he sits back down, in all the commotion of boys marching out to the front and swearing and marching back, the whisper starts spreading about him. By now Donnelly is actually jerking his thumb at Laff behind the back of the boy in front so everybody but Big Chic can see.

Ah think it wis him, he's hissing.

I've never had much time for Donnelly, anyway, and now I hate his guts. But soon enough nearly everybody is sneaking looks at Laff. I keep trying to catch his eye, but he just sits there, his mouth set tight, staring in front of him.

When Whelan gets back to his seat, Big Chic stands there looking at us. He stands there a long time, dead dramatic, milking his moment. When at last he speaks, his voice has gone that hushed and serious it feels more like we're in church than at school.

Well, boys, he says. Now I believe you have all acted in good faith, except one boy, and that boy is damned, believe me, because anybody who would lie in the face of Our Lord in his last agony on the cross is bound for the flames of Hell and good riddance too. For not only has that boy lied, Big Chic says – his voice louder now, getting tense – that boy has cast doubt on the good faith of every boy in this class. That boy has caused suspicion to fall on every one of you and he has sat through it all in silence. Does a boy like that deserve to be protected? I don't think so, and any boy who protects him is as bad as himself.

Now, boys, he says (quiet again, almost friendly-sounding), I want you to look into your consciences before you answer this. Think hard about the consequences for you and your fellow pupils, and for your immortal souls. Does any boy here think he knows who might have been responsible? Even if you swore you didn't know, you did it in good faith. But some of you might have an idea, or a suspicion, maybe about one boy in particular? Hands up anybody who has even a shred of a suspicion.

We're all looking around hoping to God he doesn't pick on us. Some of the boys are looking at Donnelly to see what he'll do.

Donnelly? Have you got any idea? Big Chic says.

Big Chic's not slow, you have to give him that.

You can see Donnelly doesn't like being singled out.

I might, sir, he mutters.

Good boy, Donnelly. Put your hand up. Any others?

Now somebody's led the way other hands go up. They're all boys sitting near Laff.

Big Chic nods. Thank you, boys, keep your hands up.

97

Now, Donnelly, he says. Would you tell us who you think it could have been?

Donnelly looks around at the other hands that are up, checking for support, then he nods his head towards Laff.

Please, sir, he says, pointing now. Ah think it wis him.

Big Chic nods. Thank you, Donnelly, for having the courage to speak out. Do the others feel the same?

They all nod, Yes, sir, and look at Laff. Paler than ever he looks back at them, hurt and bemused, and he's like some big harmless dog that's been caught in a beartrap.

Thank you, boys, Big Chic says, all of you. You've done the right thing. You've acted in good conscience.

His face is grim as he turns and stares at Laff.

Lafferty, he says. Come out here and face the class.

Nobody says a word as Laff gets up and walks out to the front. He stands up straight and looks Big Chic in the eye.

I didn't know I made a noise, sir, he says. I didn't even hear a noise.

You're a liar, boy, Big Chic says, and Laff blushes. It's an awful thing to see, because it makes him look as guilty as hell.

I am not a liar, sir, he says quietly, but with emphasis.

All this does is make Big Chic even angrier and he makes another speech to us all about lying in the face of the crucified Christ and through it all Laff just stands there with his face burning and his eyes cast down to one side as if he's the one to be crucified. And in a way he is.

Big Chic reaches under his gown at the shoulder and pulls out his strap. He always carries it there, dead gallus, like a gun in a shoulder holster. It's not the worst strap in the school, not a thick springy one like Wee Jazza's or McKinnon's, but Big Chic is a tall man and he has a vicious swing on him so it's no joke either. He makes Laff hold his hands out one on top of the other in front of him with the palms up and he starts to swing. His face is grim and he swings down harder than we've ever seen him swing before and the strap whips down and whacks Laff on the palms and after each whack he mutters: Change! and Laff has to put the other palm on top ready for the next stroke. We all think it'll stop when he gets to six because nobody ever gets more than six of the belt but no, Big Chic just says: Change! and swings again. You can see him watching Laff's face after each whack, looking for signs of tears, and you get the feeling that if Laff starts greetin' the punishment will stop. But though all the colour has drained out of his face the only sign he gives that he's in any pain is that sometimes he doesn't bring his hands back up quick enough. So Big Chic starts hitting them again on the upstroke, on the nails and the knuckles and hissing: Hurry up, boy! I haven't got all day!

Watching this we're all feart and angry at the same time, thinking, It's not fair, Laff doesn't deserve this, he only made a mistake any of us could have made. I watch him, standing out there pale in the face, and it's as if he's in shock. Nocky looks scunnered. He catches me watching him and jerks his head in contempt towards Donnelly and Cantwell and co. and though you can see from their faces they're sorry now they said anything, Serve yiz right, ya bastards, I'm thinking, and I know Nocky's thinking the same.

Anyway, Laff gets twelve of the belt, which is a new record for the Academy as far as anybody knows, and through it all he never makes any sound except a sharp indrawn hiss through his teeth at each stroke. And there's nothing any of us can do but watch as the strap keeps swinging up and down, up and down, and his swollen hands get redder and redder and his grim, set face gets paler and paler.

Cynics though we were, or affected to be, most of us in the class were shocked by this display. Not only did we think Laff was innocent, anyway, but such punishment for a minor misdemeanour was out of all proportion. Even so, I was shocked at the strength of Laff's reaction on the way home that day. It was as if he was angry at the world.

Big Chic was a bigoted so an' so. (Laff never swore: he was oddly puritanical that way.) The way he'd hammered him – and for what? Some daft noise he'd imagined he heard. But that wasn't the worst of it. It was the way he'd used religion to justify it. All that stuff about us being the cream of the Catholic community. What a hypocrite . . . !

He went on like this for some time. I'd seen him angry before (though not often), but I'd never heard him express it aloud like this: he was an intensely private person. I got a sense of turbulence long suppressed forcing its way to the surface.

Honest tae God, he said, finally. Sometimes Ah cannae stand this bloomin' place. Ah've got to get outa here before it gets me down completely.

I felt a bit hurt he hadn't said 'we', included me, but I couldn't tell him that, naturally.

Well, that's probably gonnae happen anyway, I said, happy to change the subject. Chances are we'll all be gettin' called up for the Army one day. Ye know – National Service? That'll sort us oot.

We. Us. I was dropping hints. Meaning, you and me, Laff.

Suits me, Laff said. Cannae come soon enough if ye ask me.

I was surprised and secretly pleased. I'd always liked the idea of National Service myself – with its promise of new experiences, maybe even a posting to the far side of the world. But most of our classmates seemed to see it as a black cloud looming on their horizon: a two-year prison sentence at the mercy of sadistic sergeants from the Regular Army (one boy, Gribben, had a big brother serving with the forces in Cyprus and he couldn't wait to get out). At best they saw it as an interruption to their career plans.

When I mentioned this to Laff, he just gave me a look.

Oh aye? he said, bleakly. Whit career's that?

I wasn't sure how to take that.

An' gi'e me a real sergeant any day, he said. Better than Big bloomin' Chic relivin' his Army days and takin' it oot on us.

D'ye fancy National Service, then? I asked him, warily.

How no'? he said. Chance to get away, see a bit o' the world.

Join the Navy, see the world, eh? I said, and to cheer him up, added: Hello, thailor!

It was my best Kenneth Williams voice, and not a bad imitation, though I say so myself. He didn't even notice.

Aye, he said. Get away fae here, see places like Cyprus, Hong Kong . . .

Hong Kong! Just the sound of it, its boom and echo, was enough to make the hairs on my neck tingle. But I was still trying to lighten his mood.

Catterick . . . ? I said.

He looked at me, startled. Then he grinned.

Aye, well, Ah wis thinking more of Cyprus, Malaya . . .

And let's not forget Aldershot, old bean . . .

Oh aye, definitely like the sound o' that, Laff said. Always fancied a couple o' years in exotic Aldershot.

Let's face it, I said. Cannae be any worse than this.

We walked on down the gritty Renfrew Road, slanting into a headwind, towards the Feegie busstop and our dreams of distant Empire.

TEN

On the walk down to the busstop after school Laff and I were joined sometimes by a third boy, Gribben, the one with the brother in the Army. He lived in Gallowhill, and our busstop was on his way home. He latched on to us one day along the Renfrew Road, then stopped to chat with us at the busstop until the Feegie bus came. This began to happen more often and after a while it settled into a routine.

Gribben was the tallest boy in 3A by a long way: at fifteen he was already well over six feet. It was probably the first thing you noticed about him – not that there was any shortage of striking features. He had a gaunt jaw under high, prominent cheekbones, and sandy hair cut in a rough crewcut (though not, crowed the jeerers in the class, by any qualified barber). He was also painfully thin, and walked with a stoop as if ashamed of his height. As a result, his school blazer, not in any case one of the more expensive models, hung loose and baggy from his thin shoulders, like a rag on a scarecrow. This comparison was even more apt in the winter months when he wore an old overcoat (his father's, as it turned out) that was far too roomy for him and flapped about his lank frame like a cloak. He had two nicknames, both inspired by a typical crack from Joe Duffy in his Class Clown mode.

Ah walked intae the classroom this mornin', gentlemen, Duffy said to a group of us, assuming the manner of a copper reporting an incident in court. And behold, 'twas empty save for a heap of old clothing at the back of row three. Imagine my surprise when this heap suddenly arose and addressed me thus: Is it the day we're tae hand in wir French homework? The heap of old clothing, gentlemen of the jury, was none other than our friend Gribben here!

Duffy could be very funny sometimes. In fact he'd said it without malice – he liked Gribben, probably saw in him a fellow outsider – but he was never one to let friendship get in the way of a witty remark. Gribben took it in good part but the damage was done: the name stuck. From then on he was known to the Ministry of Sneer as the Heap, sometimes shortened to Uriah. His other nickname was Grim, and at first glance you could see why – he did have a fairly gloomy cast of feature – though it made no sense when you got to know him, and especially when you saw him smile. He had big horsy teeth and when he grinned it completely took over his face: Grin would have been a better name for him. But he was a bit of a lone wolf, and not entirely by choice as far as I could see. I was put off at first by his odd appearance and these unflattering nicknames. He seemed an object of ridicule and a lost cause, definitely not someone I was eager to be associated with, I felt vulnerable enough on my own account. But none of this seemed to bother Laff; he obviously liked Gribben, and always defended him in our conversations on the bus home. And over the weeks that followed I came to appreciate the good things about him: his gentle nature, literary pretensions that mirrored my own, and a philosophical approach to jokes against himself. He knew about both his nicknames and seemed unfazed by them; and he dealt with the jeerers by ignoring them.

I tend to agree with the great Oscar, he said. (He read a lot and liked to let you know it: he was constantly coming out with big words and literary quotations.)

'The only thing worse than being talked about is not being talked about.'

Well, I thought, you've got nothing to fear on that score, pal.

When we talked about him on the Feegie bus afterwards Laff started calling him Grib for short, and I soon picked up the habit. It didn't seem to bother him – at least it was an improvement on the other two – and as far as we were concerned he became Grib from that day forward.

It never entered my head at the time, but it seems clear to me now that it was my friendship with Laff that opened the way for others to follow. I'd met Nocky through Laff; I'd met Grib through Laff. Maybe it was just the fact that we were mates that made us more approachable, in the way that two people on a night out together in a pub are more likely to get into conversation with strangers than the solitary drinker is; they exude the aura, the comfortable glow, of the pair. But I think there was more to it. When I was on my own, I had dragged my teenage angst around with me like a cross, or worn it like a crown of thorns, in plain view for all to see. I even played up the angst sometimes, persuading myself that it made me more interesting: the martyr, the sensitive soul in torment. I must have known in my heart that this was not exactly an attractive feature, but I couldn't help it; I felt I needed some disguise, a mask to hide behind, and in its way it had been effective, keeping other people at a safe distance. Laff shared many of my fears and insecurities; he was every bit as mixed up as I was. But any mask he tried to wear was transparent. Whatever he was feeling – hurt, embarrassment, wariness, fear – it shone through. It was like that blush of his; he was one of the few boys I'd ever seen who blushed so easily and so visibly. There was no disguising it. At first sight this lack of guile, this naivety of his was almost comical and made him the butt of jokes among the cynics, but it also hinted at the childlike innocence that lay at the heart of him, and it seemed that others were drawn to that as I had been. He offered no threat; he was totally approachable. And because I was his friend, he became the channel through which I could finally connect with others and they with me, beyond the barriers, past the tangle of thorns.

Years later when I read the story of Billy Budd, a simple sailor lad of such innate goodness that the glow of it could soften the hearts of hardened crewmen, an image flashed into my mind of Laff and his telltale blush. I had only ever seen one other person who blushed like that, and I would never forget her either.

I'm at the clinic in Causeyside Street for a chest X-ray, waiting my turn on a bench in the corridor. There's three women sitting opposite me. One of them's a beauty. She must be about twenty-five: lovely face, dark hair, big eyes, glorious smile. Delightfully plump, as the saying goes. She just sits there chatting and smiling; she cheers the whole place up. She's radiant, there's no other word for it. I keep sneaking furtive glances at her; I can't help it. I'm sure she never even notices.

When they call out my name the nurse shows me into a wee cubicle. It's got a door on either side: one leads back into the corridor, the other into the X-ray room. There's pegs and hooks for your clothes and a wee mirror on the wall. Strip to the waist, son, she tells me. Just go in when ye're ready. So I take off the school tie, the shirt and the vest and hang them up and go in. It takes no time at all. A bossy wee man with a Hitler moustache turns me this way and that, sighing and tutting, takes my X-ray in double quick time and sends me back to get dressed. When I get to the door I see there's another door, exactly the same, right beside it and for a minute I'm worried I'll get it wrong. But I've left mine slightly open and I recognize my shirt on the peg. So I go in and shut the door behind me.

While I'm getting dressed I can hear wee Adolf talking to the next patient, calling her Mrs McKendrick.

Over here, Mrs McKendrick. Deep breath, Mrs McKendrick. That's the way. Perfect.

This must be the woman I saw in the corridor outside: she's got the same cheery voice and manner. Adolf's in no hurry to get rid of her, by the sound of him. But eventually he says: That's fine, Mrs McKendrick. Thank you. Thank you very much. You can get dressed now.

I'm standing at the mirror wrestling with the knot in my tie, thinking, Ah don't remember ye thankin' me, pal. Then I hear her footsteps hesitating outside my door, and I remember how confused I'd been a moment earlier. But I don't give it much thought, I'm too busy fiddling with the tie – until suddenly my door opens wide. And there she stands, Mrs McKendrick. She's outlined in the light from a big window on the far wall, and she's naked to the waist. It's as if she doesn't see me, she's looking right past me, frowning, bewildered, staring at my school blazer hanging on the hook. But I see her all right. I can't take my eyes off her. I've never seen a woman's breasts before, not the real thing. And here they are, in the flesh: full, white, round, alive . . . Perfect. It's as if my breathing has stopped, and hers, and the two of us just stand there like statues for what feels like ages, and then slowly, very slowly, in slow motion it seems to me, she shifts her gaze and at last she sees me.

And she blushes.

It's a blush like nothing I've ever seen before. It floods her cheeks and then spreads down her neck to her shoulders and seeps on down to colour those beautiful breasts. And at last she speaks.

I'm sorry, she says.

She's saying sorry! To me! And she smiles, a shy, lovely smile. And then she steps back, in no hurry, and shuts the door.

A lifetime later, that memory is with me still . . . Mrs McKendrick and her blushing breasts. To this day I am disarmed by a blush; I can never understand those who scoff or jeer at it. It seems to me, as it always did with Laff, to be a rare manifestation of our essential nature, undisguised by guile or artifice. It calls to mind the eyes of some alcoholics I have met where the protective pigment of the iris seems to have been bleached away, whether by alcohol or pain or my own fervid imagination, leaving wide open the window to their souls. What it called to mind then – and made me feel doubly protective towards Laff – was the way the rural Irish I'd encountered during a childhood stay on Achill island used to treat the local simpleton. (Laff was no simpleton, of course – far from it – though he had something of the same transcendent innocence.) *Touched* was the word they used.

Ah, he can't help it, they'd say. He's a bit touched, God save the mark.

In hushed, almost reverent tones that implied: touched by God.

Gennlemen, said Laff, in his Mississippi gambler drawl. Time to place yor bets.

Five of us were sitting at the back of an empty classroom during the dinnertime break. Laff and I, Nocky and Grib, and a boy called McGonagle who'd begun to attach himself to us. We weren't supposed to be there, of course, you weren't allowed inside the building during the breaks, but we'd set up an illicit card school, playing Three Card Brag, betting with pennies. We knew we were taking a chance, because McKinnon, the Headmaster, might have been on the prowl in the corridors, but we'd shut the door, we were huddled in a corner out of sight of the glass spy-panel, and talking in whispers.

So when the door suddenly opened and stayed open, pushed back on its catch – McKinnon's trademark entrance – there was a frantic scramble to hide the cards and the money. We looked up and saw, not the Boss, thank God, but a boy called O'Hanlon from the year above us. He stood framed in the doorway, one hand still resting on the handle. He looked only mildly surprised to find the classroom occupied: nothing ever seemed to faze O'Hanlon. I think one eyebrow went up about half an inch.

Shut that bliddy door, Nocky hissed at him. Quick!

O'Hanlon looked at him, then at the rest of us, then at the stray cards on the desktop in front of us, sizing up the situation. Taking his time, he turned, released the catch with his foot and closed the door.

Keep the head, lads. He grinned. Don't panic.

Don't panic: it could have been his motto. I'd noticed him in the yard. You could hardly miss him: at times he seemed to move in his own personal spotlight. He was only about medium height, quite skinny and ordinary looking – an Irish face, with freckles and dark curly hair. The striking thing about him was he always looked relaxed, no matter what he was doing. And he always seemed to be smiling. You'd see one of the football games going on, boys charging about everywhere like maniacs, yet whenever the ball came to O'Hanlon, even in the middle of a mêlée, he always seemed to have loads of time. He wasn't one of the obvious stars, like McGinlay or Sheridan or Jackie McGrory, but I never saw him make a mistake. He'd turn, shield the ball, look around him, pass. Or shape up to pass, then twist around suddenly and ghost through the boys around him, leaving them stranded and bemused. Where the fuck did *he* go? you'd hear them muttering, and I knew how they felt. I used to stand there watching him sometimes and wonder: How does he *do* it?

It was the same with any game he played. There was one game, King Ba', where you had to catch a tennis ball and either pass it to one of your own team or hit some-body on the other team with it to get them out. But if you were tagged when you still had the ball, you were the one that was out. At this game, O'Hanlon was definitely a star. At King Ba', he was king. He often won, and even when he didn't he was always one of the last two or three left in the game. I saw him once jumping to take a pass when he was surrounded. About three boys from the other team jumped at the same time. If he dropped it, he was out. If he caught it, he'd be tagged. O'Hanlon just reached up and before anybody could touch him he'd flicked the ball over his head with his fingertips, cool as you please, straight to one of his team-mates, who then had his pick of easy targets from the bodies falling back to earth around O'Hanlon. It wouldn't have surprised me if he'd stayed up there, airborne.

In those days we never used the word 'cool' in its modern sense. We might talk about somebody having a cool head, not being easily flustered. O'Hanlon was all that, but he was also cool in the modern sense of laid-back, effortlessly stylish, long before the word aquired those meanings.

Now, however, we sat watching him resentfully – he was the one that had caused our panic, after all; even worse, he'd witnessed it. He strolled to a desk in the row near the door, opened the lid, and took out a book. He was in no hurry at all.

We kept watching him. We weren't going to restart the game till he was gone.

Come on, hurry up, Nocky said.

O'Hanlon turned and gave him a look as of mild reproach, but decided to let it go. He let us see him deciding that. He lowered the lid on his desk, taking his time. Then sauntered towards the door. At the front desk he paused. I'd kept my milk from the mid-morning break and I'd only just drunk it. I'd left the empty bottle on that desk to remind me to get rid of it when we left. O'Hanlon now picked up the bottle and looked at us in mock-enquiry.

This was too much. He was playing with us.

Leave that, I said. You don't get money back on the empties, ye know.

Grib tittered and so did McGonagle. I have to admit I was quite pleased with my quip, putting somebody like O'Hanlon in his place.

O'Hanlon was not amused. He looked at me, his head slightly to one side, as if pondering what to do with me. Then, holding the bottle by its neck, he mimed a dart-throwing action with me as the target. He was smiling, but his expression said: Watch yourself, laddie, you're pushing your luck. It was a playful warning, but it was a warning, and that was enough. I couldn't let him away with that.

Go on, then, I said. Just you try throwin' that! Ah dare ye!

As soon as I said it I knew it was a bad mistake. O'Hanlon gave an odd little shake of the head, as if in sorrow, as if to say: I don't want to do this but you leave me no choice. And with a flick of his wrist tossed the bottle in my direction. He was probably throwing it to me rather than at me, there was no force at all behind it, but I was already on edge and this was enough to push me over. The bottle bounced harmlessly off a desk in front of me and rolled along the floor into the next row. Enraged, I charged after it. The card school scattered, anticipating mayhem. I grabbed the bottle and turned, in a red mist of rage, looking for O'Hanlon, my arm back ready to throw.

I didn't have far to look. He had lightly vaulted over a desk into the same row and now walked right up to me, staring up into my face. He really wasn't very tall. His face looked slightly paler under the freckles but he showed no other sign of stress.

Now listen, he said quickly. Don't be silly. You dared me to throw that. You asked me to do it, an' I did it.

112

Nobody got hurt, there's no damage done. So don't be silly. Put it down.

I was still in a rage, but I was also beginning to understand that I'd been outmanoeuvred. I could hardly throw the bottle now, he was standing right in front of me. I could either hit him with it, which would be madness, or punch him in the face, which would be totally out of proportion: his manner was so reasonable; what he was saying made such sense. The only course he had left open to me, I slowly realized, was to do what he said. For a few seconds more I struggled with a collapsing sense of myself, then I stepped back, lowered the bottle and stood it on a desk.

You don't know how lucky ye are, I said, desperate to salvage something from this humiliation.

Aye, I know, O'Hanlon said. But it's for the best, isn't it? No harm done. Shake on it?

His tone was reasonable; he was smiling, his hand extended. I stared at it. Then, bemused, I shook it. To be honest, I had absolutely no idea what else I could do.

See yiz, lads, O'Hanlon said. Sorry about that.

And he was gone, the door closing quietly behind him.

The others sat there in silence, avoiding my eyes. I was mortified, still trembling with rage.

McGonagle picked up the cards and started shuffling.

Aye, well, he said, clearing his throat. Might as well get on wi' the game, eh?

It was one of those remarks designed to break tension that only make it more obvious. The other three laughed, but warily, watching me.

McGonagle looked at me, shrugged, and started dealing.

That bastart O'Hanlon, I muttered, sitting down. Who dis he think he is anyway?

Nocky shook his head, ambiguously. He was still looking at the door.

Ah don't know, he said. But ye definitely picked the wrang cunt there.

Coming from Nocky, there was no higher praise. Grib was grinning now, and so was Laff. McGonagle was still trying to figure out what was going on.

I struggled for a while longer with my dented pride, then I had to laugh.

Christ, I said. Whose side are yiz oan, anyway?

That O'Hanlon, Grib said, shaking his head. He's a case, eh?

I couldn't believe it. It seemed we were all members of the O'Hanlon Fan Club. No shame in losing face to somebody like him seemed to be the consensus.

Grinning, Laff picked up his cards. OK, gennlemen, he said. No more gunplay. This here game is five card stud.

ELEVEN

We're all sitting in the classroom waiting for Riley, our English teacher. He's been called away to the Boss's office for some reason. He's a nervous wreck at the best of times but he looks really worried when he leaves this time; we've got no idea what for.

He's told us to look over a chapter of *Pride and Prejudice* while he's away, and he'll ask questions about it when he gets back. And he's asked Wee Davie Muir to keep order.

If any boy gives you any trouble whatsoever, Riley says, just chalk his initials on the blackboard and I'll deal with him when I get back.

That's a laugh, for a start, especially the idea of Wee Davie keeping order. He's as big a tearaway as anybody in the class. And the thought of Riley dealing with anybody is funny as well. You'll sometimes see him muttering away to himself, even when he's sitting up there in front of us. How he imagines we don't notice is beyond me.

He's an Englishman, quite good looking in a way, a bit like that filmstar Stewart Granger. He's got a great head of iron-grey wavy hair. He keeps himself quite fit – he's very good at tennis, so they say. I wonder how they know: I don't even know anybody who plays tennis. And he's terribly well spoken. God only knows what he's doing in a dump like the Academy. Whatever it was that brought him here, it doesn't seem to have done him any good because the nerves are the first thing you notice about him, the way his face starts twitching sometimes and him muttering away to himself.

Hold hard, he'll shout out sometimes when he's lining us up to go somewhere, the canteen or fire drill or something. Stand fast!

Hold hahd. Stend fahst. Dead dramatic. We all laugh at him behind his back. He must have been in the Navy, and acts like he still is. Captain Riley, we call him sometimes.

Come to think of it, the last time we looked at *Pride and Prejudice* he had us reading on our own as well. He'd been asking us questions about the story and the social significance and all that, and getting nowhere with it, especially when he asked Nocky. Nocky said he didn't think this kind of book had any social significance at all for people like us, you couldn't even compare their lives with ours.

Riley likes it when we show an interest, even when we're disagreeing with him.

So you don't think this kind of thing goes on nowadays? he says.

What kinda thing d'you mean, sir?

Well, for example mothers, families, marrying off their daughters for money?

Ah don't see anybody getting married for money round our way, sir.

We all have a good laugh at that, but you can see Nocky's not trying to be funny. He looks genuinely angry that we're being made to read a book like this.

Riley tries a wee joke to get the class on his side.

Oh come now, McNocher, somehow I don't think Jane Austen is writing about people in Gallowhill, is she?

A few boys laugh; and it is quite funny, you have to admit, the idea of Jane Austen knowing anything at all about the kind of people you get in Gallowhill.

That's just it, sir. She's not. The people in this book are nothing like us. So how come we're supposed to be interested in them?

To broaden our minds, surely? Come now. That's one of the functions of literature, after all, McNocher. To broaden our scope, make us think about things beyond our experience?

Aye, well, Ah just don't see the point of it. It's borin', sir.

Everybody laughs at that, it's so typical of Nocky: dead stubborn, and a very blunt way of speaking, even to teachers.

Riley looks at him. It's a funny look. When he talks his voice has gone quiet, as if he's talking to himself, not Nocky.

You don't see the point, he says. *You* don't see the point!

Then he laughs, but there's nothing funny about the laugh.

I don't hold out much hope for the future of literature if everyone has your attitude, McNocher, he says. And to our amazement, that's it: he suddenly turns away, shaking his head and muttering to himself. It's as if he's given up on the argument. Nocky's as surprised as anybody else; he's left just standing there. He looks around, shrugs as if to say: what did I do? Then grins at us and sits down.

Riley stands at his desk for a while, still muttering, then he tells us to get on with some reading: he's got some correcting work to catch up on.

Now I want total quiet and concentration, he says. D'you hear? Woe betide any boy I find talking.

Woe betide. That's the kind of daft expression he comes out with.

So there we all are, reading through *Pride and Prejudice* – or letting on to: we're at the really boring bit about the young sister eloping with Mr Wickham – and Riley's up in front, leaning over his desk, one hand up to his forehead, poring over a pile of exercise books. But as far as I can see he's not really working on them at all, he's just hunched up there muttering to himself. Then I notice something: he's spying on us from behind the hand he's got over his eyes. I catch Laff's eye and jerk my head up towards Riley. Laff grins and shakes his head. He's seen it as well. We can hardly believe it, a grown man acting like a wee wean, keeking through his fingers – and he thinks we haven't noticed.

Anyway, the next thing we know he jerks up ramrod straight and points at Donnelly.

Right, he says. I saw that talker! Come out here.

Donnelly looks at him, bemused.

What for, sir? he says.

I saw you, Riley says. Don't deny it, boy. Come out here!

So Donnelly walks out looking hard done by, which he does a lot of, and Riley gives him two of the belt.

Now let that be a lesson to you, he says.

That's another laugh, because he's all flushed after it; in fact by the look of him it's taken more out of him than it has out of Donnelly. Sometimes you get the feeling that the old joke 'This is going to hurt me more than it hurts you' is actually true with Riley. His strap's a joke as well. There's all sorts of daft theories about it. He got it for his

Christmas, in a toy Teacher's Set. He made it himself, out of cardboard. Bought it secondhand – it was a reject from the Sisters of Mercy. All we know is it wouldn't hurt a fly. As if that wasn't bad enough, there's a trick that always works with Riley. He always checks your face for a reaction after each stroke. If he sees you wincing, you can be sure he'll stop. Naturally Donnelly's put on a Royal Command performance after two of the belt, and he's got Riley looking worried. It's a shame, it really is.

Then Riley goes to rummage for something in the cupboard behind him, or maybe he's only pretending: any excuse not to face the class when he's flustered. He stoops low but without bending his knees – he always does that; it's some daft keepfit exercise or something – so his backside sticks up in the air under his gown. As if that's not funny enough Joe Duffy leans out into the row to kid on he's looking up his gown, and soon two rows of heads are leaning in, from right and left, squinting up Riley's bum. It's hard not to laugh out loud. The Ministry of Sneer are in stitches.

Watch out, chaps, Duffy hisses, behind his cupped hand. He's got a Seebackroscope!

This sets the whole class off. A Seebackroscope is this daft device you see advertised in the small ads in the papers. There's this guy sitting on a park bench and you think at first he's got a huge black eye, because the drawing's that bad. Then you see it's supposed to be some kind of reversed periscope he's got jammed in his eye, and he's spying on a courting couple behind him.

Anyway Riley whips round but of course by this time we're all bent over *Pride and Prejudice*, choking back giggles.

Riley gives us this suspicious look he does, the noble

head tossed back, his captain on the quarterdeck look, checking for signs of mutiny. Then he goes back to his desk and stands hunched over his exercise books. The hand goes back up to his eyes. We can't believe it: he's going to try the same trick again. Then Joe Duffy puts his hand up to his eyes, the same way, and starts keeking through his fingers at the rest of the class, mimicking what Riley was doing a few minutes earlier. It's dead funny. So before long every boy in the class has his hand up, and we're all squinting through our fingers at Riley. Of course we're concentrating on Riley's hand, to see if he'll try his masterspy act again, peeping through his open fingers. Sure enough, after a while the middle two fingers come slowly apart, we can see his head moving furtively to get a better view . . . the suspense is killing us . . . then the head suddenly jerks this way and that and he whips his hand away as if it's been burnt, because he's just seen every boy in the class peering back at him the same way. It's dead funny. The whole class is like a pot simmering, heaving with the effort of not laughing. Every now and again, wee smothered giggles and splutters burst out, like bubbles bursting on the surface, so it must be dead obvious what's happening, but the stroke of genius here is that Riley can't accuse us of anything without admitting that he was doing the same. We've got him.

The truth is, poor old Riley doesn't know what the hell is going on half the time. It's pathetic. You'd nearly feel sorry for him sometimes.

Anyway, this day he's been called away to the Boss's office and he's left Wee Davie in charge.

It seems like an odd choice, right enough, but I've noticed before that Riley's got a soft spot for Wee Davie, because he's quite clever and he loves to debate and argue, putting his hand up, asking questions. If we had a debating society – that's a laugh for a start, in a dump like the Academy – he'd probably be in charge of it. So at least Wee Davie shows an interest, which is more than most of them do in Riley's class. Apart from Grib, Joe Duffy, Nocky, Laff and me, and one of the ringleaders from the Ministry of Sneer, Big Don Brennan, who's usually top in English, hardly anybody else bothers.

The weird thing is, Wee Davie seems to be taking his duties as class supervisor quite seriously. He's a bit dramatic at the best of times, as I know all too well from our long-ago playacting sessions in the yard, and he seems to have got it into his head that he's doing his tough cop act again and we're a bunch of no-good hoodlums who have to be kept in line. So when Riley's gone and everybody starts talking at once he shuts us up with one of his tirades like he used to do in the yard, with his Jimmy Cagney voice. It's quite funny at first; we're all having a good laugh. But then it starts to go on a bit and we get the idea he's maybe taking this too seriously. A few of the boys get restless and start passing remarks.

Hey, come aff it, Davie. Who d'ye think ye're kiddin'?

Whit are ye? The teacher all of a sudden?

Teacher's pet, mair like it.

Aye, Riley's bumboy, eh, Davie?

It's Donnelly who says that, and everybody laughs. Wee Davie doesn't like it, you can see that.

Right, Donnelly, he says, in his own voice. That's it! You're for the high jump!

And he turns round and chalks T D up on the blackboard. We can hardly believe it.

I say, Davie, says Joe Duffy. That's a bit thick, isn't it? A joke's a joke, old bean, but this is ridiculous.

Ah'm warning you, Duffy, says Wee Davie. Another crack and you're next.

He's in dead earnest. We suddenly realize this has got serious. Nobody's talking anymore and nobody's laughing, least of all Wee Davie. He looks tense, almost blushing, as if he knows he's gone too far and now he can't back down. We sit there and watch him.

Then Nocky says, Awright, Davie, fair enough, ye've made yer point. Can we get back to normal service?

He's not being sarcastic; he sounds quite friendly, even.

Wee Davie looks at him, thinks about it, then nods, OK, if that's how you want it, turns to the board and chalks up J McN. Then turns back to face us. He's really got himself into a corner now; no way he can back down.

Nocky stares at him. He can't believe what he's seeing.

Wipe that aff the board, he says.

Not a chance, says Wee Davie.

Nobody else says a word. We're all watching Nocky.

Nocky gets up, walks out to the board, picks up the duster and rubs out his initials. Thinks about it, rubs out Donnelly's as well. Everybody cheers. Nocky grins at us, puts the duster back on its shelf and walks back to his seat, smacking the chalk off his hands.

Wee Davie just stands there, watching him. Then he goes over to the board, chalks up J McN, picks up the duster and stands facing us again.

Nocky sits for a minute, thinking. Then he sighs, gets up and walks out to the front.

Gimme that, he says.

Not a chance, says Wee Davie. He moves the duster behind his back.

Nocky looks at him, weighing up the options. Then he

shrugs, walks to the board and starts wiping his initials off with the flat of his hand.

Leave that board alane! Wee Davie shouts.

Nocky looks at him.

Not a chance, he says. He turns back to the board to finish what he's doing and Wee Davie rushes him. They scuffle for a moment in front of the board, then Nocky pushes him away. Off balance, he staggers back and has to steady himself against Riley's desk; the chalk falls from his fingers. Somebody laughs, and he goes wild altogether: slings the duster away and charges Nocky, right foot up in front of him in a wild, streetfighter's lunge. Nocky goes into the boxing stance I remember from our sparring match in the yard: feet apart, right hand up guarding his chin, left fist probing. It's a total contrast in fighting styles. Nocky takes the kick on his thigh and lands a right somewhere on Wee Davie's chest. Wee Davie half trips, loses his balance, hops and staggers a few feet to the other side, then charges in again. Same response, only this time Nocky smacks him right in the face, on the cheek; we can all hear the crack.

Wee Davie staggers back again, but now it's the force of the punch, not because he's lost his balance. There's a vivid crimson spot high up on his cheekbone. He shakes his head and charges in again, like a bull this time, head down, straight into Nocky's midriff, under his guard. They grapple and crash back against the table against the wall, knocking over the stacks of books on it, sending them flying. Then, still locked together, they crash to the floor and start rolling about, kicking and punching and gouging.

It's great to watch, dead exciting. It's a lot better than *Pride and Prejudice*. Most of us are sticking up for Nocky, but that's only because Wee Davie was being a pain in the neck; usually he's OK, one of the boys. But it's the first time we've ever seen him fighting in earnest, instead of just acting it in the yard, and I must admit he's a great wee warrior. Dirty, not fair, but very good. It's like watching something out of a gangster picture: Nocky's the goody, fighting fair and square, and Wee Davie's the baddy, trying every dirty trick in the book.

Anyway, we're all watching the fight, half standing to get a better view, but nobody's doing anything to try and stop it. And then the school bell goes for the end of the period and we all get up and crowd round the two battlers on the floor, egging them on, and though we're vaguely aware of the usual ruckus outside, doors crashing open along the corridors and the other classes rushing out, nobody seems to notice our classroom door opening.

I don't know how it starts but everything gradually goes quiet as people slowly realize that Riley's come back: he's standing there in the doorway, staring at all this mayhem. Somebody keeps saying: Sssh! Sssh! and Nocky and Wee Davie get up looking dusty and flushed and sheepish, but nobody's really looking at them anymore, nobody's talking; we're all watching Riley. The weird thing is, he's not saying anything and he's not doing anything, just standing there staring at us all. And twitching. His face starts twitching and keeps twitching, worse than we've ever seen it before. It's not funny, I can tell you, it's a horrible thing to watch. And then something even worse happens. He starts greetin'. His face just kind of collapses and you can see big tears starting to stream down his cheeks and him still not making a sound. We're all just standing there: nobody knows what to do or say. A teacher, standing there in front of us, greetin'! Then he takes a wee step back, back against the open door, eyes cast down, as if to let us past. So that's what we do, one by one, just edge past him, not wanting to look at him, out into the corridor, join the crowds tramping past, just get out of there, walk away. And still nobody's talking; we're all too shocked at what we've seen. I fall in beside Laff as usual and at the end of the corridor we turn and risk a look back. Riley's still standing there, not moving, staring into his empty classroom.

We never found out what really happened that day, or what had led up to it. All we knew was that we had a replacement teacher for our next English period and the Boss made an announcement in Assembly the following morning: Mr Riley had been taken seriously ill and would be absent for a while. We would say an Our Father and three Hail Marys for his complete recovery. Laff and I talked about it later, on our way home on the bus; we guessed it must be some kind of nervous breakdown. And thinking back over the previous months we realized we should have seen it coming. The word in the schoolyard for days after was that he'd been called to the Boss's office that day because there had been complaints that he could no longer control his classes. Maybe it was that interview that pushed him over the edge – McKinnon could be a ruthless bastard, as we well knew. Or maybe – though we didn't much like to think about this, to be honest – maybe we were the ones who had unwittingly shown him the truth behind the complaint, when he came back from that interview to find two boys wrestling on the floor and his whole classroom in riotous disorder.

Anyway, that was the last time we saw him. A week or so later we had a new English teacher.

Talking about it with Laff brought back one happy memory of Riley. One day in the previous term the four of us, Laff, Grib, Nocky and I, had been in the classroom at lunchtime. We'd set up an impromptu game of table tennis on a wooden table that we'd moved out into the space at the front of the class, standing books on edge across the middle like a string of tents, a makeshift net, and we'd brought in pingpong bats and a ball. We weren't supposed to be there, but the exams were over, the summer break was coming up, things were a bit more lax than usual. Even so, we were worried when Riley suddenly walked in, and there was a scramble to clear everything away.

No, no, he said. It's all right, boys. It's fine. Carry on.

We were amazed, but nobody was going to argue. So we carried on playing, a bit self-consciously, and he just stood there watching, in a thoughtful pose that was typical of him, his head cocked to one side, one hand holding the lapel of his gown, his outstretched pinky touching the corner of his mouth, a nervous smile. When the game was over he asked, quite shyly, if he could have a go. I think it was Grib he played first, and if he only beat him 21–15 it was because he was getting the feel of the bat and our absurd, foreshortened table. But it was obvious he'd played before, and in much better company – even with that cheap bat he was getting terrific spin on the ball. Then he beat me easily, 21–10, and I was probably the best of us four (table tennis was the only sport I ever took to like a natural). Soon we were asking him to give us pointers, hints about spin and so on, and he looked flattered, and was pleased to help. Finally he played in a doubles match with the other three and I sat and watched. He really was a terrific player. Yet you could see he still got excited when he pulled off a smash, or used his incredible backspin to get a high, looping defensive shot back into play. For those few minutes, that day, he looked like what his background and personality probably meant him to be: a young games master at a public school somewhere, athletic, smiling, popular with his boys.

We'd never seen him like that.

September 1958

After a while I get up and walk along to the kitchen. I feel light in the head, my legs floaty under me. I push open the door and see my mammy, my old man and Mrs McArdle sitting round the kitchen table. They stop talking and turn their heads, dead slow, to look at me. Their cupsand-saucers on the green oilcloth like wee boats floating there. Everything has slowed down. It's as if we're all moving underwater. Mrs McArdle's still greetin'. My mammy stares at me and shakes her head. She's not greetin' – but she never does, at least I've never seen her. I can see she's trying to tell me something, though I'm not hearing her through the roaring in my head. I just see her lips shaping the words, writhing with the pain of them, her face pale and slack-looking.

She's saying something about Mrs McArdle's news. It's getting through to me now. There were three of them, she's saying. Off the same ship. Two of them were older fellas, should've had more sense, may God forgive them. Out drinking, the three of them, and got back too late for the transfer back. And then one of them had the notion of swimming out – they must have been drunk, she says, may

God forgive me for saying it. And so that's what they did, God help them, and when they got there . . .

I don't really hear what she's saying anymore, I've stopped listening. I already know the bit that matters.

I just nod and shrug. Gallus. Show I'm taking it like a man. Then before anybody else can say anything I walk on into the livingroom.

The livingroom. That's a good one. Nobody lives there. My mammy keeps it empty and tidy all the time. It's for visitors, she says. So nobody in the family ever gets to use it except me. I'm the eldest so I get a special dispensation.

John's a student, she tells Margaret and Frankie when they complain. They're always complaining. He needs peace and quiet to study, she says.

A student. You'd think she'd know by now it's only when you go to Uni they call you a student, but I don't tell her that. I just make the most of it. This is my domain. I go in and shut the door quietly behind me.

A sign to the world: Keep out.

TWELVE

If ye're ever tempted to get a bit big for yer boots, gentlemen, always remember this: the only qualifications ye required for entry to this particular seat of learning were to be male, Catholic and not certifiably insane!

With this brutal reminder of the Academy's anything-but-exclusive status as a school, Mr Docherty punctured any feelings of pride we might have had about making it into the rarefied atmosphere of 4A, and settling down for our first lesson in Spanish. He could have added that we were about to start learning Spanish simply because German – the usual foreign language option alongside French – was not available at the Academy. Mr Docherty was the teacher, French and Spanish were his subjects, and you took what you got. Docherty was his real name, but all the boys called him Wee Doc. He was a stocky man, about as broad as he was long, with a big, balding head and a remarkably expressive face. As the only teacher who never used the belt to discipline his class, he had quite a reputation. He didn't need the strap, was the word in the playground, because he was such a High Priest of sarcasm that a tonguelashing from him was worth at least two strokes of the belt from any other teacher. As if that wasn't punishment enough he'd then make you stand outside in the corridor where there was always a risk that the Boss might be on the prowl. The Boss, as most of us knew from experience, had no such compunction about using the strap. So you could end up being humiliated *and* belted. You couldn't win.

Sarcastic though he was, you had to admit that Wee Doc could be very funny. He had an exaggerated way of speaking that involved much armwaving and facepulling to emphasize certain words.

Now if ye want to learn to SPEAK SPANISH, he was saying, forcing his lips wide in a grimace on each vowel sound, the first thing ye have to learn to do is OPEN yer MOUTHS. LIKE THIS! NOT a sight ye see much in the west of Scotland, he muttered, pulling a sour face.

Just imagine a couple of the cornerboys ye see in Paisley, he said. Or Neds, as I believe ye call them these days. Big Andy and Wee Wullie, let's say. There they are, proppin' up a corner at Paisley Cross, discussing their plans for the weekend. And it goes something like this:

Ye gaun oot the night?

Aye. Doon the pub maybe . . .

Fancy the dancin'?

Aye, maybe.

Get a lumber, 'n' that?

Aye, maybe. Ye never know . . .

He performed this entire exchange, playing both parts, with his hands deep in his pockets and his mouth practically closed. Any words that escaped did so with difficulty, between clenched teeth and out of the corner of his mouth, with a skill a bad ventriloquist might envy.

Both characters remained totally deadpan, and the tone was a guttural drone.

By now we were all in stitches. The idea that a teacher could imitate cornerboys, and even *know* about things like *Neds* and *lumbers*, never mind talk to us about them, was funny enough in itself. And if we were not yet able to recognize ourselves in the stereotypes he was sending up, we all knew people very like them. (Years later, when I first saw Rikki Fulton and Jack McLean doing their *Francie and Josie* comedy routines on television, I was convinced that Glasgow's favourite comedians must have passed at some point through Wee Doc's hands.)

He looked at us now, clearly enjoying the effect he was having on his audience.

Why do we learn a language, boys? To keep it a secret? In here?

He clutched his breast dramatically with both hands.

To keep our mouths SHUT? NO! To SPEAK!

He flung his hands wide.

So, SPEAK! Do what the SPANIARDS DO.

He now switched the setting to Madrid and performed the same scene in Spanish, several decibels louder, this time featuring two friends he called Pablo and Diego. He was a man transformed. His whole body was in motion, his arms waved extravagantly about, his fingers were flying. His mouth at times opened so wide it practically split his jaw, and in the front row we were liberally sprayed with spittle. We didn't care. We were laughing so hard it hurt.

On the way home on the bus that day, Laff and I talked about nothing else. For a while we even tried to rerun the scenes he'd played out for us, though it was obvious that neither of us had anything like his virtuosity as a mimic.

But in those few hilarious minutes in the classroom, I realized, something else had happened. Wee Doc had opened my eyes to the existence of another world altogether. Already I had a faint suspicion that Pablo and Diego might be more fun to be around than Andy or Wullie. Someday, I was thinking, we'll make it to Spain, Laff and I. Someday we'll be joining in that conversation . . .

Sunday night. The livingroom to myself as usual, my homework books spread out on the table and the wireless on in the background. Radio Luxembourg. It's no distraction, not really: the harmless pop tunes make no demands on me. They're background, that's all. Like the wallpaper or the furniture, faded and familiar. And half the time the music is unintelligible anyway, drowned out by interference: the wireless on this old radiogram is hopeless. Now and again something scrambles through that catches my attention: a tune, clever words, a song by Hank Williams, maybe, or Guy Mitchell – I might turn up the volume for them – but the rest just washes by.

But this evening, suddenly, there's a sound like nothing I've ever heard before. A driving, pounding, rolling rhythm: sounding like drums until the real drums come in underneath and I realize it's only a piano. Must be boogie-woogie, I think at first, that always gets my feet tapping . . . but no, this is something else altogether: this is boogie-woogie boosted into another dimension, this is *dangerous* somehow – and it's taking me with it. I can hardly believe an ordinary piano can be producing this, maybe the most exciting sound I've ever heard. And then the singer starts and if anything he sounds even more dangerous than the music. It's a light, Southern-sounding male voice, singing: *Comealong ma babe-eh, whole lotta shakin' goin' on!*

Like no singer I've ever heard before. Totally relaxed, totally easy, the voice soaring and swooping, mischievous, playful, oozing suggestion. By this time I'm crouched beside the wireless, desperately twiddling the knobs to get better reception, turning up the volume – though not too much; for some reason I don't want the rest of the family to hear this. It's partly selfish – the music is inside me somehow, pounding, making my blood surge and my body tingle: it feels as if it's *for* me and me alone, setting off a confusion of sensations, like the feelings I get when I'm sneaking a read at *Titbits* in the lavvy, or the dirty bits in the *News of the World*, or when I'm near Senga Baird, or that never-to-be-forgotten day wrestling with Nessie in the long grass: excitement, yearning, infinite possibility. Such feelings are not right, I know, it's a sin to have them and I'd never dare to talk about them even if I could – and yet here's somebody doing it, singing those feelings or something very like them, singing them loud and free and clear – and by the sound of him guilt doesn't even come into it.

It's as if this American, whoever he is, is singing directly to me. He can't be, of course. All this stuff about chickens and barns and bulls by the horn . . . I don't even know what it means – though in a funny way I *do* – but I don't care. Whatever it is, it's a lot better than the songs you usually get on the wireless – stuff like 'How Much is that Doggy in the Window?' or 'Stranger in Paradise' – I know what *they* mean all right – but so what? Who cares?

Yeah, this is more like it: this is the stuff. A tremendous surge of release – *loose*, set free, at one with the singer. The music is stirring up the kind of feelings and longings I usually try to suppress, it's uncanny; and unbelievable though it seems, *it's all right, it's allowed, it must be, they're playing it on the wireless*! Maybe there's thousands out there listening to this and reacting like me. Maybe I'm not the only one! By now my whole body's possessed by it, I'm jerking and twitching in time to it, my heart's racing, my mind gone . . . And then without warning – a last flamboyant flourish on the pianokeys – it's over.

I'm left so high and dry, my whole body tingling, in such euphoria, I don't even hear what the announcer says about it. Then we're on to the next song, and it's back to normal service: just another boring song like any other boring song, with nothing of the danger or the power or the glory of what I've just experienced.

It's all Laff and I can talk about on the bus on Monday morning. He's heard it as well, and he's as stunned as I am by this record, though we struggle to put it into words.

I know what it felt like to me – like how it must feel to be struck by lightning – but I can't just come out and say that, not even to Laff: it would sound daft.

I soon find out that other boys in the class have been struck by the same lightning, and not for the first time either: it seems everyone's talking about this record. Nocky's a fan, which comes as no surprise, but the real revelation is Grib. With his literary aspirations I thought he'd be unimpressed by anything this basic, this down to earth, yet he turns out to be as keen and excited as we are. In fact, he knows a lot more about it than we do. Has he heard this music before, or what?

Sure Ah have, he says. It's called rock 'n' roll.

I look at him, and I'm almost dazed by the power of the name. Rock 'n' roll. Of course. It sounds so right. It's perfect. How could it be called anything else?

There's another station ye can listen tae, Grib says. American Forces Network. It's better than Luxembourg: they play rock 'n' roll there all the time. Did ye no' know that?

Laff and I shrug. We look at Nocky.

Are ye kiddin'? he says. Ah've been listenin' tae AFN for ages.

Anyway, says Grib, that's where Ah heard it the first time. It's called 'Whole Lotta Shakin' Goin' On'.

Aye, a' right, Grib, I say, sarcastically. Ah think we've worked that oot.

I'm jealous that he knows all this stuff, so I'm trying to take him down a peg. I'm a bit peeved, to tell you the truth. Because I'm beginning to realize that I *have* heard records like this before – something called 'That'll Be the Day', I remember, by the Crickets, I think it was, and one or two others that had me drumming the table and tapping my feet – though never anything quite like this. And yet the way Grib's talking, it's more than just records: it's as if it's part of a movement or something. Rock 'n' roll. 'Whole Lotta Shakin' Goin' On', right enough . . .

It's by a guy called Jerry Lee Lewis, Grib is saying. That's him playin' the piano as well.

Ye're kiddin'! says Laff, impressed.

Naw, honest!

There's a silence as we all take in the sheer magnificence of this. A guy who can sing like that *and* play the piano like that! This is unheard of in my experience. I don't even know anybody who's got a piano in the house, never mind playing it. The only person I know who plays the piano is Miss Deveney, our Music teacher. It's just not the same.

Jerry Lee Lewis, I repeat wistfully, savouring each word.

What a name, eh? Laff says.

Then the teacher comes in and we have to break it up. But for most of the lesson I'm not fully there, I'm still pondering the resonances of that magnificent name. Like the music, it sounds so American, so different . . . Like the music it lifts you out of the drab, grey world around you and into your head and from there to a different place entirely: it conjures up other worlds and whisks you there, like Jimmy's Magic Patch in the old *Beano* stories. Over the next few days I realize that just to rerun in my mind a few bars of 'Whole Lotta Shakin'' can transport me instantly from the racket of the Feegie bus or the boredom of a Maths or Geography lesson to a world of my own imagining: a Western saloon, maybe, with the Mississippi gamblers hunched over their poker game, the baize tables glowing green under cones of light, with cigarsmoke curling and dustmotes sparkling like diamonds, and gorgeous women looking on in their low-cut gowns, their flesh glowing palely at the edge of the light.

Over the weeks that follow we get to know all the other extravagant names: Little Richard, Fats Domino, the Everly Brothers, Buddy Holly. And Elvis Presley. Above all, Elvis Presley. Having been so shaken and jolted by 'Whole Lotta Shakin'', thrilled by it in a way I thought could never be repeated, might even be a matter for the confessional, to my amazement I get the same reaction all over again days later, when over the airwaves one night comes a voice of infinite yearning and loss, soaring clear of the underbrush of static like someone crying in a windswept wilderness.

It's a song called 'Heartbreak Hotel', and the hairs stand up on the back of my neck as if I've heard a coyote howling at dead of night across a deserted landscape. I picture a lone roadside bar on a dark plain, its flashing neon sign mirrored and distorted in the gleaming, low-slung, American automobile, fabulously finned and impossibly long, that's gliding slowly past in the starry night.

This may be the wisdom of hindsight, but I think that in those early days of rock 'n' roll we somehow sensed that nothing would ever be the same again. My mother certainly did. After an initial show of resistance she had resigned herself to this strange music that howled and hollered out of our crackling wireless set as the sound-track to my adolescence. Bill Haley, the Everly Brothers, Little Richard, even Elvis: she could tolerate them, just about. But she drew the line at Jerry Lee. She had always been nervous and ill at ease with 'Whole Lotta Shakin'' but when 'Great Balls of Fire' came along, that finished her off altogether.

Those blatant words, that sexy, sinful voice dripping with insinuation: it was all too much for her. Switch that off! she would say whenever she heard it, with something like panic in her tone. She knew a dangerous subversive when she heard one. Shrewd woman that she was, she had somehow sensed that Jerry Lee and his like were the avant-garde of some frightening new phenomenon, the sexual revolution that was even then on its way (though sadly none of us back in those grey days had any inkling of the fireworks that were soon – though not, alas, soon enough – to light up our horizons).

For us at that time, the battle of the sexes amounted to little more than a series of hesitant and inconclusive skirmishes. But at least the battle lines were clear: they were drawn on either side of the Renfrew Road.

On one side was the Academy, for boys only. The

dreaded Qually, or Qualifying Exam, had more settled your fate for life by placing you in Senior or Ju Secondary according to your intelligence and ability determined by the test. These separate streams usually meant separate schools. As the only secondary school available for Catholic boys from Paisley and District, the Academy accepted all comers – as Wee Doc never tired of reminding us.

The ability streams in the Academy ran from A to C in Senior Secondary at least up to Third Year, the D stream being a kind of limbo for borderline cases who could then either soar to the heights of Senior, or sink down into Junior, in whose lower depths gradings sank as far as J.

Three J was known as the Gardening Class.

Our Latin teacher in 4A, Mr Crane, known to us as Ichabod (*The Legend of Sleepy Hollow* was required reading that year) was declaiming to us from Horace's *Odes* one sultry summer afternoon, when all we could think about was the glorious weather just beyond the tall windows, wide open at the top for ventilation, and the thought of being out in it. Ichabod's voice had settled into a monotonous drone, and we were slowly nodding into a waking sleep and sweet fantasies of escape when a different kind of drone made itself heard. A fat bumble bee had drifted in through the open windows and was now bumbling around in our own Sleepy Hollow, creating a welcome diversion from Horace and his *Odes*.

Eventually – he could get quite absorbed when declaiming Latin verse – Ichabod became aware of this rival for our attention, which at that moment was being flapped away by Laff, waving his textbook.

Oh, Lafferty, said Ichabod, putting down his book with a certain relief of his own. Leave the poor thing alone. It won't harm you.

He sat watching with the rest of us as the bee droned around the classroom.

Poor thing, he mused. Coming in here of all places, looking for pollen, or whatever it's after . . . Not inspiration, surely. Poor misguided creature, looking for open flowers . . . and finding only closed minds . . .

He smiled as we all did at this shaft of wit. Ichabod could be very good when he was on form.

Yes, he said, enjoying himself now. Empty vessels . . . being filled against their will with the fruits of ancient civilization . . . Poor Horace, he added, glancing down at his book and shaking his head sorrowfully. He must be turning in his grave, poor chap.

Poor *chap*, sir? said Duffy. Poor *chap*?

Why not, Duffy? said Ichabod, mildly. Horace was a chap just like you or me. Well, possibly a bit more like me. He grinned, pleased with himself. Shakespeare was a chap, he said. Both pretty exceptional chaps, certainly, but chaps nevertheless.

We laughed along with him and watched as the bee buzzed back out the open window.

Maybe he's learned his lesson, sir, said Duffy, getting a laugh.

Well, I'm glad somebody has, said Ichabod, getting a bigger one. All right, he said. Diversion over. And resumed his reading.

He was banging out the metre on his desk with his fist, as much to keep us all awake, I suspect, as to underscore the rhythms of the text, when suddenly the fist stopped in mid-air.

We followed his startled gaze back to the window, where this time a gang of Neanderthals, stripped to the waist, were trooping silently past, shouldering shovels and rakes. They were low of brow and hulking of build, their pallid hides liberally studded with plooks. Ichabod, a genteel, highdomed Englishman whom the tides of a cruel fate had somehow washed up in the Academy, gawped at the sight of them.

What on earth, he whispered in awe, is that?

That's Three J, sir, said Duffy.

Three . . . J? said Ichabod, in disbelief.

Yes, sir, said Duffy, enjoying himself. Then, with all the grim relish of a man who knows exactly what effect his words will have, he added: Three J is the Gardening Class, sir.

The? Gardening? Class? Ichabod mouthed soundlessly, a man in shock. He watched them out of sight, gazed for a while longer at the window as if in a trance of wonder, then shook his head in bafflement and returned to the comparative sanctuary of Latin verse, banging the desk with his fist as he read:

> *Exegi monumentum aere perennius*
> *regalique situ pyramidum altius . . .*

On the other side of the Renfrew Road, and in many ways on another planet altogether, was St Margaret's Convent, a Senior Secondary school for Catholic girls, although all bodily signs of girlishness were carefully shrouded in the severe navyblue uniform, in all but skirt length as close to their own habit as the nuns could make it.

If it wis up tae the Mother Superior, Duffy used to say, she'd have them a' wearin' yashmaks!

In an effort to spare these delicate flowers the shock of confronting the Neanderthal hordes that came swarming out of the Academy into the Renfrew Road at four o'clock every day, the Convent released its charges ten minutes earlier. So we would emerge onto a road as free of the sight or sound of the female sex (give or take the odd shopworn housewife pushing a pram, or struggling with weans, or messages, or all three at once) as our day at school had been. The one female teacher on the permanent staff was Miss Deveney, a pleasant, lanky lady in tweeds who tried very hard, twice a week, to impart to us her obvious love and knowledge of Bach, Beethoven and Schubert and had got the job in this all-boys school, cruel rumour had it, not so much for these attributes as for the obvious lack of others, such as any perceptible bosom or bum.

For one term each year those of us who did French would have the occasional lesson with 'the French *mademoiselle*'. This was usually a student teacher from Northern France to whom the notion of teaching for a term in *une académie en Écosse* must have conjured up images of some baronial hall set amid brooding hills, with the possibility of a tempestuous romance with the Games master, *par exemple*, a dashing figure straight out of Robert Louis Stevenson or Walter Scott. What she must have made of this bleak Alcatraz-like fortress off the noisy Renfrew Road, the stark grey pebbledash of the surrounding Gallowhill scheme, and the trim but unprepossessing figure of Wee Pete, our gym teacher, God only knows. One never-to-be-forgotten term, the authorities so far relaxed their vigilance as to send us a girl from Orléans of quite startling beauty, with a slender, highbosomed figure and the dark hair, melting eyes and pouting mouth of a filmstar. Faced with a slavering mob of pustular, testosterone-packed youths whose every question was loaded with crude innuendo, it was a miracle that she lasted the three-month term. But she did, she did. I was fifteen. She was my very own Maid of Orléans. Her name was Odette, or Odile, I forget which. But O, definitely O. She filled my dreams, yet I kept her intact and undefiled throughout the most extravagant of my teenage fantasies. I loved her – chastely, anonymously – from afar. Recalling her now, I think I still do.

Laff fancied her too, and in much the same way, it seemed. The difference was that he always wanted to talk about her on the bus home after a French lesson, and I didn't. She wasn't something I felt able to discuss. I even had the cheek to feel jealous and resentful: as if Laff, my best mate, should somehow understand my feelings and leave the way clear for me. Do the chivalrous thing; lay down his love for his friend. Since my passion for Mademoiselle O was a secret I had confessed to nobody, including Laff, this was unfair to say the least. I was even jealous that Laff's feelings about her might somehow dilute the bond between him and me. I was jealous in both directions; my jealousy spoke with forked tongue. And to top it all I felt ashamed to be having such treacherous thoughts about my friend. Shame, confusion and guilt: the flawed building blocks of a Catholic adolescence.

Setting aside these rare and longed-for visits by Mademoiselle O, going to a boys-only school had other compensations. Free of the distraction of their actual presence, we could kid ourselves that lassies were no threat. We could strut and preen and project a self-confidence that we never really felt. The proof was the speed with which all this braggadocio fell apart as soon as it was put to the test in face-to-face encounters. These were at Paisley Cross, where many of the Convent girls had to change buses, and they were not always as keen to bolt straight home as the nuns would have wished. A few of them would loiter in small groups in the entrance to Paterson's shop (Electrical Appliances for the Modern Home) until Laff and I and a couple of other boys arrived, punching, jostling and generally showing off, laughing too loud at our own strained jokes, pointedly looking out for the bus we were secretly praying would not come and even, on a bad day, all inspiration gone, faking an interest in the electrical appliances for the modern home. Over a period of weeks which felt like years, we gradually managed to make eye contact with them, try out our well-rehearsed throwaway remarks, even engage in conversation of a sort.

These skirmishes turned out to be poor preparation for the main battleground, which was the dancehall. Some boys in our class had already been to the dancing on Saturday nights. Donnelly from the Ministry of Sneer was a known pervert – at least that was the word we used at the time: he seemed to have one hand permanently stuck in his trouser pocket, visibly fondling and adjusting his wullie under the cloth. At pocket billiards, Donnelly was the champ. But he didn't always stop there. Sometimes in class when there wasn't much going on, all of us nodding over our books and the teacher safely seated at the front, he would take his wullie out and casually stroke it till he had an impressive hard on, then he'd sit back, bored rigid so to speak, and casually display his achievement to anybody who cared to look. We watched with a mixture of amusement, disgust and fascination. Never one to pass up an opportunity for sexual boasting, Donnelly had assured us the dancing was 'a doddle', implying with a nod and his trademark leer that the Convent girls some of us hung around with at Paterson's were nothing compared to the talent available at the Town Hall and the Templars. Visions of sly, knowing and compliant hussies began to fill our heads and swell our trouserfronts. We decided to chance it.

THIRTEEN

Over the weeks that followed a routine was gradually established. On Friday or Saturday nights Laff and I would get the bus up to the Cross. Sometimes McArdle tagged along – he had become an increasingly solitary figure in Feegie and was no longer the acid-tongued sneerer. Now that I had Laff's friendship, I had gone from hating McArdle to feeling almost sorry for him. Besides, there were so few of us from Feegie who were staying on at school past the usual leaving age of fifteen, that we had to stick together for support.

Hey, Bile, whit's the score wi' the long troosers? Does yer maw know ye're oot?

Clever boays, eh? That clever yiz are still at school! Whit's the matter? Did yiz get kep' back?

Big wasters! Should be oot workin' at your age!

Such were the taunts, no irony intended, that greeted us from idle gangs of corner boys as we ran their gauntlet on our way to the busstop.

And we'd walk grimly on, the jeers fading behind us.

Ye know whit's really.ironic? Laff said one night. That could be ma old man talkin'!

It's funny when you think about it, I said. In any other place we'd probably be the elite!

Oh aye? he said, bitterly. Ye mean, on some other planet?

He had a point. On Planet Feegie, in the eyes of the natives, we were like lepers. In the domain of the Undesirables, we were the Untouchables.

On these trips up the town, Laff usually came to get me. He seemed to prefer it, and so did I. I rarely went to his house; it was not an experience I enjoyed. Apart from the walk down Craigmuir, past the hostile natives, his home was in a block of smaller flats of the kind that usually housed retired or childless couples and old people living alone. So the close and staircase were clean and well kept – pristine chalk-white borders at the junction of floor and wall, an odour of disinfectant – but the place had a cold, echoey feel about it. Laff's mother, a tall, sallow woman with dark rings under her eyes and something of the gypsy about her looks, was always pleasant to me and must certainly have invited me inside now and then, but in my memory I always see myself standing out there on that chill landing by the half-open door, waiting for Laff.

Sometimes a younger sister, a pale, fair-haired girl with something of her mother's haunted look, would make a wraithlike appearance in the doorway and peer out at me, then fade back into the gloom. Apparently she suffered from some mysterious ailment, or so Laff had hinted. For some reason he never wanted to talk about her; he blocked any questions about her with a curtness un-characteristic of him, and generally made it clear that he had no time for her. In fact he had told me once that he hated her, and he said it with a frankness and intensity that shocked me: she was his sister, after all. It was all the

147

more shocking because I'd never heard him speak badly of anybody before.

I hardly ever saw his father. He had a steady job as a fitter or something at Babcock's – a *tradesman*! my own father exclaimed with actual reverence the day Laff told him this, and not for the first time I had to blush for my old man – but that was all I knew of him. He was of Irish descent, and Catholic, but like other fathers who had actually grown up in Scotland he seemed an altogether harder, more cynical breed than mine. He was another subject on which Laff would not be drawn, though in this case fear rather than dislike seemed to be the reason.

And then there was the smell. Other people's houses always seemed to have a smell that was all their own – I suppose ours had one too, though of course I never noticed it – and the one in Laff's house was so distinctive I can almost recall it today. Whatever the source of it (steeping clothes? Boiled cabbage? Some stew his mother kept simmering on the back burner, topped up daily with scraps of this or that?) it was always there, seeping out onto the landing from that dim hallway, a pervasive odour of damp and decay unnoticed, or so it seemed, by Laff or his family.

I remember one time Mrs Lafferty did ask me in to wait. It was a Saturday afternoon, and I was surprised by the warmth of the atmosphere inside the house. The funny smell was still there, but seemed fainter somehow in the light of day. Laff's old man was away at his work and there was no sign of his strange little sister either. But what struck me most was the way Laff talked to his mother, and she to him.

Come on in, John, she said, leading me into the living-room. His lordship here cannae make up his mind what tie to wear. And even when he does, he cannae get the knot right.

The words may have been sarky, but the way she said them certainly wasn't. Laff turned from the mirror over the sideboard, where he'd been fiddling with his tie. She went up to him and started redoing the knot. It was obvious she'd done this before. I'd have been mortified to let my mother knot my tie in front of a pal of mine, but though Laff was blushing a bit, it didn't seem to bother him at all. And her strong gypsy face, which could look quite severe, was now lit and softened by a smile.

The problem is, she was saying, tugging at the tie now and again for emphasis, ye're tryin' to do a *Windsor* knot on a *Slim Jim* tie. No wonder it looks lumpy. What ye need is a *half*-Windsor . . . like that. There. Howzat?

The knot came out in a neat triangle. She smoothed down the tie and ran her fingers behind the lapel of his sports jacket.

Hmm, she said. About time we were getting ye that suit . . .

Are ye gettin' a new suit? I asked him. I'd been trying to persuade my mother to get me a suit for months.

Yeah, looks like it, Laff said. We were up looking at cloth in Hepworths last Saturday.

We? I couldn't imagine going with my mother to choose a suit. I couldn't imagine her approving of any style I'd want.

Hepworths, eh? I said. See anythin' ye liked?

Oh aye, Laff said. There was some nice stuff in there.

Whit colour d'ye fancy?

Ah wisnae sure, he said.

Ah thought we'd decided on the pea-green? his mother said.

149

I looked at her in amazement.

Ye're kiddin'! I said.

How did ye guess? she said, with a mischievous smile.

Ah liked the charcoal grey, Laff said.

Aye, said his mother. Ah think that'll be the one. Mind, they say bright colours are all the go now. Big long jackets, and the brighter the better.

D'ye mean – that Teddyboy style? I asked, not sure if she was still kidding.

Oh aye, she said merrily. Ye'd be the talk o' the town, then, eh? she said to Laff. In yer pea-green jacket and yer blue suede shoes!

We all had a good laugh at that. I'd never really seen them together like this before. I'd never have guessed Mrs Lafferty had such a teasing sense of humour, or that she talked to him that way. They acted more like pals than mother and son. Not many mothers, I was thinking, could have talked the way she did about things like Windsor knots and Slim Jims and Teddyboys and blue suede shoes. And standing there watching them together, so easy with each other, I have to admit I felt jealous.

O wad some Pow'r the giftie gie us, wrote Robert Burns,
To see oursels as others see us.

If I were to film a Laff's-eye view of the Boyle household when he came to get me, how might it look?

FADE IN   INTERIOR   THE CLOSE

Laff rings the bell and waits at the door. Sounds of commotion inside. John's wee brothers arguing, probably.

150

Again. Somewhere, a wireless is blaring. The football results, by the sound of it.

For the love o' God, Mrs Boyle shouts from the kitchen. Is somebody going to open that door?

Laff grins, gives his hair a quick comb. Puts the comb away fast when the door opens. It's John's sister, Margaret – for some reason it's nearly always her that opens the door whenever he comes. Does she fancy him, or something? She's a bit young for him, but quite nice-looking. John never talks about her. It seems the two of them don't get on. They don't even talk to each other these days.

Ye better come in, Margaret says. He'll no' be ready yet.

INTERIOR   THE BOYLES' HOUSE   THE LOBBY

Margaret closes the door behind him, and asks: Where are yiz goin anyway?

Och, you know, Laff says. Just up the toon.

Ah bet yiz have got a date, Margaret says. Somethin's definitely up. Must be. Ah saw John polishin' his shoes.

Laff grins at her, shrugs.

Clyde One, Motherwell Two, says the voice on the wireless.

He follows Margaret along the lobby, past the half-open door of the middle bedroom. Faint smell of pee, rubber sheets, socks. That's where the argument is going on – John's wee brothers having a fight, by the sound of it. They arrive at the livingroom door. It's shut. Rock 'n' roll music can be heard pounding through it.

Radio Luxembourg. Little Richard. 'Long Tall Sally'.

Margaret jerks her thumb at the door.

He's in there, she says, scornfully. Doin' his homework – supposed to be! And flounces away. Laff looks after her,

151

shakes his head in wonder. The female enigma. As he moves to open the door, Mrs Boyle calls to him from the next room. The Big Room, they call it. It's actually the parents' bedroom, but the door's always open: it's got its own small fireplace and two armchairs, and the family seem to spend most of their time in there or in the kitchen. They hardly ever use the livingroom except for visitors – and John's homework.

Is that you, James? she says. Come in here a minute, son.

He goes reluctantly into the Big Room.

INTERIOR BIG ROOM.

Raith Rovers Two, St Mirren, One.
The wireless is an oldfashioned set in a polished wood cabinet, perched precariously on the wee mantelpiece over the fireplace, where it's fighting for space with chipped ornaments, a big biscuit tin, an old leather handbag stuffed with envelopes, bills, sundry papers. On the wall above it, a framed picture of the Sacred Heart.

John's old man's sitting by the fire listening to the wireless, checking his pools with a stub of pencil. His mother's standing by the big bed in the corner, sorting laundry from a basket.

Hello, James, she says. How're ye keeping?

. . . *And finally*, says the voice on the wireless, *Scottish Division Two.*

John's old man nods up at Laff, his finger to his lips, concentrating.

Alloa Athletic Two, Hamilton Academicals—
Frankie and Vincent come bursting into the room.

Mammy, Frankie says, that John'll no' let us in that

livin'room . . . ! We never get to listen to the radiogram. It's no' fair, he's always—

Ah, now, says Mrs Boyle, ye know John needs that room for his homework. He's—

For the love o' Mike, says Mr Boyle, wid yiz wheest?

The boys give him a dirty look and storm out, still complaining.

Mr Boyle looks up desperately at Laff.

Did ye hear what the man said, son?

Laff shakes his head.

Ah, for the love o' God, says Mrs Boyle. Leave the poor boy alone. You and yer oul' pools. I don't know why ye bother. Sure ye haven't a cat's chance anyway. Would ye like a cup o' tea, son? Just while ye're waiting.

She goes out.

. . . *Berwick Rangers, nil*, says the announcer. *Morton versus Stenhousemuir, late kick-off. And that completes the football results.*

Sacred Heart o' Jesus! says Mr Boyle. What a house! Never a minit's peace.

He peers closely at his coupon, then up at Laff.

Ye didn't happen to hear how Cowdenbeath got on, son, did ye?

Cowdenbeath? says Laff. Naw, sorry.

He stands there for a while, stuck for something to say.

Ah see Celtic got beat again, though . . . two one.

Mr Boyle winces.

Aye, Ah know, son. Terrible, eh? Ah, well . . .

. . . *a pleasant Saturday evening in prospect here on the Light Programme*, says the announcer. *And now, Scottish dance music, with Jimmy Shand and his Band.*

Ah, now ye're talkin', says Mr Boyle. That's more like it.

He takes a limp dog-end from behind his ear, straightens

it, pats back the shag spilling from the ends, sticks it in his mouth. With an expression of sublime anticipation he raises an old steel lighter to his lips, flicks it two or three times. Barely a spark.

He shakes his head in disbelief and slumps back in his chair, the unlit dog-end still between his lips.

Ye havenae a light on ye, be any chance? he asks Laff.

Naw, Mr Boyle. Sorry.

Laff stands there, awkward. Mr Boyle tears a strip off the end of his newspaper, lights it from the gas fire, then lights his cigarette. He seems to have forgotten all about Laff. He settles back, absorbed in the music.

Laff gestures vaguely towards the lobby.

Eh, Ah'll just . . .

Eh? Oh aye, on ye go, son. On ye go.

Laff goes out, gratefully.

INTERIOR   THE LOBBY

As he opens the livingroom door a burst of loud rock 'n' roll fills the lobby. Looking back, he sees Mr Boyle rolling his eyes to heaven.

Arra suffering duck, he says.

John! Mrs Boyle shouts from the kitchen. Would you shut the door or turn that rangfandango down, for the love a God! Your daddy's trying to listen to Jimmy Shand.

The rock 'n' roll drops several decibels. The music of Jimmy Shand and his Band now dominates once more in the Big Room. The Valeta.

Ah God almighty, says Mr Boyle, with a sigh. That's a grand band!

Laff smiles back at him and goes into the livingroom, closing the door behind him.

INTERIOR   THE LIVING ROOM

John is standing by the big old radiogram – one of Mrs Boyle's famous secondhand 'bargains'. He's grinning, his hand poised on the volume knob. As soon as the door is shut, he turns the music back up. Jerry Lee comes rocking out through the crackling of interference. 'Whole Lotta Shakin''.

The livingroom table is strewn with books and open jotters. John now steps up to it and crouches over it, pounding the keys on an imaginary piano, miming the words. Laff commandeers the standard lamp as a double bass, plucking at the shaft of it, twirling it now and again for effect. At the top the fringed shade sways and lurches ominously.

John starts drumming frantically with his forefingers on the cover of a book. *Emma*, by Jane Austen.

There is a loud burst of static from the radiogram, then a whine, then the music disappears in an intergalactic screech.

Aw, for Christsake, John says. No' again!

He rushes over to it and starts twiddling the knobs. If anything, the interference gets worse.

Laff grooves on with his double bass, his body twitching awkwardly to the rhythm still pounding in his head.

FADE OUT

Up at the Cross, Laff and I would meet Grib and Nocky and sink a furtive, underage pint or two in some dingy backstreet pub where there was small risk of running into a teacher. Fuelled by the beer, we would speculate on the possibilities of the evening ahead, getting ever more fanciful and competitive, till we had generated enough bravado to head for a dancehall. And there the bravado would instantly collapse in the face of the triple challenge that dancehalls presented: the music, the lassies, and the dancing.

The music was provided by outfits with names like Jim McGlinchie's Hot Five or Andy McLure and the Bebop Band: small bands playing Big Band music that to our ears was bland and boring. Big Bland, we called it. Rock 'n' roll, the music that set our blood pounding, was still limited to Radio Luxembourg and American Forces Network and had to be twiddled and coaxed out of reluctant wireless sets through barrages of what sounded like intergalactic jamming, as if even the cosmos disapproved. Rock 'n' roll was not exactly banned, but nor was it available in any dancehall we ever went to. Like any potential troublemaker, it was not welcome.

Our first visit to the Town Hall nearly finished our dancing careers before they got onto the floor. We jooked and jostled and excuse-me-palled our way to the front of a group of boys standing at the edge of the dancefloor. The lassies stood in their own self-contained groups all around us. Lassies, lassies everywhere . . . Grib muttered, adding, more prophetically than he knew: And not a drop to drink! Somewhere beyond the dancers on the crowded floor, a crooner was wailing away to a bland, neutered arrangement of 'Your Cheatin' Heart'. All the couples we could see seemed to be waltzing and swaying around the floor with great poise and aplomb, at least to our eyes: they were not stepping on each other's feet and they managed to glide between and around their neighbours without actually colliding. On top of all that, they looked as if they were actually enjoying themselves. We stood there and watched this display with disbelief and envy in our hearts and expressions of contemptuous indifference frozen on our faces.

Christ, Nocky whispered, nudging me. Lookit *that*!

For once he was not drawing our attention – our furtive, cloaked glances – to some gorgeous girl. He was nodding towards the dancefloor, at a couple who until now had escaped our notice. They were in a corner of the floor away from the scattered lightshards of the revolving glitterball and, alone among the couples out there, hardly seemed to be moving at all, just circling barely perceptibly on the spot. They seemed to inhabit a space and a strange, spectral light that was all their own. The girl was a wee Hairy by the look of her, one of those hardfaced lassies we'd see sometimes walking home in raucous, cackling groups from their work at the mill: they scared the life out of us. This one was a peroxide blonde on high stiletto heels, wearing seamed black fishnet stockings and an impossibly tight black skirt. This breathtaking combination drew the eye unresisting to the twin bulges of her sturdy buttocks, one of them cosily cupped in the grasp of a big, multi-ringed and knuckledustered hand. Our gaze lingered with dumb wonder and longing on this sight, then travelled up the hairy wrist, past a thick gold identity bracelet, an inch or two of cuff skewered by a cufflink the size of a doorknob, and on up the jacket sleeve to the entranced face of a big Ned, as we called them then: a Teddy Boy of the type we'd only seen in newspaper photographs, usually accompanying some account of a disturbance of the peace in Glasgow. We'd seen a few watered-down imitations of the style posing around

Paisley Cross, but we knew at once that this was the real McCoy. This guy had it all: the thick black Brylcreemed hair with the Tony Curtis quiff at the forehead and the duck's-arse styling at the back, razored straight at the collar. The spatula-shaped sideburns fringing the jaw. The cutaway shirt; the Mississippi bootlace tie; the full drape shawl lapels with black velvet on the collarback; the jacket itself a shimmering electric blue, worn outrageously long, just above the knee (I'd seen shorter raincoats). And under it the drainpipe trousers, so black, so impossibly tight where they concertinaed above the grey suede brothelcreepers with the gleaming square buckles on the side and the inchthick crepe soles. Between trouser cuffs and shoes, whenever his legs perceptibly moved, which was not often, we could glimpse the limegreen neon of his socks.

What daring, what brass neck, to wear such an outfit in a public place, so careless of what people might think or say! What freedom! We moved closer, to get a better view, and gazed at him in wonder. He seemed to have his partner in some kind of wrestling hold: one hand firmly, unambiguously on her bum, the other clasping her hand and twisting it loosely behind him to rest in the small of his back, so that her chest, groin and thighs were moulded to his. I had a sudden wistful recollection of my wrestle with Big Nessie that day by the burn. Meanwhile his floozie's free hand was draped over his shoulder, just behind the neck, her fingers with their pointy, painted nails stroking but not ruffling that carefully groomed duck's arse. Both had their eyes closed, but he was much taller so we had a good view of the expression on his face. It was one of sheer, unabashed pleasure. He was *sent*, as we said at the time to describe the kind of out-of-body sensation brought on, at least in our puny experience, by listening to rock 'n' roll, though it was now being blatantly demonstrated to us that similar joys could be had through intimate contact with the female body, legally and in a public place. How else to account for the expression of sheer bliss that softened his hard, handsome face, the slow sway of his head in time to the music, the occasional quiver of his closed eyelids?

Which suddenly opened. A flinty stare was now returning ours, in spades. We couldn't look away, we were so startled, transfixed by the sudden change in his expression. And his posture: he had stopped dancing (or whatever he'd been doing) and now stood glaring at us over the girl's head. She turned to look at us, but we had eyes only for him, and he for us. It was as if she was no longer there.

Heh, youse, he said. Whit's yer problem? D'yiz wantae take ma photie, or sump'n?

Nocky flushed angrily and for a terrible moment I worried he might respond in kind. Laff, who was nearest, stepped in with his most disarming smile.

Whit? Aw, naw, he said. We were jist . . . ye know . . . watchin' the dancin' . . .

It sounded miserably lame. The Ned stood there and stared at us for about ten seconds, which felt like minutes, just to make his point. One by one we all looked away – Laff took Nocky by the elbow, to my great relief, and steered him to one side – and tried to look just as interested in the other couples.

Aye, right, we heard him say, finally. Well . . . jist watch it then.

He turned back to his partner. Out of the corner of my eye I caught the look she shot at us – one of total, bored contempt – before blending once more into his landscape.

So we stood, watching the dancing, trying to make sense of our surroundings.

Around the edge of the dancefloor stood tight little knots of young men and separate, looser knots of young women. Often the two camps were within an elbow's nudge of each other, but they acted as if they were separated by walls of bulletproof glass. The lassies seemed to spend all their time and energy taking a keen interest in talking to each other and totally ignoring us. We stood there in silence with bored, couldn't-give-a-toss expressions, under cover of which we were trying to eye them up without doing anything as crass as actually *looking*. So much energy went into all this posing and posturing, it was a wonder we had any left for dancing.

But then, who wanted to dance? As we soon found out, before repeated humiliation taught us to be more wary, not many of these lassies. To cross the invisible barrier between the groups, confront the girl of your choice and say: Are ye dancin'? without first having gone through a remote mating ritual of exchanged glances, half-nods and enigmatic smiles, as elaborate and nuanced as any Regency fan-play, was an act of sheerest folly. When the inevitable refusal came, you had an agonizing decision to make. Should I ask somebody else? And risk another refusal? And then what? Or should I just cut my losses, turn and try to swagger back to the boys (who've just witnessed my humiliation)? What can I possibly think of to say to them that will make me look any less of a clown than I do already?

By our second or third visit we were glumly convinced that some of these lassies went to the dancing just for the fun of not dancing. Or at least the pleasure of refusing. They had no shortage of victims to practise on, and they had so refined their version of the standard refusal – Naw, thanks – that the two simple words could take on an entire range of coded meanings, depending on your sensitivity quotient on the night.

Who d'ye think ye are?

Ye must be jokin', Jimmy.

Get away fae me, ya wurm, ye.

So when you finally led a lassie out onto the floor it felt like triumph. But it could be short-lived. And not only because our shortcomings, our dancing skills which rated somewhere between the duff and the non-existent, would then be painfully exposed. There were other obstacles, even tougher to surmount.

One night Grib was dancing with a gorgeous blonde shopgirl from Woolworths in the High Street. At least, he was holding her at arm's length and they were shuffling around more or less in time to the music. After the usual awkward moments at the start he had recovered his composure enough to risk a bit of conversation.

Whit d'ye think o' it the night? he asked her, flashing his best smile.

Och, it's no' bad, she said, looking languidly around through lashes heavy with mascara. Too many lassies, though.

Somehow Grib's glib way with a literary quote had persuaded him that he was a bit of a patter merchant.

Oh, well, he said, smoothly. Surely that shouldnae bother a girl like *you*.

The mascaraed eyes drilled straight through him.

Get scrubbed, ya big sook, she said.

Out on the dancefloor, our embarrassment was so intense it bordered on pain. All the timing and coordination that came naturally enough to us on the football field (except for Laff, of course) deserted us. Expecting the likes of us to step onto the floor, take a strange lassie in our arms and then swirl away in a waltz, foxtrot or quickstep was like asking Laff to weave down the wing with the ball at his feet, swerving past defenders with all the grace and artistry of Charlie Tully, the legendary winger at Celtic Park. As we'd have said in those days, it was just not on. Having managed to get up the nerve to ask a lassie to dance, we then had to face the test of the dance itself. Like Buster Crabbe at the picture serials, we had made it through one ordeal only to be plunged straight into another. Shackled by inhibition, hobbled by ineptitude, we shambled around the floor like walking wounded, holding our wary partners at arm's length.

We learned that we could rely on certain moments in the band's set to bring relief. On a bad night we even looked forward to the Drum Solo. The Drum Solo was supposed to be the high point of the evening, and probably was – for the drummer. For us it was just another irritant, another ordeal to expose and test the adolescent confusion we were at such pains to hide. Yet this was something you had to pretend to like, or risk being called a square. For the life of me I could never understand it. About halfway through their set, in the middle of a number, the other musicians would gradually stop playing and, one by one, make a great show of leaving the stage to the drummer. In the better dancehalls, he would be spotlit, alone on the empty stage. He would then lash up a lather of hysteria, thrashing the skins off his drums, shattering the cymbals. (Givin' it Laldi, we used to say at the time, though we had no idea what it meant. I've read somewhere since that it referred to an obscure Italian

162

bandleader whose extravagant, frankly demented style of conducting on a long-ago tour of Scotland had won him the kind of immortality his music was never to achieve.) Meanwhile, down on the dancefloor, one after another, couples gave up trying to dance to this racket and shuffled sheepishly to a halt.

A terrible confusion now took over. On the plus side, you could relax leg muscles that had gone as stiff as boards with the effort of not stepping on your partner. But now you had another problem: what to say, what to do with this exotic, scented creature you held in a half-embrace, now that the music, the only possible excuse for the embrace, had stopped? The gallus thing to do was to gaze knowledgeably in the general direction of the drummer, one tentative, would-be casual arm round the lassie's waist, tapping your feet and and twitching in rough time to the rhythm, nodding and grimacing your appreciation of the more deafening crescendos. The challenge was to carry this off without looking like the local nutter.

Then there was the crooner's obligatory Frank Sinatra number, which brought comparative bliss. Not that we liked Frank Sinatra – in the age of rock 'n' roll, this was no music for young men. But it always meant a slow dance, a waltz maybe, which seemed to call for little more than the ability to shuffle around the floor while gingerly holding a lassie slightly closer than usual, so close that at times you might brush or bump her thighs. If things were going well, you might find one who would let you wrestle her round in throbbing slow motion, like the big Ned and the wee Hairy we'd seen on our first visit, in that stranglehold we now knew as the Moonie, which was sexual harassment set to music. If things were going *really* well, you might even pull off the ultimate triumph and 'get a lumber'. Getting a lumber meant taking a lassie home on the bus, invariably to some outlying scheme on the far side of town. The reward was an awkward clinch in the back of the close, the stale odours of the outside lavvy just about held at bay by the heady cocktail of sticky textures and clashing aromas – her cheap scent, powder and lipstick; your Brylcreem, plook ointment and Old Spice – while you struggled to gauge the size and texture of her breasts through a brassiere so wired and upholstered it could have thwarted a burglar's jemmy. But oh what triumph, what delirium, when you managed to outwit those defences – or when the lassie, incredibly, dismantled them for you – and for a few fleeting moments those sleek and weighted globes fluttered in your hands! Like doves: hefted, winged, poised for flight. And then later – 'much later', as they used to write in the *Woman's Own* stories of the day – for time might stand still in these huddles of sweat and swoon but the last bus waits for no man, there was the anticlimax of the long trek home, bent almost double with thwarted lust, through the bracing drizzle that nature had thoughtfully laid on.

Most evenings, though, we had no such luck and we'd stand around at the Cross afterwards as if reluctant to leave the bright lights, talking amongst ourselves, eyeing the chattering groups of lassies that passed, in the vague hope that some miracle might yet happen to redeem the evening, some outlet for the energy that the dancing had stirred up and was still marking time inside us, pounding away in there with nowhere to go. Then we'd take our separate ways home, Grib and Nocky towards the Renfrew Road, Laff and I walking back along the High Street to comfort ourselves with a takeaway fish supper from the chippie at the West End before wandering back to the scheme along a dark, near-deserted Blackstoun Road, only speeding up to overtake or bodyswerve the occasional staggering drunk.

It was on these long walks home, joking or philosophizing about the events and non-events of the evening, our wild hopes at the start of it, the flat letdown at the end, that we began to have the heart-to-heart conversations that changed the nature of our friendship. Slowly we became aware, without ever mentioning it of course, that we were more than just mates: we were soulmates.

In the self-consciously macho culture of the West of Scotland at that time, your best mate was the most important person in your life outside your family. You might not take sides against your own brother for your mate's sake, but it would be a close call, and you would stand by him against all others. Girls, and certainly the casual acquaintances of one night at the dancing, came a poor second. If you got a lumber and your mate didn't, and he showed signs of being in trouble or depressed about that, you might even go so far as to sacrifice the lumber and keep your mate company instead. The girls would understand, having been brought up in the same code. In that harsh workingclass climate where homosexuals were not even talked about, except in the odd dirty joke or scathing aside about poofs or queers – in all my teenage years in Scotland, I never met one, or even had one pointed out to me – it was quite common to see two mates, clearly the better for drink, staggering home in the evening from the dancing, or in the late afternoon from the football at Love Street, their arms linked over each other's shoulders, their heads affectionately nuzzling, like a courting couple.

And sometimes at the dancing, at the fag-end of the evening, you'd see a pair of them, tanked up with drink and fed up with the constant refusals of women who seemed to prefer dancing with each other, taking the floor together in revenge and shuffling around in awkward embrace, like some defiant parody of *Come Dancing*, or some witless echo of disappointed men in another time, another macho culture, pacing out the sad geometry of the tango in the dockside bars of Buenos Aires.

FOURTEEN

It was Big Eamon Gallagher who told us about the Jack Douglas Academy of Dance. Big Eamon was an Irishman we'd got talking to at the Town Hall one night. He was a bit older than us and he came from Mullingar, in Westmeath, and he had a teuchter Irish accent that we'd made fun of at first – though never to his face; he wasn't called Big Eamon for nothing, and we'd heard he could be a rough handful when roused. But he had a broad hand-some face and a good-natured way about him and the reputation of being a great ladies' man. We all looked up to him. He was the only guy we knew who could dance ballroom so it didn't look like the cissy posturing it felt like whenever we tried it. We'd stand there, sick with envy, and watch him gliding and dipping around the floor with some impossibly glamorous girl we'd all lusted after from afar but hadn't had the gumption to approach. Then he would leave with her at the end of the evening, with a sly wink to us over his shoulder as he guided her out through the exit, one large proprietary mitt in the small of her back. The Ladykiller, we called him.

Ah now, don't knock the old ballroom dancin', lads, he

told us one night on the way home. (For some reason he hadn't got a lumber that night – maybe he needed the rest.) It's yer Open Sesame to the women. 'Tis. The trick is to make them feel good, ye see, feel they're lookin' good. That's all there is to it. If ye half know what ye're about, ye're made. For a start, your crutch is right up against hers, now, isn't it? And it's all legal and above board as well, that's the beauty of it, because in ballroom that's how it's supposed to be. Now where else are ye goin' to get a chance to suss them out like that? Forget yer Moonie, it might give ye a cheap thrill for a couple o' minutes but where does that get ye? Unless she's mad for it, of course. And how many of *them* do ye come across? It's like Fred Astaire says: Ya gotta make yer partner look good. Ah, Fred's the boy has the trick of it. Make them look good in front of their pals, and ye'll have them eatin' out o' yer hands. An' I didn't just pick it up off the floor, either. I took a few dancing lessons a while back. If ye play yer cards right, they'll give ye a free trial lesson. Ye should give it a try, lads. It'll work wonders for ye, believe me.

And that's how the four of us, Laff, Grib, Nocky and I, came to be standing one winter night outside a door whose worn brass plaque proclaimed *The Jack Douglas Academy of Dance*. We exchanged sheepish looks. What lunacy, we were wondering, could have brought us to a place like this? Nocky, who had never wanted to come, now wanted to go. But Laff shrugged, in for a penny, and rang the bell.

Jack Douglas was a portly man of middle height, with receding gingery hair and a walrus moustache soggy at the ends. He looked like an insurance salesman down on his luck, and in an earlier life might well have been. He wore a brown suit and black patentleather shoes on which he was promisingly light as he led us up the narrow staircase and into a large, darkened hall.

Come in, lads, come on in. Yiz're a wee bit early but that's just as well since it's yer first time, eh? Just hang on here a minute, he said at the doorway and twinkletoed away across the floor. I'll just lay on some amby-yonce. The amby-yonce is all important, as ye'll see.

He flicked a couple of switches and a huge, dusty chandelier in the high ceiling sputtered into dim life, lighting up the big room and its highly polished wood floor. Another light came on above the raised platform at one end where Douglas now appeared, sliding a glossy seventy-eight from its cover and putting it on a huge radiogram that stood centre stage. Any faint hopes that might have stirred in our hearts at the sight of it – it was the size and shape of a jukebox – were killed stone dead when the insipid sounds of Victor Sylvester seeped into the hall.

We always start beginners off wi' the foxtrot, he said, stepping down to join us on the dancefloor. The foxtrot's yer basic step. Slow, slow, quick, quick, slow. If ye can get the hang o' that, ye'll soon pick up the rest. Right, then, let's get yiz lined up in a row facing me, about a couple of feet apart.

Not daring to look at one another, we shuffled into line. We were all wondering the same thing. *Where are the lassies? Surely he's no' expectin' us tae dance wi' each other?* Douglas stood facing us, dapper, feet together, back straight. With surprising, almost balletic grace, he placed his arms around an imaginary partner.

This is the start position. Yer right arm circling her waist, right hand, gently does it, on the small of her back. Try and keep it nice and loose, lads, ye're dancing with her, not crushing her to death. Left arm out to the side, gently bent at the elbow, like that. Left hand open, loosely supporting yer partner's right hand. No need to squeeze, we're not armwrestling, ye know.

He moved slowly along the line, inspecting our postures, making adjustments here and there. He spent the longest time with Nocky. This was not a smart move. Nocky was our token hardnut, a hothead with a low flashpoint. Douglas had no way of knowing it, but he was placing himself at serious risk.

No, no, that's no good at all, he kept saying. Ye're as stiff as a board, laddie. This is not the Army, ye know. Ye're dancing, not standing to attention.

Seeing Nocky's resentful flush as his arms were pulled this way and that I began to fear for the man's safety. I had seen Nocky put the head on people for less provocation than this. But then Laff gave way to a giggling fit in which we all joined and even Nocky's taut mask eased into a sheepish grin.

Douglas now lined us up in single file behind him and, still holding our phantom partners in awkward embrace, we shuffled off in his wake around the floor, muttering in time with him ... Slow slow quickquick slow. Trying desperately to avoid each other's eyes we'd suddenly exchange a fleeting, mortified glance and burst out laughing. All except Nocky, who was stalking around the floor like Frankenstein's monster taking his first lumbering steps, and glowering at anyone who dared look in his direction. Having resented the absence of any girls, we were now thanking God in his heaven that there were none around to witness our humiliation.

But by the time Victor Sylvester was into his third or fourth number of the evening, the mood had begun to change. Grib, who was just behind the instructor, was picking up something of his rhythm and flow. He was starting to take it seriously, even adding little flourishes of his own. In spite of myself I could feel the music shaping my movements, too. It was the same with the others. It seemed to be turning into a competition, something even Nocky could respond to. Soon we were vying with each other to see who could come up with the smoothest turns, the fanciest flourishes. Grib was beginning to look like an old hand. Nocky was away in a wee world of his own. Even Laff was achieving something approaching co-ordinated movement. As the music played on we gradually stopped watching each other and began to concentrate more on ourselves, on our phantom partners and the intimate world of music and movement that we shared. I saw myself as Big Eamon, gliding round the floor with a gorgeous girl in my arms. My feet no longer dragged but seemed to skim across the floor; I changed direction with a flick of the head and a graceful dip of the shoulders. I could hardly wait to try out my skills on a real girl. I was Fred Astaire, I was Gene Kelly. I was dancing! We all were.

It was the look on Nocky's face that told me something had gone seriously wrong. He'd suddenly stopped dead in mid-pirouette and now stood with his hands thrust deep into his pockets, grunting out a curse. He had flushed crimson and he was glaring at me like a man betrayed. I stared back at him, uncomprehending. He jerked his chin viciously over his shoulder. I looked, and I saw. The full horror of our situation became clear.

Unnoticed by us a group of girls in their Saturday night finery had trooped silently into the hall and were now lined up along the far wall, watching us with horrified fascination. The worst of it was, they weren't even laughing. Their expressions ranged from incredulous scorn to profound pity. They had obviously been there for some time.

Mortified, we all stopped dead in our tracks and looked at one another. Then we turned to Nocky, as always, for guidance in time of trouble.

Nocky glared back at us, then mutinously at the girls.

Fuck this for a caper, he said viciously, out loud, for their benefit, and, tweaking his jacket closed at the belly-button with the approved finger-and-thumb pincergrip of the gallus man, swaggered towards the door. The rest of us mumbled our excuses and stumbled after him. Douglas came trotting behind us, protesting mildly, but we shrugged him off on the stairs. Within seconds we were back on the street and striding out in grim mortification for the nearest pub. Our brief careers as ladykillers were at an end.

Such were the great tragic paradoxes of our troubled adolescence in the dancehalls. The only dancing available was dancing we couldn't do. The only music available was music we didn't like. The music we *did* like, the rock 'n' roll that had us hopping about like mad dervishes in the privacy of our livingrooms and bedrooms, was not available to us except on the wireless at home, or on jukeboxes in coffee bars, where dancing was very definitely not on the menu. The idea of getting up in a crowded café and, in the modern phrase, 'getting down', would never have entered our heads. Sitting there as if nailed down in our Formica-topped seats, fenced in by Formica-topped tables, all we could do was listen. But all the while our nerve-ends were tingling, our shoulders twitching, our feet compulsively tapping – our bodies might be trapped but our minds were soaring: in our hearts and souls we were dancing like crazy.

The jukebox was the only chance we got to listen to rock 'n' roll in company. The effect of the music on us was still intensely private: each of us was 'sent' in his own way, into his own little dreamworld; but at the same time you could see it working the same magic on other people: there was a sense of sharing and companionship. We were like the audience at a theatre performance where the jukebox was stage, lighting, soundtrack and star.

The jukebox is in a coffee bar near St Mirin's Cathedral. The name above the door says the East End Café but everybody calls it Corrieri's. What you drink there is coffee, that's what you're supposed to order, that's the new, trendy drink, not like the boring old tea you always get at home and definitely not like Camp Coffee – that tangy, treacly-looking stuff that comes out of an oblong bottle. That's the only coffee I've ever tasted before and I think maybe it's the same for everybody else because there's always a bottle of it, half-empty and neglected, stuck at the back of the press in people's kitchens.

So we all sit there in Corrieri's, sipping this brown, bitter coffee, kidding on we like it, talking amongst ourselves and trying to eye up any lassies that are there – A' the wee Hairies go intae Corrieri's, goes the saying at the time. But most of all we're listening to the jukebox.

The jukebox in Corrieri's café was the first I ever saw, and it was love at first sight. And that was before I even heard the sounds that came out of it. I'd never seen anything like it. There it stood, monumental, mysterious, rounded and curved like the lines of the extravagant

American cars we'd all seen in *Rebel Without a Cause* and *The Girl Can't Help It*. There it stands, in my memory, outlined in neon, gleaming with chrome, shimmering with lights of many colours, and it's like some space vessel from a distant galaxy miraculously landed in our midst, a dazzling vision of otherness, a fantasy of escape. That shifting, iridescent aura around it is like a promise or a dream and all you have to do to reach it is put sixpence in the slot and press the button. Then you hear its innards working the way they do, click and whirr and click again, and 'Blue Suede Shoes' or maybe 'Twentieth Flight Rock' comes pounding and pulsing out of it, this rock 'n' roll music that lifts you out of your surroundings, out of your shackled body and into your dreams, free to roam your own inner landscapes of yearning and fantasy.

This dream machine has to be approached with due reverence. In the early days, before practice turns it almost into routine, I walk across the floor to the jukebox as if to a gorgeous girl I've at last worked up the courage to ask for a dance. The feelings are the same: the fear, the antici- pation, the excitement ... above all the crippling self-consciousness of that walk across the floor, under the critical eyes of the crowd in the café. Of course the chances are they don't give a toss about me one way or the other but that's not how it feels. It feels as if every- body's watching me, what I'm wearing, how I'm walking. The walk especially has to be just right, casual, just gallus enough so you look confident without being a showoff or acting the hardman. Usually I have to fake a big yawn halfway across the floor to unstick the lump in my throat and I only hope this makes me look dead nonchalant instead of dying of nerves, which is what I am. When you make it to the jukebox it's like docking safely in port after a rough crossing on a stormy sea. Everything slows down, gets easier: you've got your back to the café now and as you stare down into that mesmerizing glow it's as if you're drawing energy up from it, you can feel your calm and composure flowing back and you start thinking about your selection, your sweaty palms resting on either side of the fascia, your head reverently bent to show deep concentration on the business in hand. On a good night you might even risk a slow, sorrowful shake of the head for the benefit of anybody watching, to signal your disapproval or contempt for some of the selections on offer. Because for those few seconds, you're the captain on his bridge, the priest at his altar. You're the man in charge. You're choosing the music. For the next three minutes, the atmosphere in this place will be coloured by your mood.

Then there's the walk back. It's not as bad as the dancing: at least here there's no danger of getting a refusal and having to trail your humiliation all the way back across the floor. But it's no cakewalk either. It's a bit like walking back down the aisle after Holy Communion, because now you have to face the crowd. Where do you put your eyes? Your hands? And the music you choose says a lot about you. Sometimes you're so sure your choice will be popular that you wait till the record starts – 'Heartbreak Hotel', 'Whole Lotta Shakin'', 'Blueberry Hill' – and then you can walk back in time to the music, powered by the beat of it, in the groove, confident, immune. But sometimes you're not so sure: you're worried your choice might be seen as too square or too soppy – a ballad, maybe, like 'I'll be Home' by Pat Boone or 'Young Love' by Tab Hunter, both favourites of mine – and then you try to make it back to your seat before the record starts and the sneerers pipe up and your pariah status gets advertised as clearly as if a neon sign has appeared above your head with an arrow pointing straight down at you and the single word SQUARE! flashing for all to see.

One time Laff and I are sitting at a table there when this big Teddy Boy comes in and orders something at the counter and walks straight over to the jukebox. And we're watching him up there, admiring the long draped jacket and the duck's-arse haircut razored straight at the collar when Laff suddenly nudges me and makes an urgent sign towards him with his thumb, masking it so nobody can see but me. And then I realize: it's the same big Ned that stared us all down that night at the Town Hall dancing. So we start stirring our coffees and mumbling to each other, some fake conversation about anything at all, even though he's got his back to us, just in case he turns round and catches us staring. Again. But no, it's OK, he just saunters past us and sits down at an empty table and the wee lassie comes over and puts an iced drink down in front of him. And then out of the jukebox comes pouring that great long piano introduction we all know and love and good old Fats Domino starts singing 'Blueberry Hill'.

It seems an odd choice for a big hardman like this and after a while we risk another glance at him, we can't help it. But it doesn't matter, because by this time everybody else in the café is looking at him as well. He's sitting there at a table all on his own – you never see anybody sitting on his own in Corrieri's – and he's beating out the rhythm of 'Blueberry Hill' dead loud on the table with the flats of his big hands. The vibrations are making his drink quaver in its glass and the wee salt and pepper cruets jig about like mad on the hard tabletop but nobody says a word. Nobody dares. He's not even being aggressive – not staring anybody down the way he did that night at the dancing – he's just looking down at the backs of his knuckledustered hands, and he's so into the beat, into the music, into himself, he's like a man in a trance. It's as if he's not even there anymore and I look at Laff and he looks at me and we smile because we understand. He's *not* there anymore, he's been transported, 'sent' as they say. It's the effect of the music and it's so powerful that most of us keep it to ourselves, private, in our heads and in our hearts, we'd be embarrassed if anybody knew what feelings it stirred in us.

But this big Ned's not embarrassed, he's beyond that. He's not sitting in Corrieri's café at a table on his own with all these people staring at him, wondering, wary, a bit scared. He's gone. He's up there on some Blueberry Hill of his own, where he found his love and lost her and big hardman or no he's lamenting the loss and he doesn't care who knows it.

For a long time – too long a time, most of our teenage years – this was how it was. The only way you could hear rock 'n' roll in public was on the jukebox or on the wireless. And listening to rock 'n' roll without the release of dance, you felt like a loaded gun with the safety catch on: all fired up and nowhere to go.

One day all that began to change.

Posters began to appear all around the town centre advertising a live rock 'n' roll concert at, of all places, Paisley Town Hall. Somehow the home of Jimmy McGlinchie and his Band didn't seem the right venue. I can't remember what this new band was called, but the words 'Rock 'n' roll!' and 'Live performance!' shrieked at us out of posters, trumpeting praise for previous triumphs in places like Kilmarnock and Dundee. (Wow! said Duffy, with heavy irony.) It was hardly Memphis or New Orleans, but still, it was something. The word of mouth said that this was a real rock 'n' roll band, and it was live. We muttered and complained amongst ourselves at first – *Who are these guys? Nobody's even heard of them! What if it's just a bunch o' Scotsmen like us? How can they play rock 'n' roll?* – but in the end we had to go. I managed to cadge a bit of extra pocket money from my mother and somehow we all scraped together enough for the tickets.

I remember the atmosphere when we went in, the four of us. We hadn't expected the hall to be packed to the rafters. We were in the balcony, the only place we'd been able to get seats, and all around us and below us the massive crowd was heaving with speculation and expectation. It was like being on the terraces at Love Street before a big match, only more intense somehow because we were enclosed and under cover.

Only the stage area was empty of people, and unpromisingly laid out with the traditional lineup of individual stands for the musicians, each with the band's name on the front. There were some guitars, a bass, a saxophone, drums, but it all looked depressingly familiar, as if some elaborate hoax had been played on us.

Jist you wait, Nocky said. Any minute noo Jimmy McGlinchie and his Band'll come walking oot on that stage. What's the bet?

Sure enough, when at last they appeared they looked very similar to Jimmy McGlinchie and his Band. They were all older men in jackets and ties. The bandleader cracked a few jokes that went down badly; the atmosphere was too tense, the packed audience too dangerously restive. *Where's the music? We're here to hear rock 'n' roll! Live!* Then he introduced the vocalist, Danny 'Dude' Donovan! and out onto the stage to scattered applause and ironic cheers came a tallish young guy in a black and white houndstooth jacket, white shirt, bootlace tie, black slacks, patentleather shoes. His black hair was styled in a neat Tony Curtis, but there was no getting around it, he looked disappointingly ordinary. He wasn't as square as the rest of the band – how could he be? – but that was no recommendation. Whatever we'd expected a rock 'n' roll singer to look like, he was not it. All he looked was nervous, and who could blame him, facing this restless mob and their impossible expectations? He was only about our age, he could have been one of us. In fact, he looked remarkably like Laff.

Hey, Laff, I said, shouting over the racket. That singer . . . he looks a bit like you!

Whit? Laff peered down at the lonely figure in the spotlight. Then he went red, and looked annoyed. Och, away ye go! he said.

The restlessness in the audience gradually settled into a kind of wary silence, with an ominous undercurrent of anticipation and judgement suspended. *This better be good!* was the silent warning that oozed up from our ranks to the nervous-looking figure on the forestage. He had unhooked the microphone from its stand and now stood fidgeting to one side, flicking the cord clear of his feet, taking longer about it than seemed necessary, as if he was settling himself. Then he coughed once or twice, and gave the microphone a tentative but very audible tap with his finger. Somebody in the audience tittered, and for a few dangerous moments the laughter started to spread, then died out. It was too early in the evening, and there was too much at stake.

179

In a silence almost sacramental the singer turned to the bandleader and nodded. I could swear I saw his Adam's apple bulge as he swallowed a gulp and I remember feeling desperately sorry for him, a feeling I could only marvel at in the light of what happened next. Because what happened next was astonishing. He hooked the mike up towards him, jerked his head down to meet it. He shot one leg out to the side with just the polished shoetip poised on the floor, and punched the opposite arm straight out to the other side, his index finger stabbing towards the wings. He held this unlikely and faintly absurd pose for a split second in total silence – then screamed down into the mike: *WE-HEH-HEH-HEHLL!*

An almighty crash of drums, followed by a yowl of electric guitars.

Well it's Saturday night an' Ah just got paid!
Fool 'bout money don't try ta save!

As if powered by the crashing noise and the pounding beat the singer started leaping and skipping across the front of the stage, from one side to the other, then up to the band, down to the audience, back to the band. He was fizzing about like sodium on water in Pop Lynch's Science classes at school, a firecracker shooting out of control all over the stage. The musicians were still in one place, but swaying now, rocking in time to the music like men possessed. And after the first few seconds of total disbelief, nailed down in our seats, the entire audience was on its feet and doing the same.

Ma heart says Go go! – have a time
Cos it's Sadderday night an' baby Ah feel fine!

And from then on, it was mayhem, onstage and off. The whole audience was on its feet. Up in the balcony, we were swaying from side to side, our feet stamping out the beat on the wooden floor. The drumming and the vibration and the fear that the floor might collapse under us at any minute only added to the excitement.

Gonna rock it up!
Gonna rip it up!
Gonna rock it up
Have a ball tonight!

McArdle had found somebody's lost umbrella on the floor under his feet. He opened it out and began waving it over his head. Then, egged on by the rest of us, he launched it off the edge of the balcony, out into space. We watched it float down like a parachute onto the heads of the seething crowd below, where it was passed, in a series of slow, leapfrogging jumps, from one section of the audience to the other for the rest of the evening.

The next day the *Paisley Daily Express* ran a report, under the headline 'Town Hall Rocked by Teenage Hysteria'. 'At one point', the report said, 'the air above the heaving, swaying audience was filled with open umbrellas launched from the balcony, like a parachute drop into a warzone.' (Or words to that effect I may have exaggerated their exaggeration.) McArdle was briefly a star in the close in Blackstoun Road and in the pub. The Umbrella Man, we called him. Laff was telling anyone who'd listen that quite a few people had commented on the striking resemblance between him and Danny 'Dude' Donovan. We were ecstatic. We had seen the dawn of a new era. Rock 'n' roll had arrived in Paisley at last. Surely now they would start playing decent music at dances. There would be many more such concerts.

They didn't, and there weren't – at least as long as I was there. That was the first, and the last.

September 1958

I stand at the livingroom window, looking out at Craigmuir Road.

And I see Laff walking away down the road in his charcoalgrey suit, that day he turned up out of the blue with the new suit and surprised us all at St Fergus's at twelve o'clock Mass. The draped jacket, the tapered trousers tight at the ankles: toned-down Teddy boy was what we called that style and Laff was the first of us to wear it and we were all mad jealous at him. I see him passing through the Undesirables, head up, the broad shoulders square in the new suit, no fear about him now. He's quite tall, about my own height, that mad mop of hair tamed at last in a great Tony Curtis, the D. A. at the back, the lot.

He looked different that day, in that suit. It wasn't just the style, I don't know what it was, to tell you the truth, but he looked terrific, there was no other word for it. Watching him, I felt proud and jealous at the same time.

And I realized: he'll be a man soon. He's growing up. We're all growing up.

FIFTEEN

On the bus one morning, there was a shout from one of the Toerags sitting at the back:

Hey, Boyle! Lafferty! Yiz better watch it! Ah hear Sconey's lookin' for yiz!

From his tone, and the raucous cheers this drew from his mates, you'd have thought he was giving us good news.

Sconey was an older boy who'd already left the Academy. He lived up at the far end of Feegie, but Laff knew him well from their primary school days. His name was Connelly, but everybody called him Sconey. Like most of us in those days, he'd had problems with headlice in primary school and it seems his mother got so fed up going through his thick tangle of hair with a fine-tooth comb, she made his father crop it almost to the scalp. To hide this they made him wear an old floppy bonnet like the one featured on the Bisto packet. For a while he was mocked as the Bisto Kid but later this changed to Sconey ('scone' was our slang at the time for a cloth cap) and the name had stuck.

Laff and I looked at each other. Why would Sconey be looking for us?

We had reason to be worried. From early schooldays Sconey had had to learn to defend himself against mockery with his fists – and his head: ironically, it was usually that shaven skull of his, the cause of all the jeers, that took its own brutal revenge. For a time, Laff had told me, you could spot that head, with or without its trade-mark bonnet, in every playground fight that was going. Nobody with any sense would take the mickey out of Sconey nowadays, but at nineteen he already had the battered, blurred features of a boxer down on his luck.

Ye wantae watch that Sconey, the Toerags in Feegie used to say. He's a right nutter when he's fightin'!

For them, there could be no higher praise. For us, it only added to the menace of the message we'd just been given.

In fact Sconey had a surprisingly gentle side to his nature – he'd always genuinely liked and admired Laff, you could see that, and occasionally he'd attach himself to the two of us when we'd meet up the town. It was touch-ing, almost pathetic in a way. But that didn't make us feel any better now. We spent the rest of the bus ride trying to remember the last time we'd seen him, maybe find some clue to what the problem was.

Ah've got it, Laff said at last. The dancin'! The Toon Hall, remember?

We'd been in a long queue outside the Town Hall, Laff, Grib and I, one Saturday night about three weeks before. A uniformed doorman stood at the top of the steps keep-ing an eye on us, waiting for the signal to let us in. Then Sconey appeared, clearly unsteady on his feet, scanning the queue for faces he knew.

Hey, Laff! he shouted. Then he saw the rest of us.

Hallo there, lads!

185

The battered face lit up in a broken grin. He'd obviously had a few pints.

He stumbled into the queue to join us, provoking mutters of complaint from a group behind us; presumably they didn't know him, or his reputation – yet. We braced ourselves for trouble but, amazingly, Sconey was feeling too mellow even to argue.

Och, who wants tae wait in a queue, anyway? he announced, to no one in particular. Ah'm away up to have a wee talk wi ma pal up there. He nodded towards the uniformed doorman. The Commander, he said. Herr Kommandant. Fine figure o' a man, eh? Me and him are best mates. Watch this.

And he lurched away and up towards the impassive figure at the top of the steps.

For a minute or so it did seem that he knew the doorman: their conversation looked friendly enough. But as it turned out the man was only humouring a drunk: when Sconey tried to walk past him into the Town Hall, his way was firmly barred. Then there was more talk, not so friendly this time, then a minor scuffle and for a while the two of them were waltzing precariously to and fro at the top of the steps. The upshot of all this was that two uniformed police came along in a squad car and took Sconey away, still protesting his innocence but going quietly, unresisting. Before he disappeared into the squad car he'd shot a hurt glance in our direction.

That must be it, I said. He thinks we should've given him a hander, or at least said somethin' to the cops.

Ah think ye might be right, Laff said. We're in trouble.

For days after that we were looking over our shoulders whenever we were up the town, ready to duck into a doorway at the first sign of Sconey. I was the one whose luck ran out first. I was walking up Wellmeadow one Saturday afternoon when I saw the familiar cropped head bobbing towards me along the crowded pavement. Thank God, I thought, he hasn't seen me, and I skipped across the road and down the stairs to the public toilets under the clock.

The place was deserted. I was standing at the urinal – when I heard heavy footsteps coming down the stairs from the other entrance. I knew before his face came into view that it was Sconey.

Heh, whit's this? he said, spreading his hands in an aggrieved way. If Ah didnae know any better, Ah'd think ye were tryin' tae avoid me.

Whit? Aw come on, Sconey. Whit would Ah dae that for?

Well, anyway, said Sconey, Ah'm dead relieved tae see ye.

He meant it. He was smiling his crooked smile.

Whatever I'd been expecting, it wasn't this. It turned out he'd been charged with being drunk and disorderly that night at the Town Hall, and also possibly with breach of the peace: his case was coming up soon. Legal Aid had advised him to get hold of some character witnesses if he could, and we were the only friends he could think of that might be appropriate.

Ah mean, you and Laff and Grib, ye're clever – no' like me – ye're respectable, doin' well at school an' that. Wid yiz speak for me in court?

I was so touched by his obvious sincerity – and so relieved that I wasn't after all going to be duffed up in a public toilet by one of Feegie's most notorious hardmen – that I agreed without hesitation.

When I approached them Laff and Grib were more than

happy to do their bit, not least because it meant a morning off school. (I suppose the defendant is a former pupil of ours? McKinnon asked wearily, and when we confirmed it he gave a philosophical shake of the head, like a general noting the latest in a long list of casualties.) Though none of us would have owned up to it, I know they were as excited as I was at the prospect of taking part in a real-life courtroom drama, even if it was only Paisley Sheriff Court.

I think it was this, on the day, that was at the root of all our troubles. The prosecutor was a posh lawyer with an impressive vocabulary and a fluent way of speaking that we all envied. We disliked him on sight. From what little we were able to gather, Sconey's defence was that he might indeed have had a pint or two on the evening in question, but he had merely been engaging the doorman in a bit of friendly conversation to relieve the boredom of waiting in the queue. He himself was a simple, friendly soul who would not dream of causing any trouble – there had been no disturbance at all, in fact, just a mild difference of opinion – and here to prove it were three character witnesses of undoubted integrity and respectability to speak for him.

In fact, we were three overgrown schoolboys with foolish notions of being Perry Mason for a day. So determined were we to show that we were undaunted by our surroundings, so intent on showing off our command of words, that the prosecutor handled us, one by one, like a skilled matador playing a charging bull. He kept playing our own words back to us, with only the faintest shift in emphasis, so that we ended up condemning the man we had come to defend. At one point I found myself protesting that yes, of course there had been a disturbance, since Connelly was about to be run down the stairs. As soon as I said it I recalled Sconey's plea that there was no disturbance to speak of. Laff was tricked into admitting that he had seen the defendant getting into many a fight in the past. But only when he was provoked, he added, lamely. But the prison door was slammed well and truly shut by Grib, at his most dangerously loquacious. Connelly is well known, he said at one point, to have a rather pugnacious nature. Then, realizing he might have gone too far, he continued: But only when he's inebriated, of course!

Sconey sat in the dock listening to all this and I watched his expression fade from a kind of wistful, trusting optimism to the fatalistic contemplation of a lifetime behind bars. As it turned out, though, we had done him some good just by turning up. It surely says something for this defendant, the judge said at the end, that these three senior schoolboys have taken time off from their studies to come here today and speak for him.

There may have been a hint of sarcasm in his tone, but at least he stopped short of saying what must have been obvious to everybody in court: that we'd have done more to help our friend's case by saying a lot less.

In the end Sconey got a six-month suspended sentence, being bound over to keep the peace for that period. For the moment, he was free to go. It wasn't as bad as we'd begun to fear – certainly while Grib was in full flow – but it wasn't exactly Case Dismissed either. Afterwards, as the three of us were heading back to the Academy, we took our leave of him on the pavement outside the courtroom. Good-natured soul that he was, he tried his best to thank us for coming to support him. But he couldn't hide, nor could we fail to notice, the disappointment in his eyes.

Thanks for nothing, they said. Some help you three turned out to be.

About my social life, such as it was, I never told my mother anything I didn't have to. I never told her we were going to the pub. I never even told her we were going to the dancing, unless she asked. I certainly never told her if I was going out with a girl.

Are ye going out? she'd say, watching me in my good suit, with my foot up on a kitchen chair, polishing my shoes. I hardly ever polished my shoes, so I suppose this was a bit of a giveaway.

Aye.

Oh? And where are ye going?

Jist oot.

And she'd look at me.

Oh? Going out on a date, is that it? she'd say, the word sounding awkward, oddly formal coming from her.

Och, naw! Jist oot.

Silence.

Aye, well, she'd say. Just mind yer p's and q's.

Whit's that suppposed tae mean?

Ye have to watch these girls. They can trap ye, ye know.

Whit are ye talkin' aboot, they can trap ye?

Ah, never you mind. Ye're not as smart as ye think. Just remember that.

Remember whit?

Just you mind your p's and q's.

And that was it: that was the extent of my sex education.

I don't know by what intuition my mother knew it, but by now I had a girlfriend. Her name was Rosemary Clancy, a plump, pretty girl from St Margaret's Convent.

We'd met in the group that congregated outside Paterson's after school and after weeks of tentative and oblique soundings – she was very well spoken and her family lived in a big house near Ralston – I'd finally got up the gumption to ask her out to the pictures. I can still remember my astonishment and relief when she smiled at me and said: Yes, why not? As if it was the most natural thing in the world, and why had it taken me so long to get round to asking?

I take Rosemary to the pictures at the Kelburne or the La Scala then see her home on the bus to the house where she lives near Barshaw Park. There's a tenement block on the other side of the street and a handy close on the corner where we go to say goodnight so nobody can see us from the big bay window at the front of her house. We have to go to the back of the close now because when I gave her a goodnight kiss in their front porch on that first night (encouraged by the warmth of her thigh against mine in the picture house and later on the bus, pressed closer than we needed to be in a double seat upstairs) we were soon hugging and clutching at each other with such sighs and moans, we couldn't help ourselves, that Rosemary got scared her folks might hear us. And so, over the weeks and months that follow, in the dark and the damp and the lavvy smells at the back of that close, we gradually seek out and explore the secret places of each other's bodies. Rosemary's a Catholic like me and she always tries to stop me but it's no use, we can't help it, neither of us can, even when we're supposed to be going to communion the next day. If anything the thrill of this touching is even greater because it's forbidden; we're ashamed to be doing these dirty things to each other, altarboy and convent girl, we know we're in mortal sin and we'll have to confess it. Sometimes I'm in such a fever of ecstasy and fear that I feel we're swooning there on the very brink of Hell, any minute now we'll topple over and down into the pit, and I know Rosemary must feel the same, and still we can't help it. It seems there's nothing we can do only suck greedily on each other's tongues and clutch and grab at each other under our clothes, me clumsily unhooking her brassiere to free her breasts then cupping and squeezing them, hurting her sometimes in my urgency, or probing and frantically rubbing the mysterious wetness under the mound in her pants, she fiercely stroking the bulge in my trousers even as I unbutton my flies, then helping me tug it free for her to hold, with such tension throbbing in it that it's actually hurting me, but I don't care. The smells of sweat and secretions from our bodies in that dark enclosed space and the moans we're making are driving us wild, and all the time the dread sense of sin and doom about what we're doing is overwhelming and still we don't care. But when I try to put it in her she pulls away, her elbows hard against my chest, then turns her back to me and leans heavily into me and Stop, she whispers, stop, please stop, it's too dangerous. Please. And so we have to stop and clumsily, reluctantly, I cram my swollen lust back into its cage and help her refasten her brassiere from the back and she buttons up her blouse and adjusts her panties and suspender belt under her skirt. We stand there for a while just getting our breath back and I try, I really try just to hold her in a chaste embrace, my arms loosely around her waist, my hands linked over her stomach. But even this safe position is not safe at all, with the curves of her warm bum pressing into me and the smooth under-curves of her plump breasts in their satiny halter within such easy reach now of first my tentative thumbtips, then my hungry hands, that within minutes we're at it again with renewed frenzy, I've shoved her brassiere back up and I have those slick heavy globes in my hands again and I'm kissing her arched and fugitive neck, her delicate ears, till, in spite of herself, with such fearful guilt, such abject surrender, she turns her face to me again, yields to me her wet and moaning mouth and we're back on the brink, swaying there on the edge of doom and damnation till Stop she says again, pleading. Oh stop, please stop.

On the long walk home at night after these encounters in the close I would still be stiff and quivering with thwarted lust. After leaving Rosemary, and on many another late night walk through the scheme when lust had me similarly in its grip, I could scarcely pass a girl or a woman on the way without imagining us both in some sexual encounter. Such were the frustrations, the impossible hopes, the fears and fantasies of a teenage Catholic boy in the grey, forbidding fifties, in the wet wild West of Scotland. Of course I never dared to say a word to any woman that passed me in the night, or to approach her in any way: it was as much as I could do to risk a furtive glance at her in passing, in the daft, doomed hope that some forlorn longing in my eyes might transmit to her what I was thinking, make her aware of the swollen lust held concealed and captive under my cupped hand in its sheath of pocket lining, but bursting, bursting for release. What was I hoping for? That somehow, impossibly, she might understand me without a word being spoken, instinctively understand and take pity on me as if she were some alter ego, some female other half in thrall herself to the same mad urges, and acting on this unspoken pact between us would go with me to the back of a close somewhere or behind a high wall and let me do to her the thing I hardly dared to dream about, it was such a sin, shove it into her and shag her savagely up against the wall, or on the rough ground, anywhere, and thus be relieved of this terrible burden, free at last of this crippling tautness and tension. *Shag*. That was a terrible word, the kind of thing Big Hendry said all the time, or Wee Shuggy. *Wee Shaggy!* It was a word I'd never said out loud, yet it seemed the right word for the kind of act I was imagining now. An act stripped of all mystery, all emotion, a brutish satisfaction of appetite. Physical relief at its most basic, like having a pish – treating a girl like a toilet. And yet I could think such thoughts about every likely girl I passed, as long as she was more or less the right age, and more or less regardless of what she looked like: in fact the uglier, scruffier and more stupidlooking the better. You'd be ashamed to defile a nicelooking, respectable girl. No, far better some slag you could shag stupid and then leave, just walk away from all the mess and the guilt and the shame of it, with no desire ever to see her again, except maybe by secret arrangement in some secret place known only to you and to her.

With such images constantly seething in my brain I used to wonder sometimes if I were not some monster unfit to live among humankind. In the language of the firebrand priests who came on regular missions at St Fergus's, such foul lusts could belong only to slouching, slavering beasts and my punishment would surely be to spend eternity in the pit of Hell surrounded by their kind. But then I'd reflect that if a convent girl like Rosemary, a Catholic girl of good family, could go down with me as she did into these dark depths of the soul, even wallow with me there in the slime, then surely I was not the only sinner? Other people must be prey to the same dark urges?

I could never talk to anyone about any of this; not even to Laff. There were limits to the things you could talk about, even to your best mate. Even in the confessional you never actually talked about them or analysed them in any way: you simply owned up to them – and even that ordeal was made just about bearable by the formality of the language.

I have committed the sin of impurity, Father, in thought, word and deed.

In deed – was it alone, or with others?

Alone, and with others.

How many times?

Gulp. Erm, about three times, Father. Maybe four.

Well? Which is it?

Five?

This simple formula with its air of clinical detachment somehow disguised and diluted the intensity of the acts in the back of the close, and the awfulness of the other, secret lusts that flickered again in my mind even as I knelt there, in another enclosed darkness. Then the priest would pronounce the penance, like a judge passing sentence, still in this language of stilted formality. I would kneel and say my penance prayers and walk out of the church almost lightheaded with relief – almost, because always there remained the dread undertow of suspicion that I had somehow made a bad confession, not told the whole story: one day, there would be hell to pay.

SIXTEEN

We're all sitting in the café at Barshaw Park one night. It's a place Rosemary and some of her Convent pals go. There's a jukebox there and it makes a change from Corrieri's so I start going there with her, and after a while Laff starts coming with me, then Grib, then Nocky. It's a bit like it used to be at Paterson's shop at the Cross, except that here there're tables and music. But you still get all the usual posing and showing off.

The place is quite busy this night and we're all crowded round the one table: me, Laff, Nocky, Rosemary, and two of Rosemary's pals from the Convent, Noreen and Big Elaine. We're keeping a chair for Grib, because he said he'd be along later.

Perry Como's singing 'Magic Moments' on the jukebox and the lassies are getting on our nerves, swaying and singing along, even though they know we hate it.

Talk aboot a waste! I say. They get a jukebox in the place, then they go and put stuff like that on it!

Laff looks at Big Elaine.

Aye, he says, grinning. And then some balloon goes and picks it.

Elaine just smiles back at him, not bothered at all. She's a big posh lassie who lives in a bungalow along the Glasgow Road. They've been out to the pictures together a couple of times but they seem to be more pals than anything else.

Just to annoy us and drown out our comments they start singing even louder.

Nocky shakes his head in disgust.

Ah don't think there's a decent rock 'n' roll record on there.

Oh, that's not fair, says Noreen. They've got Tommy Steele, 'Singing the Blues'.

She's in dead earnest. Nocky looks at Laff and me as if to say: whit can ye do?

Across the café I suddenly catch sight of Grib. He runs up the few steps outside and pauses in the doorway. He looks a bit flustered, even more rumpled than usual. And he's got a very obvious black eye. He looks around the crowd in the café, sees us and heads for our table. As he passes a table by the window, a fair-haired guy with a crewcut looks up and shouts after him, for the benefit of his mates.

Aye, aye!

His mates all find this very funny, and so do some other guys at the next table, especially when they look at Grib and get the joke. Grib turns and glares at the guy but keeps coming to our table. His eye looks quite bad.

Whit happened tae you? Nocky says.

A slight difference of opinion wi' the brother, Grib says, sitting down. Flash bastard, saving your presence, ladies! He's just back on leave from Cyprus, actin' the big man. Tryin' tae boss everybody—

There's another burst of merriment from the table by

197

the window. He turns round and glares in their direction.

Thae clowns are askin' for it.

Take it easy, Grib, Laff says. It was quite funny, ye have to admit.

Aye, maybe, Grib mutters.

The guy with the crewcut has started singing in a low voice, and his mates are joining in. It sounds like 'Jeepers Creepers', but they've changed the words. They're singing about 'keekers' – taking the mickey out of Grib's black eye.

Grib's furious. He jumps to his feet and points at them.

Right, you lot! Ye've had yer fun. Now cut it oot!

The singing trails off. The five guys at the table look at each other.

The guy with the crewcut turns in his chair to look at Grib.

Oh aye? Goin' tae try and stop us, are ye?

There's one of those awkward silences. Grib hesitates. He looks at Nocky. Nocky shrugs, as if to say: what did you expect?

You can see Grib is not sure what to do next. He doesn't want to make something out of nothing but he doesn't want to back down either. Finally, he just shakes his head and sits, trying very hard to look like a tolerant parent dismissing a toddler.

Bunch o' balloons, he says to us, but loud enough to be heard.

There's no response, but after a while we hear somebody singing in a low voice. It's 'Jeepers Creepers' again, and there's another burst of laughter from the table. Grib whips round to see who the singer is. Crewcut.

Grib jumps up again and marches over to their table.

Right, he says to Crewcut. You and me, outside!

He stalks past them and out. As he does, Crewcut ostentatiously shoves his chair back, gets up and follows Grib. His mates follow him out. So do some other guys at a table nearby. There's general commotion in the café as people get up and scramble to the windows for a view.

At our table we all look at each other. We're a bit taken aback by how quickly it's happened.

Nocky gets up, grimly.

Daft bastart. But we've got tae gi'e him a hander.

Laff and I glance at each other again and follow him outside. The lassies come after us and stand on the steps by the door, watching.

Outside Grib is standing a few yards from the steps, facing the five guys. Crewcut is making a great show of throwing off his leather jerkin, loosening his tie, flexing his shoulders, rubbing his hands together with exaggerated relish. The others don't look anything like as sure of themselves, but they soon cheer up when the guys from the next table come out and line up alongside them.

Nocky, Laff and I walk over and stand behind Grib. Nocky takes off his jacket, folds it carefully on the low wall that borders a narrow shrubbery and starts deliberately rolling up his shirtsleeves. His shirt is a brilliant bluey-white in the fading light.

Laff and I just stand there, not sure what to do next. In our hearts we're appalled at finding ourselves facing ten guys, but we're even more afraid of losing face. Most of them are as unsure as we are, at a guess, though one or two look threatening. To give myself something to do, let them see I'll be no pushover, I pick up a half brick from under a bush in the garden and heft it in my hand. Crewcut is still strutting back and forth in front of his group, doing his elaborate warmup act. Nocky's out in front of us, just standing there, not moving, staring at him.

Grib looks at the newcomers.

Hey, what's all this? he says to them, pointing at Crewcut. Ah was talkin' tae him!

That's your funeral, bigmouth, Crewcut sneers. You're the one that called us oot. They're oor mates.

Silence. Grib looks completely at a loss. Nobody moves.

Crewcut is still playing to the gallery, smiling and cracking his knuckles.

Nocky hasn't stopped staring at him since we came out. Now he steps forward to face him.

A' right, Nocky says. If that's how yiz want it. But there's ten o' you and only four o' us. That's no' a fair go. So we'll take yiz on in groups o' four. Right?

He says this in such a reasonable tone and with such total conviction that it throws everyone off balance, including me, Laff and Grib. The other guys look at one another, mystified. Nobody says anything.

We'll work through ye in groups of four, Nocky says. Just pick oot yer first four. We're ready.

He stands there, not moving. Behind him, me and Laff are doing our best to look hard, as much for the lassies watching on the steps as for the guys in front of us.

Crewcut looks warily at Nocky, then back at his mates. He's not so sure of himself now.

Hey, wait a minute, he says. He hesitates, then points at me. That guy's got a brick in his hands. That's no' fair either!

Nocky turns his head to look at me.

Drop that.

I hesitate, not wanting to lose my only weapon. Or to be seen to take orders, even from Nocky.

Chuck it away, Nocky says.

Still I hesitate. Then he throws me a lifeline.

Ye don't need it, he says.

Aye, ye're right, I say defiantly, to cover my embarrassment. And, dead gallus, taking my time, I toss the brick back behind the wall.

Nocky turns back to face them.

Right, he says. Yer best four. We're ready.

Crewcut is now standing among his group and for all his earlier bravado he looks as much at a loss as they do. Encouraged, Grib now steps forward and stands beside Nocky. Nocky looks at him, sidelong, then stares back at Crewcut.

Or Grib here'll take on yer best man. Or Ah will. Square go. Any way yiz want it.

Grib goes pale and I sense that this was not at all what he had in mind. But he can't back down now, can't undermine Nocky. We're all getting the feeling that he's got these guys worried.

Crewcut looks from Nocky to Grib, sizing them up, then turns round to confer with his pals. He'll be their choice of champion for single combat, that's obvious. But you can see he's beginning to ask himself why he should be the only one to fight. He's looking a lot less sure of himself.

They all go into a confused team huddle and start arguing among themselves.

Nocky just stands there, staring.

Then the café door opens and the manageress comes out onto the steps. She's a motherly-looking woman, and she's not happy.

Now you lot listen tae me! she says. Ah'll no' stand for this carry on. Yiz are like a gang o' big weans! Ah've just

201

phoned for the polis so you lot better get aff yer marks and quick aboot it. Ah'm warnin' ye, Ah've phoned the polis. Ah'm no' kiddin'!

She's talking mainly to the other guys. She knows us by now, knows we're with the lassies. There's a standoff for a few more seconds. Then Crewcut's mob starts to break ranks. Most of them look as relieved as we feel, though they try to disguise it with sneers in our direction. But still, nobody says anything. They start picking up their jackets from where they left them and walk away towards the park gates. Some lassies that were with them in the café follow them, whispering amongst themselves. Crewcut hangs back for a moment. He looks as if he's going to say something but in the end he doesn't. He picks up his jacket last, his flash leather jerkin, hooks a finger through the tab, slings it over his shoulder, dead gallus, and saunters away after the others.

The manageress calls after him.

And don't bother comin' back, either!

Laff and I are still trying our best not to show how relieved we are. Grib walks back to join us, looking very pleased with himself now.

Nocky's still standing there, watching the other mob leaving.

The manageress sees him and wags her finger at him.

And it'll be the same for you lot as well, if ye don't watch yersels!

She goes back in, shaking her head. The lassies come down the steps to join us. Nocky starts rolling down the sleeves of his spotless white shirt.

Walking along the Glasgow Road later, we're nearly giddy with excitement and relief.

That was great, Nocky, Laff says. The way ye bluffed them. Magic, so it was!

Nocky gives him a look.

Who wis bluffin?

Aw, come ON, Nocky, I say to him. Ah mean, a' they had tae do wis rush us and it wis all over. It was ten ontae four. We were dead men.

Nocky shakes his head.

Says who? See that flash blond bastart wi' the crewcut! Him that was daein' a' the struttin' aboot? If anythin' startit Ah wis gonnae stick the heid on him. Just run ower there an' wallop! The rest were a bunch o' big lassies. Nane o' them wanted tae fight.

We all look at him. It's as if he's really disappointed that the fight never happened.

Grib's relief comes out as bravado.

Aye! he says. Bunch o' big weans. If ye . . . rifted at them, they'd fa' doon.

Even Laff gets in on the act.

Aye, they were running aboot there like . . . chooky hens!

This sounds so daft and childish and not like him that we all burst out laughing, even Nocky.

I look at Laff, bemused. He shrugs at me and grins, as if to say: Well, if ye cannae beat them . . .

Now that the danger is past, it seems we're all warriors.

I'm at the back of the close with Rosemary. The only light is the dim moonlight filtering in through the small cracked panel above the back door.

We're standing with our arms loosely around each other, because we're still talking about the standoff at the café.

All I could think about was Nocky's shirt, Rosemary says. It was like . . . that poster for Persil Washes Whiter! It was so white it was blue! I just kept seeing that spotless white shirt getting spattered with blood.

Och, Nocky would'a been a'right. Don't worry.

I tell her about the first time I met him, the boxing in the playground that I thought was in fun, and he decided was in earnest.

I was worried about you back there, though, she says.

What d'ye mean? I ask her, touchily. Is she suggesting I wouldn't be any good in a fight?

I meant I was concerned about the rest of you as well. You were outnumbered, let's face it.

Oh. Aye, well . . . Grib is all talk, mind. And Laff, well, he's not exactly a warrior either . . .

No. Poor Laff. He's such a sweet, gentle soul . . . I was really afraid for him . . .

Och, we could've handled thae bas— balloons.

I'm sure you could, she says, snuggling in. But I'm allowed to worry about you, amn't I?

You can worry aboot me any time you like, I say, dead gallus, and draw her in and kiss her. Within seconds we're into the heavy breathing and fondling. She tenses and takes my hand out of her blouse and pushes me away, gently.

No, no, please . . . I'm going to communion tomorrow.

Oh, right . . . So am Ah.

And that's that. We kiss again: chaste, regretful.

Me and Laff are sitting in Corrieri's when he tells me. It's a quiet night, not many people in the place, and out of the blue, just like that, Laff's telling me he went to the pictures last night with Rosemary.

High Society, he says. As if the name of the picture matters. It wis quite good, he says.

I stare at him. I'm in such shock, I don't trust myself to speak.

On the jukebox, somebody's just put on the King Brothers, singing 'A White Sport Coat'.

It's a song I usually like. But what Laff's just said is still hanging in the air between us, spoiling it, like a bad smell that won't go away.

Whit're ye sayin'? I say at last. I have to force the words out. Ye're kiddin' me oan, right?

By now he knows. Something's seriously wrong.

Naw, he says, warily. Naw . . . Ah saw the lassies at Paterson's yesterday efter school. She told me she fancied seein' it and Ah said so did Ah.

I'd had to go straight home because there was some rehearsal at St Fergus's for a big funeral on the coming Saturday. So I hadn't gone to Paterson's.

I can hardly believe what I'm hearing.

Whit are ye sayin'? I ask him. She's ma girlfriend. Ye know that. And ye asked her oot?

For the first time, he looks really uncomfortable. His whole face has gone deep red.

Och, naebody asked anybody oot, he says. We jist went tae the pictures. Just like, pals, ye know? Ah mean, whit d'ye think Ah wis . . . ?

What do I think? I don't know where to start, my thoughts are in such turmoil. What I'm thinking is what taking Rosemary to the pictures means to me. The kissing and fumbling at the back of the picturehouse. Squeezed together in a double seat on the bus home, hardly able to keep our hands off each other. The breathy, urgent, sweaty embraces in the dark at the back of the close. I see

Rosemary's neck arching away that way it does, her fingers on the hand that's on her breast, trying to pull it away at first then yielding to it, pressing it closer to her, her head turning back to the shadowy figure behind her, but not me now, not me, her mouth sighing open, helpless, giving in, giving in . . . Had she done all that stuff with Laff? Let him do that to her? How far had they gone?

There wis nae harm in it, honest! Laff's saying. He's still blushing, and the blush is as bad as I've ever seen it. Is it because he's lying? Or because he's realized at last how bad I'm taking this?

How could ye dae that? I say to him. You're ma mate! Rosemary's ma girlfriend! How could ye dae that?

Ah'm sorry, John, he says. Ah'm sorry, honest. Ah'd never've done it if Ah thought ye'd take it bad. Ah didnae see any harm in it. Ah mean, we jist went tae the pictures!

I don't say anything because I don't know what to say, and I don't think I could get the words out anyway. The scenes in the back of the close are still racing in my head. Laff starts explaining, something about three of them at first wanting to go to the pictures; Big Elaine wanted to go – in fact it might have been her idea – but then she couldn't, typical Big Elaine, some problem at home, so when he turned up at the Kelburne there was only Rosemary. And so they saw the picture and he walked her home, and that was that.

He walked her home. Did she take him to the close? It's all I want to know. It's all I care about. But I can't ask him that question. I look at him, seeing him as if for the first time in years: the shy face, the blush fading now, as if he's recovering. Maybe he thinks it's OK now, it must be – I haven't gone mad with rage, after all, haven't hit him or anything. If only he knew. In my mind it's all happened already: I've already swung a wild punch at him across the table, smashed him in the mouth. The table's gone over, glasses, cups and all, and he's lying on the floor, spitting blood, and I'm standing over him, screaming.

Ya fuckin' traitor! I'm shouting, and for some reason I'm in tears. Ah thought ye were ma mate!

These scenes are flaring in my head, vivid, all the time I'm listening to him. Rosemary turning; that helpless yielding. The shadow behind her: Laff, not me. Me exploding with rage; Laff bleeding on the floor. And then me standing there, greetin' like a wean.

Laff keeps on talking. I suppose he reckons anything's better than the terrible silence that came between us after he first told me. Of course, it was all Big Elaine's fault, he's saying. If she'd been there, it wouldn't have been a problem, would it? Three's a crowd, eh? Big Elaine. Bloomin' typical. Probably some argument with that mad mother of hers. They were always arguing. That was it: her mother must have kept her in.

Half listening to this, I'm recovering at last. I desperately want to believe him. I can't bear the thought that my best mate and my girlfriend might have done the dirty on me. How can I face either of them again if that's true? How can I come out of this with honour? I can't let anybody, not even Laff – especially Laff – see the damage this has done to me.

Aye, well, I say to him, and for some reason I have to cough. As if I'm clearing my throat. But . . . kin ye no see how it looked tae me?

Looked. Past tense. As if it's over. But it's not. Oh no, it's not.

Oh aye, Laff says. Sure Ah can. It's jist – at the time Ah never saw any harm in it, honest tae God.

I look at him. That innocent face, the blush still lingering under the skin. Why? But I have to believe him.

A' right, I tell him, and I start coughing again, I can't help it.

Are we OK, then? he says.

Yeah.

Thank God for that, anyway, he says.

The King Brothers stop their wailing about white jackets and carnations and being stood up at the dance and in the sudden silence I realize we've only been talking about this thing for about three minutes. That seems amazing to me. It feels like hours. We sit on for a while, Laff doing all the talking, relieved now it's over, or so he thinks, telling me about Grace Kelly, how beautiful she is, and this great song Bing sings with Frank Sinatra . . . I'm still only half listening, still trying to block out the scenes whirling in my mind. I force myself to concentrate on the solid things around me: the Formica table top, the steel sugarbowl with a brown teardrop stain in the white crystals; my glass of lemonade that I've hardly touched though normally I'd have gulped it down by now; Laff's coffee half full, gone cold probably; an empty, crumpled crisp packet. Then he runs out of things to say and there's a silence. Nothing on the jukebox now. The place has an empty, dead feeling about it that matches my mood. I take a few sips of my lemonade. Laff picks up the crisp packet, starts fidgeting with it. That crackling noise it's making is dead irritating, but it doesn't seem to bother him and I don't say anything. He looks inside it, then flattens it out on the table, straightens the edges with his thumb. *Crackle, crackle.* Then he picks it up and chokes the neck of it, holding it to his mouth as if it's a balloon. His eyes smiling at me over the top of it, trying to cheer me up, maybe. Playing this daft wee game to fill the silence. Then he starts blowing into it. I look away, faking an interest in the lemonade in my glass. I swirl what's left of it around in the bottom, trying to get it fizzing again, then raise it for a last swig . . .

. . . and jump to my feet at a tremendous bang right in front of my face. I'm jumpy at the best of times, but in that silent café, in my turmoil of mind, I jerk up as if I've been shot, knocking my chair over, spluttering lemonade all down my shirt and onto the table. Laff's just burst the blownup crisp bag between his hands and he's sitting staring at its crumpled remains. He seems almost as shocked as I am at how much noise it made. Except that he's laughing. He's laughing! At the noise, my reaction, the mess I've made of my clothes and the table. Then people at another table start laughing too, and that's more than I can take. I'm so enraged at Laff for doing this to me, making me look a fool on top of all the other stuff that's still seething in my brain, that on instinct, without thinking, I try to throw the dregs of my lemonade in his face. But my glass is so slippery with spill that it flies out of my hand. I watch it as it hits him on the shoulder as if in extreme slow motion, showering his shirt and jacket with drops so bright and clear and individual I can almost count them, then clatters onto the table, rolls off it, and falls to the floor. Amazingly, it doesn't break. In real time, Laff goes white with shock and fury and jumps to his feet and now the two of us are standing there glaring naked hatred at each other. We're exactly the same height and our faces are inches apart and I swear I can see my own blood-rage mirrored in his eyes.

*

I don't know what it was that stopped us having a fight that night. Oh, the old Italian behind the counter came rushing out making noises, half-indignant, half-conciliatory, but even before he got to us we'd decided to back off. I saw it in his eyes; he saw it in mine. Just before that I'd been shocked by the transformation in Laff's face, all the shyness gone, the fearful aggression that took its place, and he must have seen the same in me. And now we watched the blood-rage dying in each other's eyes, being replaced in its turn by something vague and foolish and furtive. And again that feeling of looking through a mirror into another soul. And thinking, Wait a minute! This is your best mate! What the hell do you think you're doing?

And so the madness passed.

I had to forgive Laff, had to believe that in his innocence he had seen no harm in what he'd done. The alternative did not bear thinking about. But I never quite forgave Rosemary. Because in one crucial way she knew me better than he did: we shared the secret and the intensity and the shame of what we did together at the back of the close. How could she not have known what fears and jealousies her sortie with Laff would provoke in me? Not that I had ever told her. I just felt she should have known. We tried to talk about it but I was hopelessly inept, choked by fear and embarrassment, and so the incident was just put away, ignored but never forgotten. It was like a force suppressed, a turbulence beneath the surface that would surge up now and again in heated arguments that burst out of nowhere, about nothing at all. We kept on going out for months afterwards, but it was never the same. In our sessions at the back of the close I became ever more insistent on going all the way, finishing what we had started. I was sixteen and desperate to lose my virginity. But now I also wanted to punish her, bury in her all my resentment, all my pain, mark her as my territory in the crudest way. And she, who must instinctively have known exactly what was going on, became ever more resistant, ever more determined. We were acting out, though it never entered our heads at the time, the oldest cliché in the world: boy desperate for sex, girl set on engagement and marriage. But we were on a path that had already forked; eventually we faced up to that and went our separate ways.

SEVENTEEN

I suppose everything began to change that day, not long before Laff turned seventeen, when we were standing as usual at the front of our close in Blackstoun Road, just the two of us, telling jokes, speculating about lassies (though the shadow of Rosemary still fell across such conversations, or hovered at the edge of them), passing the time. We were drifting towards the end of term and I was relishing the thought of the summer break, nearly two months ahead of us with nothing to do except whatever we took it into our heads to do, and one special highlight in prospect.

The hoalidays, eh? I said. Bugger all to do and weeks, nay months, in which to do it. Hey, whit aboot that ATC summer camp at Kinloss, eh? That'll be great. They say it's even better than Aberdeen . . .

We'd joined the Air Training Corps, of all things, the year before. It was Laff's idea. He'd heard about it from somebody or other, how you got to go up in a plane – something neither of us had ever done or would otherwise have had a chance to do – and the great summer camps they had every year, at various airbases around Scotland.

He was so enthusiastic he'd soon persuaded me, and so every Wednesday night for months we'd been going along to a draughty drill hall just off the High Street, walking along Wellmeadow self-conscious but proud in our RAF uniforms and polished boots, then tramping around on dusty floorboards for two hours under the bellowed orders of a sadistic sergeant who acted as if we were all in training for an imminent airlift to some troublespot in the distant Empire. It was worth it, though. We'd qualified for the summer camp at Aberdeen that first year, and we'd made our first flight in a small plane they used for training, an Aston – I'd only just stopped myself throwing up and letting the side down altogether. We'd been up several times since then, most memorably in a Shackleton bomber one sunny day, Laff and I crouched in the nose bubble like Biggles and Ginger as the giant plane skimmed at zero feet over glinting, choppy waves in the Upper Clyde Estuary, frightening the life out of passengers going 'doon the watter' on a passing pleasure boat.

We were reminiscing about this, or at least I was, laughing at the memory of their terrified faces, when it struck me that Laff was hardly listening, in fact hadn't said anything for a while. I looked at him as if to say: Come on, mate, your turn, but he didn't respond, just kept staring out at Craigmuir Road, where nothing much was happening that I could see. Bare patches like scabs on the porridgy pebbledash of Nessie's old house across the road. The same old sagging hedges on the corner, the wrecked fences. Oh, and a few ragged-arsed weans wheeling a car tyre almost as big as themselves, whacking it along with a paling ripped from a fence.

Look at them, Laff said suddenly, out of the blue. Wobblin' doon Craigmuir. On the road tae nowhere.

I didn't know what to say. He was in a funny mood, no doubt about it.

Remember that black American that time at the Prestwick airbase? I said, after a while. I was still trying to get him going.

One Saturday afternoon our squadron had gone on a bus run to the American airbase at Prestwick, and after showing us round the base they'd let us into the recreation centre used by the airmen when off duty. Just to hang out with the guys for a while, as the host officer told us. We couldn't get over the American accents, or seeing the black faces among the white – up till then we'd only ever seen black people on the screen at the picture house. Most of them were crowded round a pool table, playing or smoking or lounging on a bench nearby, waiting their turn. They looked so casual, so relaxed, wearing great clothes – gear, as we called it then – tightfitting T-shirts and blue jeans, like James Dean, or loose Hawaiian shirts with baggy trousers tapered at the ankle.

Crikey, Laff whispered. It's like a scene fae *Rebel Without a Cause*.

We hadn't even noticed the jukebox: it stood glowing in a dark corner well away from the lighted area round the pool table and it was only when the familiar rhythms of 'Blue Suede Shoes', the original version by Carl Perkins, suddenly came pounding out of it that we realized it was there. It was even bigger and more spectacular than the one in Corrieri's, but that wasn't what caught our attention. We were watching the black guy who'd played the record. We couldn't take our eyes off him.

He was dancing. He was dancing all by himself, on the spot, jiving with an imaginary partner with incredible fluidity and rhythm. His hand movements were so precise, so subtle, it was as if he was conjuring her shape out of the air: you could almost see her there, twirling in his orbit, ponytail bobbing, wide skirt swirling. We'd seen people jiving before, at Paisley Town Hall or the Templars (Big Eamon, wouldn't you know it, was quite good at it), but nothing like this. This was the kind of style you only saw on the big screen. He danced with a total lack of self-consciousness, as if no one was watching him – and in truth, apart from two goggle-eyed cadets who'd never seen anything like him before, nobody was. For all the attention the poolplayers gave him, this might have been something he did every night. He seemed lit by the glow from the jukebox. The blues and reds and ambers shimmering up and down its sides were caught and reflected in the shirt he wore, a dark-coloured number in some satiny material, now adazzle with strobe effects, and in the film of perspiration on his jetblack face there were rainbow highlights. It was as if he occupied his own personal spotlight. His shoulders rolled and twitched in perfect time to the music, his hips shimmied, and beneath the loose black trousers pegged at the ankle his feet were flying. And there we stood, constricted and awkward in the coarse, itching stuff of our ATC uniforms, even more inhibited than usual by the unfamiliar surroundings, and we watched in wonder and admiration till the record was done.

Talking about it afterwards on the bus back to Paisley, we agreed it was one of the most stylish things we'd ever seen. And though we were only talking about the way he danced, I think we sensed there was more to it, somehow – we had seen a nonchalance, a freedom of spirit, so far outside our experience that it seemed hardly attainable. Yet the glow of it was still out there in the distance, like a promise. Someday. Maybe.

Normally any mention of that black airman would have been enough to get Laff enthusing, but not today. He gave me a sudden, sideways look, like a startled bird. It was as if he'd just noticed my presence.

Ah'll no' be goin' tae the summer camp, he said, suddenly.

I stared at him. He wasn't joking.

How d'ye mean, ye're no' goin'? I said. That's whit we joined for, intit?

Ah'm chuckin' school, he said, with that shy, offhand defiance of his. Ah'm no' goin' back next year.

Whit d'ye mean?

The aul' man's got me fixed up at Babcock's.

I looked at him in shock. He was taking the mickey. Had to be.

You *are* joking, of course, m'lud?

He shook his head.

Naw, he said. It's true. Ah'm tae start there as an apprentice draughtsman in September.

Babcock's was the big boilermaking firm where his old man worked. This was a bombshell. I was hurt and resentful that he'd come out with this news so suddenly: the decision must have been talked about for weeks beforehand, yet he'd never given me, his best mate, even a hint of it till now. And I was appalled at the thought of going back in on the school bus every day to the Academy without Laff there to keep up my spirits.

Oh aye? I said. Whit d'ye reckon tae that?

I tried to make it sound gallus and offhand but I could hear the strain in my voice.

He still wouldn't look at me. He was staring doggedly down Craigmuir Road, his mind made up. At least that's the impression he was trying to give, but there was a furtive, frightened look about his eyes. He shrugged.

Och, whit difference dae ye think that makes? he said, sounding bitter, even angry. Then he realized he'd given the game away and tried to laugh it off. Aboot time Ah wis oot earnin' some money, eh?

Oh aye, big bloke like you! I said, sarcastically. High time ye left school anyway. What's the matter wi' ye, did ye get kept back or somethin'?

This was below the belt, the kind of stuff the Toerags shouted at us on the bus, or on our way through the scheme. Laff gave me a look.

Go easy, eh? he said, quietly. Ah get enough o' that in the hoose.

I felt worse than if he'd shouted at me.

Is it yer aul' man? I asked him, in a different tone. He shrugged.

Who else wid it be?

He said it in that dismissive way he had; you knew he didn't want to talk about it. Laff hardly ever talked about his old man. He never talked about his mother, either, but he got on well with her, you could see that. In an odd way they were pals, or near enough.

His old man was a different story. He was a quiet man who never had much to say for himself: what in the West of Scotland they called a man's man. I'd always admired him for that, though I kept that to myself, especially since I had the feeling Laff was a bit scared of him. He seemed to me at the time to be the way a father should be: he had a natural authority, there was no nonsense about him, as my mother would say, and he had definite opinions about things. He went out to his work, kept himself to himself. He smoked, I knew that, and he liked a drink now and again, but Laff had never seen him drunk, and I'd often thought how great that must be, to have a father like that. Not like my old man, staggering home scattered drunk sometimes, putting us to shame. Though I'd never mentioned that to anybody, not even Laff. How could I? The truth of it was that I'd always envied Laff his father, though I couldn't tell him that either. And now I never would. For the first time I was beginning to get some sense of my old man's qualities. As a father of six, on a labourer's uncertain wages, he had so much more reason to pull his eldest son out of school. Yet he'd never so much as suggested it. This news showed Laff's old man in a different light. This put him squarely on the side of the Toerags: big hefty lads like us should be out earning a living, not filling our heads with useless nonsense at school.

Desperate by now to find some way of cheering us up, I said: *Et quoi autour de votre français, et tout ça? Vous savvy?*

Laff was quite good at French and we'd have these daft conversations sometimes – it was his idea, he'd started it – on our way from the Academy to the busstop in Gallowhill: we'd translate West of Scotland slang literally into French but in broad Scots accents. We'd be in hysterics sometimes by the time we got to the busstop. Of course we never did it on the actual bus; we weren't that daft. No point in giving the Toerags any more ammunition than they already had. We'd done it a few times at school, though, among our classmates, thinking at least they would get what we were talking about. But it was obvious we were the only ones that found it funny. The Ministry of Sneer crowd just looked at us, then at each other, shaking their heads as if in pity.

It's a shame, intit? said Cantwell, true to form.

Not that we minded much, to be honest. It made it more fun, in a way, that it was just something between the two of us.

But now Laff just looked at me and his expression said: I don't play these daft games anymore. He looked as if he'd aged five years since we started talking.

Whit aboot it? he said, and it wasn't a question.

We stayed there talking for a while longer, staring awkwardly out into the road. I learned, as much by guesswork as by anything he actually said, that his old man had had to pull strings to get him into this job: officially, he was too old; the applications had been closed; he was lucky to get this chance; there was no way he could turn it down.

The decision had been made, and that was that.

He was so downcast that by the end I was trying to cheer him up, letting on I was a bit jealous of him – and I didn't have to pretend much because it was partly true: not having to go back to the Academy, going out to work, becoming a man! And just think of the money he'd be making! All the clothes and stuff he could buy!

Laff played along with this pretence; he seemed almost cheerful by the time he left. One thing we were agreed on: this wouldn't change a thing. We'd still be best mates. We just wouldn't see each other as much during the day, that was all. But evenings and weekends would be just like before. We'd still be going out to the pub, to the dancing, with Nocky and Grib. We were mates, and that was that. Nothing was ever going to change that. We even shook hands on it when he left the close. It was Laff's idea. One minute he's walking down the path, the next he's turned round and stuck his hand out.

Shake? he said, and he blushed, I don't know why.

Anyway, we shook hands. We'd never done that before. It felt a bit daft at the time, to be honest. But it was all right.

September 1958

I hear the door opening behind me and turn round, jumpy.
It's the old man. He's just standing there in the doorway,
half in, half out, that mooching way he has.

What the hell's he doing in here? Can he not see I want
to be on my own?

Are ye all right? he says.

His eyes are watering. He's been greetin', probably. He
takes these things to heart.

Some help you are, I'm thinking, and me here tryin' to
take it like a man.

Aye, I say. Ah'm fine. And turn back to the window.

Meaning, end of conversation. I don't want to talk.
Leave me alone.

He doesn't take the hint. Never does. He just keeps
standing there. It drives me mad when he does that.

He starts telling me the same thing my mammy just told
me. All over again. In that slow, plodding Donegal way of
his. That's the kind of maddening thing he does.

D'ye think that's what happened, right enough? he asks
me at the end of it. He'll wait a long time for an answer.
That's the old man all over. Always wanting to talk about

things, even when you make it dead obvious you don't want to. He just won't leave you alone. Honest to God, I don't know why he bothers, because the thing is, my old man thinks I'm odd. At least that's what he always says when we've got visitors and I go to my room for a bit of peace and quiet and he comes in and finds me stretched out on the bed there with all my clothes on, the curtains half-drawn, just staring up at the ceiling, not even reading. Are you odd? he says then, tossing his head back, and his eyes flicker up that dead annoying way they do so you can only see the whites; it'd scunner you to look at it. He can't understand why I won't talk to him. I don't know either. I don't care. I don't even want to think about it.

I can practically feel the damp of the old man's gaze on the back of my neck, reproaching me. I don't feel too good about it myself, to be honest, but still. I don't say anything, don't turn round. Just stand there at the window and hope to hell he'll go away.

Old Slim Whitman's still giving it Laldi in Big Nessie's house across the road. He's beginning to get on my nerves.

After a while I hear the old man doing that sharp indrawn sigh of his, the one that means: Ach, what's the use? The way he tosses his head back and up when he does it. I'm standing there with my back to him and I swear to God I can see him doing it, plain as day. Then I hear the door creaking. I force myself to wait a bit longer then turn my head to look.

He's away. Thank God for that. Peace at last.

EIGHTEEN

I wanted to think of that handshake with Laff as a token of our undying friendship, but soon I came to see it instead as a kind of goodbye. Now that he'd left the Academy, I saw him less and less. I should have seen that coming, but I didn't. Didn't want to, I suppose. We'd still see him occasionally up at the Cross, Grib and Nocky and I, on our way to the dancing, and we'd always stop to talk, but he ran with a different crowd now, other apprentices from Babcock's, young working men like himself with money to spend. They were better dressed than us, talked about different things, somehow looked and acted older. I had no time for any of them, to be honest, and couldn't understand why Laff did.

Our paths still crossed now and again at St Fergus's on Sundays, when chance would bring us to the same morning Mass, usually the twelve o'clock, and afterwards with Big John McPaul or McArdle (he was the only other Senior Secondary boy in Blackstoun Road, and I'd fallen back on his company again now that Laff had moved on) we would stroll back through the scheme. But for a while the reality was that Laff was fading out of my life: whole weeks could go by without seeing him. I resented it at first, feeling abandoned and hurt, but eventually I got reconciled to it: I had Grib and Nocky, after all, and Duffy had become a good pal. Maybe I had sensed by then that I owed these friendships, at least in the beginning, to Laff's innocence and good nature. Why should I now resent him for doing something he had no power to avoid? Our lives had taken separate paths and there was nothing either of us could do about it.

I remember the jolt we all got the day he turned up at twelve o'clock Mass for the first time in a while, wearing a smart new charcoal-grey suit, draped jacket, trousers tapered tight at the ankles, the whole thing astonishingly well cut by our standards. My own first suit, which I was also wearing that day, was a special offer from the Fifty-Shilling Tailors, made to measure from a remnant of cloth in an iridescent slate-blue that my mother hated on sight but I quite liked. Or at least I did, until I saw Laff's. His was from Hepworth's, definitely a cut or several above mine, and set off by a dazzling white shirt with sharp cutaway collar and a grey and red striped Slim Jim tie. We teased him about all this, of course, but our hearts weren't in it – he looked terrific, and he seemed unnervingly sure of himself. To tell you the truth, I felt a bit jealous of him. He even had a girlfriend, though we only found that out through a chance remark of Big John McPaul's and Laff tried to deflect our questions about her with a combination of the old shyness and a new, quiet self-possession that I found hard to deal with.

Her name's Jean McKinnon. Went tae St James's.

Oh aye, I said. An' her aul' man goes tae St Mirin's!

It was a reference to the Boss at the Academy, a feeble

attempt at the old banter. But he seemed too grownup for that stuff now.

Och naw. She's jist . . . a lassie I used tae know years ago. Met her again at the dancin'. Nuthin' serious. Ye know how it goes . . .

I didn't know how it went, far from it, but I could see clearly that some kind of metamorphosis was taking place: the Mohican hairstyle had grown out; the face had strengthened; the old, awkward Laff had all but gone. I wasn't sure how to deal with this chrysalis that was changing almost before our eyes yet remained somehow familiar – the same shy smile, the same fugitive charm.

To hear him talk he was making the most of the money and the novelty of freedom, but later as we stood at the corner of Craigmuir with McArdle he started reminiscing about the old days at the Academy, and even as he laughed at the memory of some of Duffy's witticisms it seemed to me that there was a shadow about his expression, a ghost of lingering doubt. He walked away down Craigmuir that day, with his smart suit and newly confident stride, and he looked so out of place in those surroundings that he seemed to be moving in his own aura. I took some bittersweet satisfaction in the thought that he was missing us, his old mates. I realized that his four years in Senior Secondary with mandatory exposure to English Literature, Latin and French – no matter how much, like the rest of us, he had resisted or resented them at the time – had sown yearnings in him that were not being nurtured by the rigid routines of the boilermaking industry.

Somebody at Babcock's must have reached the same conclusion, because a few weeks after we'd seen him at St Fergus's, we heard that he'd left the company: he'd been called into the office one Friday afternoon and told that his apprenticeship was not to be renewed.

We saw more of him that summer: like us, he now had time on his hands. For a while he tried to carry on as usual, going up the town on Saturday nights with his new pals from Babcock's. But that became a strain: he had even less in common with them now and he no longer had the kind of spending money he needed to keep up with them. And so, gradually, we resumed our talks in the close.

Ah've got myself a wee part-time job, he told me one day, in a tone that tried to be offhand, and didn't quite make it. He seemed to have lost much of his new confidence along with his job. I felt sorry for him and relieved at the same time – at least now he was back among us, where he belonged: he wouldn't be going anywhere for a while.

Oh aye? I said. Whit's that?

Och, it's just . . . floggin' the *Evenin' Times*, ye know? Might be a laugh . . . They're still lookin' for people. D'ye fancy it, by any chance?

Sounding more like the Laff I knew, defiant and wary.

Usually I'd have jumped at any chance to spend time with Laff, but now I wasn't so sure. I'd already tried my hand at paper and milk rounds when I was younger. It had been my mother's idea: with six children to raise she was always looking for ways to get more money coming into the house. And I'd been fooled by the soft-focus image we'd seen in countless Hollywood pictures: cheery, tousle-headed urchins delivering their wares to sun-dappled front porches in leafy suburbs of middle America. In Paisley, as I soon found out on my milk round, it was very different. It meant getting up in the freezing dark, in what felt like the middle of the night, and then running – always running: walking was seen as an act of criminal provocation – back and forth, through puddles, up and down dank tenement stairs, my hand practically frozen to the steel crate, at the mercy of some embittered sadist who made it clear that he hated his job and his whole life and held me personally responsible. It was not the ideal start to the school day.

On the other hand this was something I'd always longed to do as a boy, when I used to watch the paperman under the lamplight at the top of Galloway Street: to stand on a street corner with a wad of papers under my arm, shouting *Eelast-ray-ace!* (the last race!) and *Eelast-race-feeno-oh!* (the last race final!) at the top of my voice. And I'd be doing it with Laff. We'd be a double act. It would be like old times.

Still I hesitated. I was a Senior Secondary boy, about to go into Fifth Year. How would this go down with my classmates? What if the Ministry of Sneer got wind of it?

Are we no' a bit old for that game? I said, hedging.

Och, naw, he said, too quickly. C'mon. It's only part-time, anyway.

And he blushed as only Laff could blush and I knew then that he was desperate for me to say yes, to keep him company in this. That he had his doubts as well, but didn't have much choice. And now that I knew, neither did I.

So that was us, every Friday and Saturday night, standing up at the Cross or Gilmour Street station, selling the late editions of the *Evening Times* with the results of the last race. We had separate pitches on opposite sides of the street but we kept within sight of each other, for company. The only trouble was, as we soon learned, that when you've been shouting *Eelast-race-feeno-oh!* for a couple of hours, the novelty starts to wear off. There were nights when we'd be standing there for what seemed like ages in the wind and the wet and nothing much happening in the way of custom. One dreich Friday night I was standing in County Square by the station entrance, so I was getting a regular trickle of business. Laff's pitch was on the far corner of Gilmour Street and from what I could see nobody was going anywhere near him. Every so often he'd let out a call as if to remind an indifferent world that he was there but the calls were sounding increasingly plaintive. After a while, I got the impression they were sounding *different*. I couldn't quite place it. It *sounded* like *Eelast-race-feeno-oh* but it wasn't quite that. What was he saying? I gave my own call, and listened again for Laff's response.

There was definitely something odd about it. Was it . . . but surely it couldn't be? Surely Laff couldn't be standing out in the street selling the *Evening Times* and shouting *Dandy-Beano*?

Yes, he could. I checked his next call and there was no doubt about it.

Ee-Dandy-Beano-oh!

I had to laugh. What a brilliant way to relieve the boredom. Of course I couldn't let him get away with it: I had to respond in kind. So I waited until there was nobody around then took a deep breath and chanced it. Out it came, loud and unclear, and I must admit it sounded great. *Ee-Dandy-Beano-oh!* There was an exultant answering cry from the opposite corner as Laff realized I'd picked up his signal. We had a hilarious duet for the rest of the shift. I had a hard job not laughing out loud the first few times some grim-faced working man or some big Ned came up in response to my cry of *Ee-Dandy-Beano-oh!* and said: Right, son, Ah'll take wan, but after a while I was handing them over no bother, deadpan.

It was such great fun we were bound to get carried away, and we did. Our shift on the Saturday was quite busy, with people coming back from the football at Love Street, so we were shouting *Ee-Dandy-Beano-oh!* practically into our customers' faces. And still nobody noticed. Then I started to show off, and add in variations.

Hot-spur-Rove-eh-er!

There was a long pause while Laff pondered the implications. Then came the response, echoing across the street.

Wiz-ard-Adven-ture!

This was terrific. I was beginning to think we could do no wrong. We carried on with this new call and response for a while, and all the time I was trying to think up new, witty variations. It was only when I'd tried *Tit-bits-Revalley!* two or three times without getting a response that I began to think maybe I was overdoing it a bit. So I went back to *Ee-Dandy-Beano-oh!* to send a signal to my partner in crime that we were going back to normal service. Still no response. In fact I could no longer see Laff at his usual pitch. I was up on my toes and straining to see where he might be when I heard a man's gruff voice right in front of me.

Gie's wan o' thae *Dandy*s, son. In fact Ah'll take the loat!

It was Mr Leckie, the wee man from the *Evening Times* paper shop, known to the paperboys as Speccy Leckie on account of his thick pebble glasses. He had a bundle of papers under his arm. Beside him, paperless, his hands stuck disconsolately in his pockets, stood Laff. He shrugged at me hopelessly. The game was up.

Tell ye whit Ah'll dae wi ye, son, Speccy said, in a tone at once reasonable and threatening. You gie me thae papers, an' Ah'll gie ye yer walkin' jotters. Right?

Miserably, I handed over my pile.

Now, on yer way, the pair o' yiz, before Ah change ma mind an' gie yiz a kick up the arse!

When we got over the initial shock and the humiliation, we were able to laugh about it. But it was hollow laughter, the kind you force out to cover up embarrassment, and I noticed I was doing most of it. Laff didn't seem to find it so funny, and I wondered about that at the time. Then I understood, and was contrite: what to me had always been a part-time adventure for pocket money, for a bit of a laugh, was the only job he had at the time, his only source of income.

We could spend hours loitering there in the closemouth, Laff and I, leaning on the side walls, talking of this and that, or falling silent for minutes at a time and gazing out past the teeming squalor of the Undesirables into the haze of a brighter future. He was a bit lost at this time: he had burned his boats at the Academy and now he was out of work. He'd had to sign on at the Labour Exchange (or the Buroo as we called it then), an experience he found humiliating, but he had no wish to take any old menial job in an office, something they were constantly pressing him to do. Things were getting tense at home as well. His mother never openly reproached him, but he found her hurt silences almost as hard to take. His old man, whose banal dream – son follows in father's footsteps – was now in tatters, wouldn't even speak to him, except in muttered, venomous asides on the rare occasions when their paths crossed.

Big waster, he would say. Column dodger!

It had to erupt eventually and one day it did, in a furious row, with Laff shouting at him: Whit'd ye take me oota school for? How could ye no' leave me alone?

And his old man jeering back at him, goading him: Make sumthin' o' yerself for Christsake! Dae sumthin' useful, instead o' draggin' aboot the hoose a' day like a big useless lump! Go and jine the Merchant Navy, or sumthin'! Ye're nae bliddy good for anythin' else!

I was amazed that Laff was telling me this much. It was more than he'd ever told me about his home life. And trying to cheer him up, just to let him know that things weren't exactly running smoothly in our house either, I at last confided in him about my old man's drinking, my embarrassment at his displays of emotion, the deadly silences of my mother's disapproval. During those long talks in the close that summer, when it was just the two of us, we talked about things we'd never said aloud to anyone before. I told him how I'd always dreamed of being a journalist one day, in London maybe, on the *Telegraph* or *The Times*. Or a foreign correspondent, even, in the great cities of Europe or the States. He nodded, dead serious, and said I'd probably do it, no reason why not, and there was a wistfulness about the way he said it that saddened me.

Maybe ma experience floggin' the *Evening Times* in Paisley might come in handy after all, I said, trying to lighten the mood. But he just smiled and kept nodding, insisting it would probably happen if I kept at it. He said the main instinct for him now was just to get away from here, travel a bit, see the world. He knew that with his education cut short his options would be limited. He said maybe the Merchant Navy might not be such a bad idea, after all, but he was sounding so bitter and sarcastic and not like himself that I didn't take him seriously. Looking back on it now my inner cynic reminds me that we were adolescent boys, so there was an element of posturing in there – we were best mates, no doubt about that, but we were also self-consciously playing up to that myth, at the same time trying on these projections of our future selves. Even so, our friendship had never been more honest, or more intense. It was too good to last.

Ah'm gonnae sign up, he told me one day. Ah'm gonnae join the Merchant Navy.

I knew at once by his tone that he was in dead earnest. It made me fearful and jealous: Laff would be leaving, getting away from here; he was actually going to do what he always said he'd do. And what was in store for me? I'd be left behind in bloody Paisley, with nothing but my hopes and dreams for company.

Oh, I said sourly. So ye're doing what yer aul' man telt ye?

It was a low blow, but I couldn't help saying it.

Aye, Ah know, he said simply. That's what's been stoppin' me doin' it before. Didnae want tae gi'e him the satisfaction, Ah suppose. But it's a good idea, ye have tae admit it.

I couldn't argue with that. It was what we'd always daydreamed about when we'd talked about doing National Service in Cyprus or Hong Kong. And by now we knew that National Service was being phased out: we'd both be too young to make the last call-up.

Aye, I said reluctantly. Could be even better than National Service, eh?

Yeah, he said. Ah mean, ye could end up stuck in Catterick or some bloomin' place for a coupla years. This way Ah'll be signing up on a ship and Ah'll know where it's goin'.

Ye mean, ye get tae pick and choose? I said, trying to keep the envy out of my voice, and failing.

Oh aye, he said, not even noticing. At least, Ah can pick a ship that's goin' tae South America, or the Far East. It'll be up tae me.

South America. The Far East. Just the thought of such places was overwhelming. What could I possibly say to that?

Hiv ye told yer aul' man? I asked him.

Aye, he said. Ah'm no' sure how he took it. Acted a bit surprised.

Maybe he never expected ye tae call his bluff?

He looked at me sidelong, then shrugged.

Aye, well . . . serves him bloomin' right, eh?

It was as close as I'd ever seen him come to malice.

He disappeared for a while after that, and I learned from his mother one day when I went down to look for him that he'd been going back and forth to Glasgow, making arrangements with the Merchant Navy Pool. Then he turned up at our door one evening when I was out serving at Benediction at St Fergus's, and left a message for me. He was leaving on the train to London first thing in the morning: he had to get down South to join his ship. I was distraught at missing him. I had pictured some dramatic leavetaking on the docks at Clydeside: close up on a pro- longed handshake, a searching exchange of glances, a sense of powerful feelings unspoken, then back to long- shot for a last wave as the great ship pulls away from the quay, on which for some reason I stand alone and palely loitering in the gathering dusk . . . Every cliché of the big screen was in there somewhere. Anyway, that was that. He'd gone – disappeared overnight. It was to be the last we heard from him for a long while.

NINETEEN

Weeks later I was well into Fifth Year at the Academy. I was still struggling to deal with the grim morning routine now that Laff was no longer there for support: braving the bedlam on the top deck of that hellish bus, made even worse by the dreich West of Scotland winter that was already closing in over us like a sodden blanket, so that the atmosphere on the bus, already thick with cigarette fumes, was now further enriched by hoarse coughs, sniffles, loud, unshielded sneezes and – a sound that scunners me to this day – thick phlegm noisily sniffed back and gulped down with apparent gusto.

Then the postcards began to arrive. They would turn up weeks apart, glossy, impossibly sunny cards bearing smudged postmarks, some from places I'd never even heard of. The colour photographs were of distant, unpronounceable ports, or dazzling pastel villages set against lush green vegetation, brilliant blue skies, and impossibly turquoise seas.

On the back they were festooned with alien stamps and stickers, their place names printed in several languages. And there, in blotchy biro, would be a few jaunty lines from Laff, now the seasoned voyager to hear him tell it. I kept the first ones in my room on the chest of drawers and even got my atlas out and tried to pinpoint the ports – the first time in my life I'd shown any spontaneous interest in Geography. I think I had some notion of keeping track of Laff's route by linking up the ports, like the pictures they'd ask you to make in the Fun Section of the *Sunday Post*, joining up the dots. It wasn't easy: I had no talent for map reading and I was getting nowhere till I realized that the cards didn't always arrive in the order of their sending. So then I had to check the postmarks, and some of those were illegible, and after a while I gave up. I was happiest just lying there stretched out on the bed, on my back, gazing at the cards and fantasizing about the places they came from.

From the picture on the card – some had four miniviews on the quartered surface, their contiguous corners sealed down with a jolly lifebelt dead centre, framing a jolly message (Greetings from Trinidad!) – it was a mere eye-blink to the big screen of the ceiling, my theatre of dreams, the blank space onto which I could project the fantasies it inspired. And the card I held in my hand was solid proof that such fantasies could come true. It could be done. Laff was doing it! I saw him sailing into the sheltered bay of some exotic spice island, standing at the prow of the ship, the rope held ready in his hand poised to throw to some listless, strawhatted figure on a rickety, sunstruck quay. I saw him – in a vision that owed more to Robert Louis Stevenson than to my wayward grasp of Geography, or indeed of reality – aloft in the rigging, in the crow's nest, like another Jim in another story, another time. I could hear the mainmast creaking, the canvas sighing in the warm breeze. I could see Laff, that mad mop of hair flying (the Tony Curtis presumably vetoed by the dreamweaver), magically transported now to Columbus's ship, squinting into the Western glare with a wild surmise, his face coppered by the setting sun, and shouting: *Land ahoy! Land ahoy!* I got, let's face it, a bit carried away.

And then drab reality would reassert itself, the dull familiar shapes of my room come back into reluctant focus, along with the familiar striped curtains, the old brown wardrobe with the creaky door that always, maddeningly, swung open, and I'd think back to how low he'd been in those last weeks in Paisley just before he left, how hopeless he'd felt, and I could only wonder at it. I told Wullie Logan about the cards (he was now my sole companion in the close) and he asked wistfully if he could see them. His delight was so transparent, his eyes shining as he stared at the view, his whole face lit by a daft grin, that I saw my own reactions mirrored in him and I was touched.

D'ye think he's really been tae a' these places?

Oh aye, I said, preening a bit, as if I was the one who was sailing the seas. Ah don't think ye can post postcards off a ship, Wullie.

It jist shows ye, eh? A boy fae Craigmuir Road, and here he is, travellin' the world. Good luck tae him anyway.

Then he started asking to borrow the cards, so he could show them to his pals at school.

I wasn't so sure about that, and said so.

He looked so downcast that I was immediately contrite.

Oh nae fear, John, he said, with great dignity. Ye don't have tae worry. Ah'll bring them back. Ah widnae let ye doon. No' for sumthin' like this.

That was Wullie. He might overdo the sincerity a bit,

but his heart was always in the right place. He was no Laff, but in the desolation of Laff's absence he was a friendly port.

I was walking down the Renfrew Road one Friday after school, on my own – Grib had already cut off towards Gallowhill. I'd decided to walk to the Cross instead of waiting for the bus. It had been a rare day of Indian summer and I was hoping the walk might cheer me up. I'd been feeling a bit down all day, and I was in no mood to face the bedlam on that Feegie bus without Laff. Crowds of boys from the Academy were walking down the hill and just ahead of me were two characters from my year, Donnelly and a wee hanger-on, Charlie O'Connor, nick-named Cocky by the Ministry of Sneer (his initials on the blackboard read COC. Get it?). They took the mickey out of him mercilessly but he seemed happy to put up with it – maybe he saw it as the price of admission to their clique. I didn't have much time for either of these two, to be honest, nor they for me, so when I caught up with them I just walked on.

Aye, aye, I said as I passed. (I felt I had to say something.)

Naw, naw! said Cocky with a cackle. (That's the kind of annoying wee nyaff he was.)

Donnelly found this very funny.

Oooh, he called out after me. Look who it is! Poor Boyle, all on his oaney-oh! Where's yer pal now, eh? Where's yer ping-pong partner now?

I could hardly believe it: he was harking back to an argument we'd had at the end of the last term, before Laff left. I'd been playing bookend table tennis with Laff one day in the Monitors' room (Donnelly and I were both

238

prefects, though Laff wasn't) and Donnelly and his cronies objected. It's supposed tae be for prefects in here, they kept muttering, loud enough for us to hear. So whit's Lafferty daein' here? I thought at first they were joking – I couldn't believe they'd be that petty – but they weren't. Anyway, we just ignored the comments, dug in doggedly and played out our game to the finish. But Donnelly seemed to take it as a personal insult: he kept making snide comments to me about it for days afterwards.

And now here he was, out of the blue, starting all over again.

Boyle and Lafferty, eh? he sneered. The great ping-pong champions, Ah *don't* think!

Ping and Pong! said Cocky. Maybe that's whit we should ca' them.

They both thought this was hilarious. I didn't like it, but decided to try to ignore it and walk on. I'll soon leave them behind anyway, I reasoned, I'm walking faster.

Would you believe they actually speeded up to keep the same distance between us?

Hey, Ping! said Cocky. Where's Pong these days?

Naw, naw, wait a minute, said Donnelly. That cannae be right. Boyle must be Pong, judgin' be the smell roon here.

Hey, that's a good yin! Cocky cackled. Hey, Pong! Where's Ping these days?

I was still trying to ignore them, because that's what I'd decided at the start: keep the head, don't give them the satisfaction of reacting. Now I wasn't so sure. But to turn round and start responding in kind would look like an admission of defeat. Or so I convinced myself. The truth was, my heart wasn't in it. And so it went on, all the way down that long hill, Cocky and Donnelly keeping a constant two or three steps behind me, tormenting me with their improvised comedy routine. *Ping and Pong. Hong and Kong. King and Kong.* On another day I might have found some of it quite funny. In this mood, it was unbearable. Eventually I had to shake them off by turning into Old Sneddon, which was not even on my way – and they made sure I knew they'd realized that. By the time I was clear of them I was actually sweating with embarrassment and humiliation and my ears were ringing with their jeers.

I brooded about this all weekend. I had tried to rise above it and it hadn't worked. If Laff had been there it would have been different: I'd have shot back at them with some barbed comments of my own – I still felt protective around Laff, and that adopted role seemed to give me courage – and we'd just have ignored them. Eventually, they'd have given up, and that would have been the end of it. If there had been two of us, I knew, it would have been different. But I also knew there was every chance it would start all over again on Monday. By not reacting, I had let them feel they could get away with it.

A phrase kept coming into my head: something Nocky had said one day when we were all talking about the possibility of National Service.

Ah'd go for the Black Watch if it came to it, he said. *Nemo me impune lacessit*, that's their motto. Nobody assails me with impunity. That's good enough for me.

Nobody assails me with impunity. He was right: it suited him. Nocky would never have put up with the stuff I'd taken from Cocky and Donnelly. In some odd way I felt I'd let him down. I'd let Laff down. Worse, I'd let myself down. Now I had to put it right. If they started again, I'd have to react. I'd have to finish it. And I'd have to do it on my own.

Nemo me impune lacessit. All through that miserable weekend, reliving the humiliation, dreading the coming confrontation, I kept repeating it to myself like a mantra, over and over.

Maybe it won't be so bad if I stay out of their way?

No. *Nemo me impune lacessit.*

As it turned out, staying out of their way was not an option. Mischievous coincidence (or implacable Fate, take your pick) saw to it that Donnelly and Cocky were almost the first two boys I met in the Academy on Monday morning. The main corridor was loud with the clamour of jostling boys and I decided to cut through the side passage past the gym, which was empty. Donnelly and Cocky must have had the same idea and then changed their minds for some reason because they suddenly appeared round the corner at the far end of the passage and were now walking straight towards me, slowing as they got nearer. Unbelievably for that time in the morning, there was no one else in the passage. *High Noon*, I thought.

Well, well, said Cocky as they drew level. Look who's here!

He sounded sarcastic, but then he always did, and I thought, Well, no real harm in that. I was still hoping we might just pass each other in peace. I even gave them a nod as I passed.

And then Donnelly laughed.

The message, to me at least, was unmistakable. He was laughing at me, at my lack of response to their insults on Friday, and at my readiness, even now, to let it be.

I swung round.

Hey, Donnelly, I said. Don't laugh. Ah'm warnin' ye!

They stopped and looked at each other, then at me, in mock astonishment.

Ooh! Whit's *his* problem? Cocky said to Donnelly.

Beats me, said Donnelly, shaking his head.

O'Connor, I said. You stay out of this. Ah'm no botherin' wi' you, ye're too wee. But you, Donnelly, Ah'm warnin' ye. Don't ever laugh at me again.

They looked at each other again, in pantomimed bemusement. But I could see I had them rattled. To make the most of my advantage, I added: And don't laugh at Laff, either!

Don't laugh at Laff. It came out sounding so stupid, I couldn't believe I'd said it. Cocky went into his hysterical cackle. Donnelly just grinned and shook his head, as if in pity.

Or you'll dae what? he sneered. You an' whose army?

I punched him in the face.

What hit him was all the force of the rage that had been building up in me over the weekend, stoked by the constant repetition of *nemo me impune lacessit*. It even shocked me. It caught him just beside the eye, and his head jerked back with the blow and banged against the corridor wall. He'd been holding his briefcase under his arm and as it hit the floor books and papers came tumbling out and scattered all round us. For some odd reason – maybe he'd been disorientated by the suddenness of the attack, or the effect of the punch – he seemed more concerned about picking up his stuff than defending himself against me. He'd dropped to one knee and was distractedly arranging the scattered books and papers into little piles, at the same time shooting wary, puzzled glances up at me.

Jesus, Boyle! said Cocky. Whit the hell's the matter wi' you?

Shut up, O'Connor, I said. Stay outa this. Don't even talk.

He made an odd gurgling sound. Without realizing it I'd grabbed him by the tie and was twisting my fist into his throat. He'd gone pale, and as I let go he shrank back against the wall as if he was facing a madman – and in a way he was. I turned back to Donnelly. He was now cramming books back into his bag, and watching me with an expression more concerned than afraid. Maybe he thought I'd gone mad as well. When everything was back in the bag he clutched it awkwardly across his chest and started to get to his feet.

Don't get up, I said. Ah'm warnin' ye.

He shook his head, whether in dismissal or confusion I don't know. I remember thinking how poignant he looked, kneeling there on the floor, his arms crossed on his chest, a hurt expression on his face. Like a wee boy. I'd never thought of him like that before.

Listen, Boyle, he said in a reasonable, let's-be-grownup-about-this tone, and struggled again to get to his feet. And I swear I very nearly put out a hand to help him up.

Instead I hit him again.

Nemo me impune lacessit.

Ashamed though I was to be hitting a man when he was down, I was even more scared of letting him up. Donnelly took the punch full in the jaw, swayed, and nearly fell over. His bag flew open again, strewing its contents all over the floor, pathetically, all over again. He put a hand out to the wall to steady himself. He was looking up at me in amazement. He seemed to be trying to smile, as if to make peace, laugh the whole thing off. Blood was trickling from the corner of his mouth. One eye was already puffing up from the first punch. Suddenly I felt desperately sorry for him, but I couldn't call this off now. I swear to God I was getting ready to hit him again when there was a shout from the far end of the corridor and Pop Lynch, the Science master, came hurrying towards us, his gowntails flying.

What's this? What's this? What do you boys think you're doing?

We were all called up in front of the Headmaster. The three of us stood before his desk and I gave him a summarized version of the story as honestly as I could. Nobly, I said it was all my fault. Donnelly and O'Connor were not to blame. I had overreacted. Just as nobly, Donnelly said it was all their fault. They had provoked me. I was not to blame. Surprised and impressed, I looked at him. He was a sorry sight, with one eye now swollen and discoloured and a puffiness about the jaw where the second punch had landed. The knuckles on my right hand were skinned and tingling. Our eyes met fleetingly, and there was the faintest nod between us, a tacit acknowledgment that it was over. I felt an enormous sense of exultation and euphoria. I was more than ready to take whatever punishment the Boss might choose to hand out.

McKinnon had stood behind his desk, listening to both sides of the story, his hands behind his back and under his gown, looking keenly from one to the other of us as we spoke. Now he shook his head slowly, theatrically, and heaved a deep sigh.

Now listen here, gentlemen, he said.

This was a first. He'd never called us that before.

Don't you think I've got enough trouble keeping order

in this madhouse without having my monitors fighting amongst themselves? Hmm? Don't you?

We couldn't argue with that. We nodded.

Right. Well, if you'll just shake hands like men and agree to put all this silly business behind you, I see no reason why I should detain you further.

And that was that. Self-consciously we shook hands and he showed us out.

I'm depending on you, gentlemen, he said.

I floated out of that office and along the corridor. It was the first time the Boss had ever spoken to me as an equal. I felt some important milestone had been passed.

TWENTY

In spite of all the hints my mother kept dropping, I was still resisting the idea of a part-time job. The memory of the *Evening Times* debacle could still make me wince – I had not yet mastered the adult alchemy which can turn humiliating experience into amusing anecdote – and I knew that any job I did from now on I'd be doing on my own, without my pal to keep me company. I pleaded that the homework I got from the Academy was more than enough to occupy my time, and this worked for a while – my mother could see the state I got into on Sunday nights, when I'd often be sitting up past midnight trying to finish my Maths homework for Big Paddy.

The Lord save us, she'd say. How can they expect ye to be sitting up that late and still be up bright and early for school the next day?

Of course the main reason I was still struggling at midnight on Sunday was that I'd put off starting any homework until early evening, and leave the Maths till the very end. On top of that, I was listening obsessively to the Top Twenty on late-night Radio Luxembourg. But shrewd as she was, my mother was still so mystified and intimidated by the whole notion of homework – in outlandish subjects like Latin, French, Spanish – that she never dared to challenge me.

But she never gave up on the idea of a part-time job for me, and in my heart I understood that she had little choice. Even when he was working, which was most of the time, my old man's wage was so meagre that the housekeeping must have been a constant struggle for her. And there were times when he was off work with his bad back, or had just been paid off on one site and was waiting, hoping for the next. I was vaguely aware of these little dramas being played out in the parallel world, but I was spending so much time in my head, dreaming of this and that, they might have been episodes of *Mrs Dale's Diary* on the wireless for all the effect they had on me. So, when she walked in one day, heaved her shopping bags wearily on to the kitchen table and announced that she'd found me a job, I was less than overjoyed.

Oh aye? I said warily. Whit kinda job?

Oh, it's in a café on Causeyside. A nice place. In the afternoons, after school, and Saturday mornings.

Well, that was something. At least I wasn't going to be hauled from my bed in the middle of the night.

Whit café? I mean, whit am Ah supposed tae do? Ah'm no washin' dishes, I muttered, mutinously.

Cardosi's. Causeyside Street. Just make yourself useful in the shop, keep yourself busy. Ye've to go and see Mr Cardosi tomorrow after school. He's a very nice man . . . He's Italian, she added helpfully.

We liked the Italians. They were Catholics, for a start, and we thought of them as lowly immigrants like ourselves, if anything a bit further down the social scale with their funny foreign accents, at least among the older generation. (The reality was that they were much better off than us, and while we were making fun of their ice-cream vans and fish-and-chip shops, some of them were laying the groundwork for future catering empires.) But we had something else in common: we were looked down on by the native Scots, even the poorest of them. To them we were just Paddies and Tallies, foreign interlopers, up to no good. There were several Italian names at the Academy – there was one in my class – but no Cardosis that I knew of. That was a blessing. It was bad enough that I was to be an odd-job boy; the last thing my fragile self-confidence needed was for that to become common knowledge at school.

Reno Cardosi, the café owner, turned out to be a heavy-set man with kindly eyes and a pronounced limp from some accident in childhood. From the first, he was under-standing and helpful to me, though I soon learned from the waitresses that he had a brother Renso who was a different story altogether. They all called him Rinso of course, after the soap powder popular at the time, but never to his face – all except Big Agnes, a simple soul who thought his name *was* Rinso and kept saying it that way, oblivious to his furious scowls. He ran his own café somewhere in Glasgow and came to Paisley only rarely, an arrangement which seemed to suit everybody.

At first Reno put me behind the counter, the domain of silent, dark-skinned Rosa, her blue-black hair pulled back in a severe bun. In that narrow space I felt big and clumsy and in the way as this tiny woman deftly served sweets and cigarettes and rang up brisk arpeggios on the cash register. I took refuge in restocking and rearranging the shelves of cigarettes, savouring the exotic names: Craven A, Dobies

Four Square, Sweet Afton, Olivier, Pasha, Balkan Sobranie.

I served a woman one day who asked for ten Oliver.

Ah think ye mean *Olivier*, I said, showing off the Fourth Year French.

Is that no' typical? she sighed. I used to say *Olivier* but people servin' me always called them Oliver. So I thought, Well, when in Rome – and then I get some smart alec just out of school, correctin' me.

It was days before I could speak to another customer without stammering.

At its far end the galley fanned out into the main service area which at busy periods was frantic with activity. On one side of the counter, the waitresses slammed down their empty trays with a clatter and shouted overlapping, sometimes conflicting orders: Two cappuccinos, two milky teas, one cupcake! . . .

Ten ice drinks: that's four orange, two banana, three lemon, two lime! Naw, wait a minute . . .

And on the other side, manning the hissing espresso machine, the vats of orange and lemon squash, the big chrome pumps of flavour concentrate, stood Reno, steady and methodical, the still centre of the storm.

After a busy period the kitchen would be full of the lusty gossip of busty, unbuttoned waitresses on their fag break. Coming from a boys-only school, I was like a raw recruit dropped into a war zone: I was totally unprepared for the company of young women like these and I found their forthright language frankly shocking.

The ringleader was Big Julia, an ash blonde who always leaned against a narrow round pillar just inside the door, casually blowing perfect smoke-rings through lips of bright scarlet. Her magnificent, upholstered bust under the flimsy overall protruded at an angle that seemed to me mathematically impossible, and created such a distraction that I found it almost impossible to look her in the face. She'd stand there smiling at me, puffing at her fag, brazenly enjoying my discomfort. On my first day in the kitchen she turned round to face the pillar and twirled round it flirtatiously, as if it were a dancing partner.

Hey, d'yiz like ma new boyfriend? she said to the other girls. He's Polish!

They all had a good laugh at that, and I managed a grin to show that I got the joke.

Is he no' a wee bit skinny for ye, Julia? said another girl.

Aye, said Julia. He might be skinny, but he's dead *smooth*.

She stroked the glossy painted surface suggestively with one hand.

And he's *long*! she said.

Cue raucous merriment all round, and sly, sidelong glances to see how the token male in their midst was taking this.

I tried for a while to assume a mask of seen-it-all-before world-weariness, until I realized that they were not fooled for a second. It's not easy for a gawky sixteen-year-old to act the sophisticate in a world of older women, and it's no help when he's up to his elbows in greasy dishwater. My worst fears had come true: while I was not officially the dishwasher, dishwashing was undeniably part of the deal. But I cut such a pathetic figure at the sink that sooner or later one of these brassy girls would bustle me aside and take over, masking her good nature behind a barrage of scorn for the benefit of her mates.

Oota the way, ya big lump ye, ye're useless!

The one I liked best was Isobel, and not just because she

was the one who usually took pity on me. She was a lot quieter than the rest, with dark hair cut in a pageboy style and a glint of mischief in her blue eyes. So I would stand there, ineptly wielding a teatowel to justify my existence, while Isobel built a gleaming stack of dishes in the rack between us. After a while I grew to like this arrangement, which settled into a routine whenever we were on duty together: Isobel washing, me drying, and the banter flowing – I liked her, could relax in her company and began to give as good as I got. I was almost sorry when Reno, whose soft brown gaze missed very little, reprieved me from kitchen duties altogether.

A narrow alley ran from the kitchen door along the back of the premises, past the storeroom, and on to another building at the end which turned out to be the Cardosis' own ice-cream factory. This was to be my domain. Reno had noted my ungainliness in the shop and my embarrassment in the kitchen; here, he must have reasoned, was a backroom boy if ever there was one. The work was menial: helping Reno keep the factory clean and getting new stock from the storeroom, but at least I was out of the glare of public scrutiny.

I had just finished mopping the factory floor one day when there appeared in the doorway a powerful, sallow man in a smart suit and highly polished shoes, flanked by two strikingly pretty girls, one about my own age, the other younger, both in the uniform of St Margaret's Convent. Behind the glower on the man's broad face, I could see enough of a resemblance to Reno to realize that this must be the notorious Renso. He now set about justifying his reputation.

Hey! Who-ah you? he barked. Whatta you doin' here?

Eh, ma name's John, I said politely. Ah work here.

Oh, so you're this *Johnnie*! he said with extreme distaste. You're this . . . boay my brother took in!

He meant took on, but I resisted the temptation to correct him.

Hmmph! I no' like boays, he snorted, superfluously. Boays . . . they like glass, they break!

I smiled wanly at the girls, affecting an offhand manner. Renso was still looking around with obvious mistrust. Whatta you doin' here anyway?

Thinking a little dumb insolence might help me save face with the girls, I looked pointedly at the mop in its bucket, propped against the wall, and then at the wet floor.

Moppin' the floor! I said, wittily. I was showing off a bit. Jist aboot finished, I added, looking at the gleaming linoleum tiles with some pride.

Renso scowled at the floor, his massive head twitching, nostrils flaring, clearly peeved that there was no obvious fault for him to pick on. Suddenly a spark of hope glimmered in the coalblack eyes. He grabbed at the door which was jammed back tight against the wall, tugging hard to free it, then shouted in triumph as he spotted something behind it.

Ha! Whassa thees? he cried triumphantly, kicking a soggy Craven A packet and some indeterminate grit all over my clean floor.

Looka thees, eh! Feelthy, he cried, pointing accusingly at the toe of his shoe, its shine now perceptibly dulled. You ca' this a-washin' the floor?

I could feel my ears burning. The two girls were clearly embarrassed for me, which made it worse.

Well . . . Ah hadnae got tae that bit yet, I lied, bluffing desperately.

Donta gimme that-eh! he shouted, his accent thickening as his excitement mounted, and for a moment I was afraid that this powerful man was about to lose control altogether. But I had got Renso precisely wrong: his was one of those suspicious, combative natures that always need something or somebody to pick on. Now that he had found it, I was looking at a genuinely happy man.

Ye goattae try harder if ye wantae work wi' Cardosi's, he said, by now so pleased with himself that he sounded almost friendly. Nae rooma here for stupid boays.

Ah'm no stupid! I said resentfully. Ah'm in Senior Secondary at the Academy. Ah'm in Fifth Year!

Feeth Yee-ar? he yelped in disbelief, with a glance at the older girl. You? In Feeth Yeear? Like-ah ma daughter?

I had a powerful urge to tell this flash Tally that for all his fancy suits and shiny shoes, by any local reckoning he ranked below me on the social scale. But I also had a feeling that these might be my last words on earth.

Aye, Fifth Year, I repeated, sullenly.

The big sallow face suddenly split in a startling grin.

Feeth Yee-ar! he mocked. Aye. Eesa good name for you. Okay, clever-boay, Feeth Yee-ar. You cleana the floor, eh? You clean it a-right!

Andiamo, he said, with a gesture to his daughters and the three of them walked down the alley towards the goods entrance, Renso still muttering in Italian. The only words I understood were *Feeth Yee-ar!* flung over his shoulder one last time with a derisive snort. And as far as Renso was concerned, that was my name from that day forward.

Fortunately his brother was made of gentler stuff. Reno seemed to take it as a personal challenge to find a job where this willing but awkward adolescent could be of some use. Soon I was spending practically all my time between the factory and the storeroom.

It seems to me now that my time in Cardosi's storeroom, in my own home town, was my first taste of foreign travel. I even had some sense of that at the time. I was missing Laff desperately, and maybe it was that recurring image of him sailing into foreign ports on the far side of the world that made me try to find some parallel in what I was doing. It was a pathetic fantasy, but it was a way of keeping alive the idea that one day I would get away as well. So the moment I stepped inside the storeroom and began to climb the narrow wood stairs, I would start self-consciously to breathe in the atmosphere of alien, exciting odours. Ground coffee was the first scent to reach me; an ancient mechanical coffee-grinder stood at the top of the stairs and the mixed residues of ground beans that layered its funnel and bowl gave off a dark, musky aroma that permeated the whole room. On the rows of shelves were cigarettes of all brands, pipe tobaccos, various makes of sweets and chocolates, powdered vanilla, cones and wafers, spices, peppers. And there was much to stimulate the other senses, too: *olio de oliva, sardinas, spaghetti, vermicelli, tagliatelli*; row upon row of boxes, packets, cans, most with their names and descriptions in this exotic language; some, like the heavy oblong cans of olive oil, with colourful, other-worldly illustrations. I loved these cans, the look of them, the heft of them. The pictures on them made me think of the views on Laff's postcards, and triggered the same daft fantasies, the same unfocused yearnings.

Reno's instincts had proved right: I loved going to that storeroom. The problem was that once there, I'd drift into daydreams. When eventually I got back to the café my cardboard box would hold an order that was incomplete, or bore only a faint resemblance to what had been asked for. And Reno would shake his great head, his mild eyes clouding with reproach, and send me back, insisting that next time, please, you write it-ah doon, eh? Sometimes, sitting there among the stacked cartons, munching drowsily on a filched chocolate bar from a 'broken' packet of Fry's Chocolate Cream, whose dark chocolate coating and milky, minty core I found irresistible, drugged almost by the blend of flavours and the aromas in the air, like some cowled Arab in the souk, hunched over his hookah, I would lose all sense of time and be gone so long that Reno had to send out a search party. Yet his good nature adjusted even to this.

Johnny, he used to say to me, we needa some tings from the storeroom. We need ... eh ... mo' coffee, you remember how to grinda the coffee? We needa two can olive oil – you writin' this doon, OK? Two carton Players, two Capstan, two Woodbine. One Craven A. Two carton Fry's Turkish Delight, two Chocolate Cream – and donta break them, OK? Two Cadbury's Hazelnut. You goddit-eh? You writin' it doon, eh?

Right, Mr Cardosi, I think I've got that.

Are ye sure? Right-o. Away ye go. Oh, and Johnny ... Wee smile, playful wag of index finger. Donta forget to come back, eh?

One Saturday there was a big delivery of stock to the storeroom and Reno had asked me to work the whole day, rearranging shelves and carrying boxes up the stairs.

Donta worry, he said, smiling. We give ye somethin' to eat-eh. We no letta ye starve.

I was expecting a cheese sandwich with a tumbler of

lemonade, if I was lucky, sitting on a box in the store-room, but he told me to come up to the family kitchen above the café. It overlooked the narrow courtyard at the back and I'd often heard them up there at mealtimes, with the window open for the cooking smells and them talking away in Italian – arguing, it sounded like, since they seemed to be talking very loud and all at once.

That's how it was when I walked into the kitchen that day, but they weren't arguing at all – they were all smiling, even Rosa, who was usually so serious. She was setting plates on a table already laid with a patterned cloth and cutlery, chatting away in Italian to Eva, a quiet young woman I'd seen in the chip shop on Well Street. Eva was standing on the other side of the table grating a big lump of white cheese into a bowl. It was the first time I'd ever heard her talking. An older lady I'd sometimes seen struggling up the back stairs laden with shopping bags – I took her for Reno's auntie, though I was never sure – was standing at the cooker fussing over some big, steaming pots. She turned round when I came in and smiled, wiping her hands on her apron. She said something in Italian to Reno, sitting at the head of the table, and he patted a chair next to him.

Come in, Johnny, he said. Donta be shy. Ye can sit here.

I sat down, awkward. I hadn't expected this, sitting down with the family at a table so formally laid. The kitchen was cramped but cosy, and full of interesting smells, though none familiar to me. Whatever they're cooking, I was thinking, I hope it's not too foreign – I might use the wrong knife or something and disgrace myself altogether.

The old auntie placed in front of me a shallow bowl, steaming hot, filled with a pale oily-looking liquid with odd, coloured vegetables and beans and things floating in it. I didn't like the look of it at all.

I peered down at it, very conscious of Reno and the others watching me.

It's *minestrone*, Rosa said.

Aye, I said, confused. But *whit is it*?

They all had a good laugh at that.

Eesa soup, Reno said, smiling. Italian soup. Ye no like-eh soup?

Doesn't look like any soup *I've* ever seen, I was thinking. The thick soup my mother made at home was probably my favourite meal. It had lentils in it, and barley and split peas and sometimes potatoes, leeks and onions. But the way she made it, all these things seemed to blend into it, so you weren't really aware of the individual ingredients.

Oh, Ah like *soup*, I said, staring down at it. But *whit's in it*?

More laughter. The old auntie turned back from the cooker and asked Reno a question in Italian. He answered her in a discreet undertone, for my benefit, I guessed. She threw up her hands and began to run off a long list in rapid Italian, counting the items out on her fingers. The first word, and the only one I understood, was *macaroni*.

All I could think of was the messy, lumpy macaroni cheese we sometimes got at school dinners. My stomach lurched.

Ah'm sorry, Mr Cardosi, I said. Ah don't like macaroni. Honest. Ah cannae eat it.

There was a hush, and obvious dismay all round. Eva relayed the gist of this to the old auntie.

Reno looked at me with mild reproach.

Ye no even goanae try? he said. Go on, Johnny, just a wee taste-eh. Try.

They were all looking at me. I realized I had to try, to be seen to make the effort. Gingerly I picked up my spoon. Warily I stirred the steaming liquid, with all the alien bits and pieces floating in it. I took a spoonful that had as few solids in it as I could manage, and raised it to my lips. I blew on it lightly, then put it in my mouth.

What I tasted was like nothing I'd ever tasted before. I looked again at the foreign-looking vegetables floating in the bowl before me, and now it seemed to me that I was tasting each one of them separately, and yet somehow all at once. A small explosion of delicious sensations had gone off inside my mouth. It was so intense, for a moment I think I actually forgot where I was.

Then I realized they were all still waiting, watching me.

Well? said Reno. So whaddaye think-eh?

I looked at him. I was so overwhelmed I didn't know what to say.

Oh Mr Cardosi, I said at last. It's . . . That's the best soup Ah've ever tasted in ma life!

This came out sounding so heartfelt that they all burst out laughing.

Ye see? said Reno. Eesa no just soup, eh? Ees Italian soup. Ees *minestrone*!

As if this was some kind of signal they all picked up their spoons and dipped them into their bowls. The old auntie came over and joined us at the table, and soon they were all babbling away happily in Italian. It didn't bother me. I was too busy gulping down spoonfuls of this *minestrone*.

Ye wantae try? I heard Eva say at my shoulder.

She was standing beside me with the bowl of grated cheese.

Whit is it? I asked her.

Eesa *parmiggiano*, she said. Ye put in the *minestrone*.

I hesitated. I didn't want to do anything that might alter the sensations in my mouth.

Ye put *cheese* in *soup*? I asked, dubiously, and that set off more laughter, and another ripple of Italian around the table.

So. Ye goanae try it, Johnny? said Reno. Or no?

It sounded like a challenge. I shrugged and Eva sprinkled the creamy flakes into my soup.

Again they had all stopped to watch, as if waiting for my signal, as I stirred it in and raised my spoon to my mouth.

If anything, it tasted even better. There was a general sigh of relief when they saw my reaction.

Ye see? said Reno, grinning. Eesa no just cheese. Ees Italian cheese. Eesa *parmiggiano*!

More laughter, more clattering of spoons and plates, more cheerful slurping. Looking around me, my mouth still tingling with these foreign tastes, listening to their chatter in this alien tongue, I felt a surge of euphoria, as if I were an actor in some foreign picture. Like *Bitter Rice*, that Italian picture Laff and I had gone to see one day because Silvana Mangano was in it. And the way they all kept looking at me you'd have thought I was the star turn and they were so pleased with my performance they might burst into applause any minute.

We stayed there much longer than I'd expected and I had two more bowls of minestrone. And wee baked rolls of a kind I'd never seen before that tasted even better than my mother's homemade sodabread. And Reno gave me a taste of wine. And when I told them I'd tasted it before, used to take a wee sip sometimes after Mass when I was supposed to be emptying the dregs from the cruets in the vestry, they let on to be shocked that an altarboy would do such a thing but they were only teasing me. The old auntie had put the light on because it was gloomy outside and I looked up at one point and saw our bright reflection hazy in the window, all of us huddled there in that cosy kitchen, talking, laughing, eating this marvellous food, and I thought how well I fitted in – with my black hair and brown eyes I knew I looked as Italian as they did, because friends of the family had come into the café one day and started speaking to me in Italian, assuming I was one of them. Aye, no doubt about it, I thought, I blend into the picture all right, and I was glad, because what with the food and the company and the exuberant bonhomie around that table, at that moment I felt there was nowhere else on earth I'd rather be.

TWENTY-ONE

One day Wullie Logan knocks on our door with great news: he's heard Laff's back in Paisley, on leave. I don't believe him at first – I've heard nothing from Laff for weeks – but it seems it's true enough. He's been seen up the town; he's been seen on the Feegie bus with Eddie McConval, a pal who lives near him down Craigmuir. Where is he? I wonder. What's he playing at? How can he be in Paisley and not come to find me?

And then the very next day he turns up at the close. I'm walking back from the busstop at the roundabout and I see a small group standing by our fence. Wullie's there, and McArdle, and somebody I don't know at first then recognize as Eddie McConval, and a fourth man with his back to me who looks like a foreigner, tall and dark and wearing a brilliant red silky jerkin with a tiger emblazoned in gold on the back. And at first I think they must be giving directions to some stranger who's got lost in Feegie, of all places, then Wullie sees me coming and points and as the man turns to look I realize with a jolt that it's Laff. He's taller and thinner and he's smiling, his teeth dead white against the tan, and he's looking like a million dollars in that brilliant jerkin.

Hey! he says. Great tae see ye!

He sticks out a hand and I shake it, and this time I'm the one feeling self-conscious. To cover it I give him a big slap on the shoulder.

Great jaiket, I say, and my voice comes out too loud for some reason. Where'd ye get it?

Bought it aff a mate on the ship, he says. He got it in Singapore on his last voyage. Dead cheap, as well. He had tae bargain for it, though.

And he starts telling us the story: how the stallholder had wanted so many Singapore dollars, but his shipmate just kept bargaining with the guy, kept beating him down.

Know how much he got it for in the end? he says, and looks around at us. Two dollars! he says. And that's all Ah paid ma mate for it.

Two dollars! Wullie says, whistling through his teeth, though I'm sure it has no more meaning for him than it does for me.

Is that where ye got the watch as well? I ask him. There's this big, chunky gold watch and matching bracelet sparkling on his wrist, looking great against the tan.

Is that real gold? Wullie asks him.

Aye. Well, so they telt me anyway. Laff smiles and shrugs, looking at the watch. Naw. Ah got that in the West Indies. That wis another story, Ah can tell ye.

And away he goes into the story. I'm only half listening, to tell you the truth, I'm that dazzled at the sight of him, and I can't get over how he's talking about these places as if they're just up the road, like Glenburn, or Barrhead. This is Singapore he's talking about, this is the West Indies! At the same time I'm watching him, we all are, to make sure he's not getting above himself, acting the

Bigshot, bummin' his load. It would be terrible if he let all this go to his head. And I must admit there's definitely a hint of that – he gets that worked up as he's telling us the story, with his tanned face lit up and his hands waving about, he's like one of the Italians in the Cardosis' family kitchen above the shop, all of them talking and laughing and gesticulating at the same time – but the funny thing is, it doesn't matter. He's joined the Navy and he's seeing the world and he's full of it. Of course he is. Wouldn't you be?

Watching him standing there, lit up somehow by the tan and the brilliant jacket and some aura that I've never seen on him before, I begin to understand why I haven't seen him until now. It's probably been like this ever since he got back to Paisley. Everywhere he goes, with that tan, that silky jacket, he's bound to be the centre of attention, a local hero: everybody he knows, relatives, neighbours, schoolmates, workmates, they'll all be queuing up to hear about his travels. I can see that, but it doesn't make me feel any better. I feel like I'm just one of the audience, and that doesn't seem fair, considering how close we've been. I've got so much I want to talk to him about. I feel even worse after about twenty minutes when Eddie starts looking at his watch and says they've got to get going, because they promised his mother they'd be back for their dinner. And that's when I find out that Laff's leaving tomorrow, up to the Merchant Navy Pool in Glasgow first thing, then away to join another ship. I feel badly let down, to tell you the truth, though I try my hardest to cover it up, and just join in with all the kidding and joking. But I know Laff knows, because at one point he catches me staring at him and falters, and he gives me this look and a wee hopeless shrug that says: Sorry, mate, what can I do?

Nothing, that's what we can do, I'm thinking, and I feel sick to my guts as he and Eddie smile and wave and start walking away down Craigmuir. And then, before I know it, I'm walking after them, nearly running, I can't help it, and shouting: Laff! Laff! I nearly forgot. There's something Ah forgot tae tell ye!

He stops and turns round, looking bemused, and walks slowly back towards me. I lead him away to the side, onto the pavement outside Nessie's old house. Eddie lingers at the top of Craigmuir, waiting.

Whit is it? Laff says.

Now that I've got him to myself I don't know what to say. I want to tell him about my job at Cardosi's, and all the waitresses, and especially Isobel. I want to tell him about Cocky and Donnelly that day and how I stood up for both of us, even when he wasn't there, and put them in their place. I feel I've got so much to tell him, so much I want to ask him, but I can't. Not here, not now. The time's not right. The mood's not right. His pal Eddie's standing there watching us, wondering what's going on. So are Wullie and McArdle.

Och, it's nuthin', I tell him, in a low voice, and it comes out sounding melodramatic, ridiculous, like a wean whispering a secret. It's jist . . . Ah wanted tae talk tae ye on yer ain for a minute, withoot everybody listenin'!

Aye, Ah know, Laff says. Ah'm sorry, John. Ah couldnae help it. Honest.

I stand there looking at him. I can't think of anything to say.

Well, I say at last. Cannae be helped, Ah suppose. Ah just wanted tae . . . wish ye the best o' luck. Honest.

It comes out sounding really lame and daft but I don't care. I stick out my hand. He looks at it, and I can see I've got him embarrassed as well now, but he shakes it just the same.

A' the best, eh, Laff? Take it easy. Keep thae postcards comin', a'right?

Aye, he says. Sure.

And I turn away because I don't know what else to say and I'm that choked up I don't think I could say it anyway. They're all standing there watching me. I walk right past them and go straight into the house. I feel like an eejit, but I don't care.

I go through to the livingroom and stand well back from the window so nobody can see me from outside and I watch Laff and Eddie walking down through the grey desolation of Craigmuir, Laff's silky jacket shining like a dab of Technicolor in an old black and white film. I don't know what made me run after him like that. Like a wee wean. I made a fool of myself. But still, I'm glad I did it.

I watch them out of sight, till that brilliant red glow blurs and fades.

We were nodding over an analysis of the 'Waverley' novels in the English class one afternoon when after the most peremptory of knocks the classroom door flew open, crashing back on its hinges: the unmistakable calling card of McKinnon, the Boss.

Hands up any boys here who have part-time jobs, he barked, after the merest nod at our startled teacher.

A few hands went reluctantly up, mine among them. The Boss then asked each boy in turn what he did and at what time of the day. There was the usual collection of paper rounds and milk rounds, but I was the star turn.

Ah work in an ice-cream factory, sir, I said, careful not to mention the café. No suspicion of dishwashing must be allowed to enter the heads which were now turning to look at me.

Really? said the Boss. Obviously this was a new one on him. And what exactly do you do there?

I paused and looked around, savouring my moment.

Help to make the ice cream, sir, I said, a cool statement of the fairly obvious that was calculated to win the admiration of Grib, Nocky and co. without qualifying as actual cheek. No boy with any claim to sanity would willingly provoke the Boss.

He glared at me for a second, suspiciously, then, Hmmph! he grunted at last. To my enormous relief, he looked slightly at a loss. He'd read some scare story in the papers about the harmful effects of part-time jobs on the academic prowess of schoolchildren and, man of impulse that he was, he was now storming around the school to check how many of his boys were affected. He made a brief admonitory speech, spent a few minutes talking quietly to the teacher – shoot first, reason later, that was always his style – and then clutched his gown about him and swept theatrically from the room. At the break, my job attracted a lot of interest and even, when I passed on a few extracts from the waitresses' gossip, some envy.

The reality was very different. I was only an odd-job boy and not even a good one, but Reno continued to stick by me, though there were times when this must have demanded the patience of a saint.

I would sometimes help him pour the powdered vanilla and milk into the gleaming mixer where the ice cream was made, or pour the flavour concentrates for the ice lollies into vats to be diluted and then transferred to trays for storage in the huge walk-in freezer. One day, after I'd been there a few weeks, he decided I could be trusted to do the ice lollies on my own. He left me in the little anteroom outside the freezer with the two steel cylinders of flavouring concentrate, one strawberry, one orange, and simple instructions on how to proceed.

You OK to mix them on your own, Johnny?

Aye, sure, I said cockily.

You donta wantae write it doon? he said. He was joking, surely: what he'd told me was so simple a wean could have done it.

Och, away, I scoffed. He smiled and left me to it.

I blame Elvis for what happened next. He was singing 'Blue Moon' on the old wireless in the factory as I settled down to work. It was a song Laff and I used to sing on our long walks back from the dancing, late at night, down King Street and along the deserted Blackstoun Road. The haunting, echoey sounds were enhanced by the acoustics of the empty factory and I turned up the volume and sang along as I slowly stirred the concentrates in their separate cylinders, thunking out the rhythm with the long wooden spoon against the steel sides.

When the song was over, I emerged as if from a trance and contemplated the two cylinders in front of me. Reno had said to mix them. But did he mean mix them together, or mix them separately? I giggled. This was an intriguing linguistic nuance we were dealing with here. But one was strawberry, the other was orange, so logically they should be kept apart . . . On the other hand, mix meant mix, and what else were they to be mixed with if not with each other? I stared at them, amused and befuddled. Maybe better go and check. Then I thought, No, that's stupid, we've already had a laugh about how easy it is, I'll look like an idiot if I go and ask him now. Mix means mix. And scorning my own confusion, giving myself no more time for hesitation, I hefted one cylinder and poured it deliberately into the other.

As soon as I saw the deep, brilliant red of the strawberry bleed into the thick orange concentrate, my instinct was to stop. But to stop was to admit the unthinkable and so I kept doggedly pouring. An opaque rust-coloured sludge now filled one cylinder. As I looked at it, and at the two unused cylinders of water which had somehow come back into focus in front of me, a profound depression settled over me. Orange and Strawberry do not mix. Strawberry into Orange will not go. And I knew, with all the dread certainty of the condemned man at his first sight of the black cap, that I had made the most monumental cock-up of my short career at Cardosi's.

I had to face Reno. This could not be covered up. Held together only by the desperate hope of a last-minute miracle – maybe he *had* wanted me to mix them, after all – I made my nervous way down the alley to the kitchen and, in a faint voice that I barely recognized, asked for Mr Cardosi.

He came out smiling.

Yes, Johnny, whit is it?

For some reason I felt that a show of bravado and some loading of the question might improve my chances.

Eh, ye know thae two flavours ye told me to mix? Orange and Strawberry, right? Ye did mean for me to mix them together, right?

He looked at me for a second, uncomprehending. Then a light of something like panic appeared in his eyes. He stared at me, almost pleading.

Whit? Ye don't . . . Ye didnae mix them up, did ye?

I wanted to say no. At that moment I would have liked to say no more than anything in the world. But all I could say, hopelessly, was aye. And for a moment Reno looked as frightening as his brother in his worst rages.

Imbecile, he said in Italian. Ya bliddy stupid wee foo—!

Ah'm sorry, Mr Cardosi! I cried, shrinking back.

He stopped himself and stared at me like a man betrayed, as he had every right to. Then he looked away, shaking his head, breathing heavily through his nose.

Ye betta show me whit ye've done.

We walked in silence back to the scene of the crime.

He stood for a long while looking at the sludge in the cylinder, shaking his head, making a soft, hopeless whistling sound through his teeth. Then he turned to me.

How ye no aska me, Johnny? Eh? Ye coulda asked me.

All my false bravado was gone.

I didnae like tae ... I felt that stupid. I'm sorry, Mr Cardosi.

How can that be stupid, eh? When ye're no' sure, ye ask. It's when ye don' ask that ye're stupid. And see, ye see whit happens?

There was nothing to be said to that. We stood there side by side, sorcerer and apprentice, united in gloom.

We havtae make upa the mixture, he said at last. We cannae just throw it away. Ees over thirty poundsa stuff here.

The full weight of what I had done now descended on me. Thirty pounds was a fortune. I was close to tears and Reno sensed it.

Ah well, he said briskly, no use cryin' aboot – how you say?

Spilt milk, I said, miserably.

Ecco! he said. Spilta milk. Gimme a hand to separate this stuff, eh?

He stirred the brown sludge with the wooden spoon

and I helped him pour half of the mixture into the empty cylinder. Then we added water to the two cylinders, which was what I should have done in the first place. The diluted mixture came out a kind of dull amber, which didn't look too bad, considering. But by now I was in full penitential mode.

Disnae look very good, does it? I said.

Eh well, Reno sighed. Havetae do . . .

But – whit flavour will it be?

Who knows? We see whit comes oota the freezer, eh?

Ah mean . . . whit'll ye call it?

Heh . . . ? he said with a shrug, spreading his hands. Then suddenly he was smiling. I know! he cried. We call it-eh Johnny Special!

I tried to see the joke but my mood was suicidal.

Ah'm awfu' sorry, Mr Cardosi, I said.

Eh well. Cannae be helped, eh? And he gave me his rueful, wise smile, shaking his head. Eh, Johnny, he said. Johnny Special. Whatta we gonnae do wi' ye?

When the batch was finished, he really did call it Johnny Special and to my enormous relief it sold, well, like ice lollies. It was quite funny, in fact: some wean at the front counter would ask for Strawberry or Orange flavour and Reno or Rosa would look down into the freezer compartment and shake their heads sadly.

Sorry, son, nane-eh left. Only Johnny Special.

And most of the time the wean would take the Johnny Special. We even got repeat business, with weans coming back in and asking for Johnny Special by name. They enjoyed it, you could see that: it made them feel in the know, somehow, insiders, ordering this flavour you couldn't get anywhere else. After a few days of this my cockiness had so far recovered that I dared to suggest we might make a repeat batch. Good sport that he was, Reno smiled at the notion, but waved a slow finger at me in warning. The flint in his gaze that I had seen once before was there again and I realized that even the gentle people have their limits and you cross them at your peril.

And then came a day of Indian summer, a day forever branded in my memory, when Mrs McArdle came grieving to our door. When my daydreams began their downward spiral into nightmare. And a pattern was set that would be repeated for months to come.

September 1958

I turn back to the window and now the words Mrs McArdle said when my mother opened the door are echoing in my ears.

Oh, Missis Boyle, is that no terrible? Terrible news. Terrible. Poor James Lafferty drowned! Drowned dead in the Manchester Ship Canal!

Outside the window I see nothing but a pale haze with dim shadows shifting in it, like shapes that loom up at you suddenly out of thick fog. And I see his big, awkward body struggling underwater, not swimming anymore, not doing that long, reaching crawl he was so proud of, the only physical exercise he was ever any good at. I see the blurred shape sinking in filthy water, canal water, thrashing as it sinks, that obstinate way he had, never give up, never give up, except this time I know it's no good, won't be enough. And keeps sinking, in slow motion, down and down and down, all that dogged determination of his at last no longer enough.

The weird thing is, I'm not even sad. I'm angry. It's not fair, I keep thinking over and over. It's not fair. If it had to happen it should have been in clear blue-green water: the

Caribbean, or the Indian Ocean. Surely that's the least he deserved. But a canal? The Manchester Ship Canal? What the hell was he doing there? I picture black, sluggish water, the surface slicked with oil. The black, rusting hulls of big seagoing cargo ships. Heavy chains and cables sagging down into murk and slime. A skyline at night – I see it at night – jagged, crisscrossed with cranes and girders. What kind of place was that to die? He might as well have drowned here, in the Clyde, or the dirty old Cart. He might as well never have left Paisley. And that's the thought that gets me angry: angry at his pigheaded old man, angry at bloody Babcock's. Angry at God for letting my best pal die in a mucky place like that.

TWENTY-TWO

Trying to make sense of it afterwards, piece the story together from the scraps of information we'd heard, I could imagine it all too easily. Laff going out drinking with two older shipmates on their last night onshore. Like me, he didn't have much experience of drinking. Like me, he'd have done anything rather than admit that. I remembered a Saturday afternoon when we were up the town and we'd bumped into Big Eamon. We were standing chatting at the Cross and he said: Fancy a drink? I exchanged a panicky glance with Laff: we were under age, and we'd only been to pubs once or twice, at night, before the dancing. Going for a drink in the middle of the day was something that would never have occurred to us. But we just nodded as if it was the most natural thing in the world and followed Big Eamon into a pub, the Long Bar I think it was. Then he turned to us and said: What're yiz having, lads? and again we panicked, not remembering what to order, and desperate not to show it. For a few seconds it was stalemate. Then I caught sight of a sign up behind the bar, 'My Goodness, My Guinness', and casually, to mask my relief, I said, Ah think Ah'll have a

Guinness, and Laff said, Aye, good idea, so will Ah. And Big Eamon looked at us with great respect, it seemed, and said: Oho, ye're Guinness men, are ye? and ordered three bottles. Then of course we had to kid on we were enjoying it, though it tasted that strong and bitter it's a wonder to me we got it down without gagging, and after a couple of sips I was wishing to hell I'd remembered what we'd had before because whatever it was it tasted a lot better than this.

So I can just see Laff on that last night onshore, in some rough dockside pub in Manchester, trying to keep up with these older shipmates, pint for pint, determined not to let the side down. And when they were on the quayside and they'd missed the boat out to their ship and somebody suggested swimming out (or so the story went), although all his natural caution would have told him, drunk or no, that it was a stupid idea, and dangerous, he wouldn't have wanted to admit that and risk looking like a sissy. For all his gentle nature, he was a West of Scotland boy: if anybody backed down, it wasn't going to be him.

I'm in the livingroom one night and my mother sticks her head round the door, saying there's a reporter at the door to see me.

I think it's about James Lafferty, she says. He wants to talk to you anyway.

A reporter! My dream job! Even though she tells me it's only the *Paisley Daily Express*, I'm excited. But whatever I'm expecting, the wee baldy man in the greasy raincoat that my mother shows into the room is not it. He's carrying a bunnet. I thought at least he'd be wearing a soft hat.

My mother tries to take his coat but he keeps it on and says no, thanks, to her offer of tea.

Well, I'll leave you to it, then, she says.

He sits on the couch and looks into the empty grate.

A sad time, eh, son? he says, fitting his bunnet on his knee, his old raincoat sagging open on either side of his trouserlegs. He fishes a notebook and biro out of his raincoat pocket. Terrible news aboot – eh, James, he says, glancing at the notebook.Were yiz good pals?

Oh aye, I say. We were best pals. We've been pals for years.

He scribbles a line of shorthand and I watch him, impressed. Great, I'm thinking, I'm going to be in the paper. But I'm a bit nervous as well. I've never been interviewed by a reporter before. I tell him what I've heard: about the two older shipmates, the decision to swim out, Laff not making it to the ship.

Naw, son, he says. There wis a bit mair tae it than that.

And he tells me a different story: that there were only two of them, Laff and his mate, and it was the mate, not Laff, that didn't make it to the ship.

For a second I think he's come to tell me it's all been a terrible mistake: maybe it was just the mate that drowned. Could Laff still be alive?

Ye mean tae say Laff—?

He reads my expression and interrupts quickly.

Naw, son. Unfortunately, naw. Yer pal drowned all right. The pair o' them did. The way it happened . . . was James a good swimmer?

Oh aye, he was. Definitely.

It was the most surprising aspect of Laff I'd ever seen, the time Wee Pete took our PT class to Paisley Baths to grade our swimming for an exam. I was useless, as usual, floundering in the shallow end – I'd nearly drowned once in those same baths on a school trip from St James's, and

I will never forget the green, choking horror of it. But Laff was a revelation. Awkward and shambling at every sport I'd seen him try on land, in the water he was transformed. Somewhere he'd learned to swim, not the breaststroke like most of the boys, but the crawl, and he did that stroke like nobody else I'd ever seen. To this day – I am still a poor swimmer – the image of Laff moving through the water is fresh in my memory, the goal I aspire to if ever I learn to swim properly: that flat, leisurely glide, not fast but rhythmic, smooth, seemingly effortless; one arm lifting lazily out of the water by his side then arcing forward to dip his outstretched fingertips, with barely a ripple, under the surface an arm's length ahead. Then that powerful, rhythmic kick and the body's deceptive surge forward, barely disturbing the water, and the whole languid cycle would start again. Freestyle, they call it these days, and the word gives a much better flavour of Laff's flowing stroke. The contrast with the effortful threshing and churning of the swimmers around him was something to see. Even the best of them looked like what they were: adolescent boys straining to propel themselves along as fast as they could in a noisy swimming pool. Laff seemed a creature apart, some pale amphibian gliding through the green water as if in its natural element, the big, perfect physique at last set free, fulfilling all its promise, as if it were coming home.

Anyway, the reporter is saying. Anyway, Ah think James went back for him.

Tae try and save him, ye mean?

Aye, that wis it, probably. His mate got intae trouble, and James went back tae save him. And then, they must have struggled, or somethin', and . . . well, James never made it back.

Ye mean . . . Laff was a hero?

The wee man looks at me, as if he's weighing me up or something.

Aye, son. Ye could say that. He wis a hero. Tried tae be, anyway. Look, son, ye havenae got a picture o' him, by any chance?

Naw, Ah don't think . . . Hey, wait a minute. Ah think Ah might.

For some reason I had, in the top drawer of the chest in my room, an old black and white snap of Laff, taken when he was about thirteen. How I came by it I don't remember. Did he have one of me? Did we one day, during one of those intense, self-conscious talks in the close about always being best mates whatever happened, attempt to seal that bond by exchanging snapshots, in some naive and timid parody of blood brotherhood? I don't know, and memory won't help me. Whatever the reason, I had this photo and I mentioned it to the reporter.

Could ye let me see it, son? he says.

I go out and rummage in the chest of drawers in my room and after a while I find it. A black and white snapshot, blurred, Laff looking like a wee boy, with the shy smile, the untamed mop of hair.

I take it back to the livingroom and show it to the reporter.

Are ye gonnae print it? I ask him.

Och, no, Ah very much doubt if they'll use it, son. It's too old. It'll just be for reference, for the file, ye know?

Oh, right. But will Ah get it back?

Oh aye, son. Never fear.

Of course they did use it, and I never got it back. The article said nothing about Laff being a hero, a young man killed in an attempt to save his drowning mate. Only that he never made it back to the ship. Just the thought of that could bring tears to my eyes for months afterwards, though I could feel nothing but jealousy and resentment for the mate, whoever he was, who had drawn my pal to his death. I cut out the article and kept it for a while in the drawer where the snapshot had been, though I could never look at it without a pang of guilt – as if Laff was there with me, looking over my shoulder, reproaching me. How must he feel, being remembered in Paisley as this wee blurred blackandwhite schoolboy, and not the tanned young worldwanderer in the red silk jacket of his last incarnation?

I'm underwater, struggling, choking, sinking. I know I'm going to drown. Then it's all right, I'm calm again. I'm floating on my back, still underwater. The water is nearly black but I can see daylight glimmering through the surface high above me. Light. I'll go back up there eventually. No hurry. I drift along in the dark depths, dreaming now, rested, at ease. At ease! shouts the ATC sergeant in the drill hall, and Don't shout, Laff says, don't shout, you're disturbing the peace. I hear his voice but I don't see him. A slow shadow moves onto the surface above me. The light scatters and a heavy black weight comes plummeting, plunging towards me.

I scream, but no sound comes out.

I can barely remember the funeral Mass. I was still an altarboy at that time and for the life of me I cannot remember if I served Mass at Laff's funeral. If I did, I'd have been holding the crucifix as usual atop its long pole, standing there at the head of the coffin and facing the

279

congregation. I suppose it's possible that the strain of getting through the ceremony without breaking down in tears and letting myself down altogether was so intense that it wiped the memory from my mind. Whatever the reason, only one vivid image of the ceremony has stayed with me. At a funeral Mass the draped coffin was always placed on trestles at the front of the main aisle, just below the altar rails. That day, the outline of the coffin under the heavy purple drape seemed impossibly small, like a child's coffin, surely too small to hold Laff's big body. When I mentioned this later to McArdle and Big John McPaul we speculated in a hushed and wondering way that maybe the body had never been recovered at all, maybe some kind of prop coffin lay under the cloth that day to enable the priest and the rest of us to act out the rituals of grief. But we were Catholics, brought up in a tradition where mysteries were to be accepted, not questioned, and like all those other unexamined mysteries it gradually faded from our minds.

And the burial itself? Did we move on then as usual in a slow procession of cars, following the hearse to the open grave at Hawkhead cemetery? Not that I can remember. Did I stand beside the priest at the graveside as usual, watching as he intoned the burial prayers, and sprinkled the holy water on Laff's coffin? Surely memory would have retained an image like that? But no, that perverse trickster has no such slide to show me.

Here are the only pictures he deigns to produce.

We're at Laff's house for the traditional reception for family and friends – though even here the image is hazy, as if the watcher is dazzled by the sacrilegiously bright sunlight that floods the packed room, threatening to wash out completely Laff's ashen mother and his pale, waif-like sister. My most vivid recall is of Laff's old man being overly pally with me, Nocky and Grib, his dead boy's mates. He knows we're under age yet he keeps filling our glasses and listening with piteous devotion to our most banal reminiscences about Laff, transparently desperate to be thought of as 'a good bloke', to make up for everything that's gone wrong, everything he's done wrong. But he's trying too hard; it's too much, and it's too late. I'd never have thought I could feel sorry for Laff's old man, but that day, in spite of everything, I do.

Now Laff's mother is talking to me about the article in the paper.

Did ye see the picture they showed of him? she says. Like some wee schoolboy in his first pair of long trousers.

She laughs, but it's a bitter laugh. I look at her, feart she might know where they got it. Then I have to tell her the truth, about the reporter who came to the door and took the photo, promising me they'd never use it.

She shakes her head.

What would they want it for if they weren't going to use it?

I'm downcast at the implied rebuke and it must show, because she puts a hand on my arm.

Ah, God, she says. They'd say anythin' to get what they want out of ye. It's all right, John, don't worry about it. How were ye to know?

She falls silent then, and her daughter isn't saying anything either, so I stand there trapped and awkward for a while till some woman starts talking to them and Mr Lafferty comes by and refills my glass, again, and I see a chance to escape to a splash of sunlight by the window.

After too many glasses of McEwan's ale, looking on as if from a great distance at this improbably sunny scene, all edged with brightness and loud with the chatter of people getting on with the business of life, I became aware of something else. Not a presence, but an absence. And not just the obvious absence – the sheer unreality of being in that house and not seeing or hearing Laff. The smell – the dank, distinctive odour that had always lurked around the place – was not there. As if, I remember thinking, it had not been invited to the feast. Or as if, like the banshee, it had claimed at last what it was always waiting for, and taken it away.

Standing out there on the rim of things, I suddenly thought of Laff's girlfriend, Jean McKinnon. I looked around but could see no sign of her. When I started to ask I soon realized that nobody in the family knew anything about her. And then when I thought about it I could hardly believe I'd been daft enough to ask. Of course they didn't know. Laff never told them. How could he? Girlfriends to us at that time, no matter how innocent the connection – and despite all our clumsy efforts at seduction it was usually fairly innocent – were like guilty secrets you kept to yourself. Like dirty jokes, or the nude pictures you'd look at in *Health and Efficiency*, or tossing off in the lavvy. Not the kind of thing you'd talk to the family about.

And that's when I realize Jean McKinnon might not even know Laff's dead.

I knew she lived up at the far end of the scheme, the Red Road end, and so the next day I set off to look for her. It was another of that Indian summer's impossibly long, sultry days and I walked the slow length of Ferguslie Park Avenue, through the weans playing on the pavement, past groups of teenagers idling on corners, or leaning on wrecked palings. For once I passed through without incident, and more or less without comment. Maybe they were just too sluggish in the heat to bother, maybe the message I was carrying so weighed on my mind that I was projecting some aura of immunity. Immersed in the drama of the situation, in a perverse way even enjoying it, I was already rehearsing my role in it. I could see myself as if in flash-forward, breaking this tragic news to Laff's girlfriend, comforting her in her distress. Her grieving head bent on my shoulder. My hand gently patting her hair. There, there.

When at last I found her, recognized her bottlegreen St James's skirt, she was out in the street playing skipping ropes for a laugh with some younger lassies. As I came near they stopped and turned to watch me, whispering among themselves, speculative, appraising. And, safe there among her sly juniors, she was laughing merrily.

Hey, Jean? I called to her. Kin Ah talk tae ye a minute?

Somebody snorted, smothering a giggle. And now they were all tittering, muttering ribald encouragement.

Oh aye?

Whit's this, eh?

Gaun yersel', big yin!

Aye, sure ye can, Jean said, still laughing. Whit is it?

In my confusion I forgot whatever it was I'd planned to say.

It's . . . eh . . . well . . . Ye know James Lafferty?

This set them off again and now I had to smile myself to cover my embarrassment. What a daft question. Of *course* she knows him.

Oh *aye*, she said with playful emphasis, smiling with devilment, and in spite of myself I could not get rid of my idiotic grin.

It was all going wrong. I was getting desperate. Stop

this. Just tell her, quick.

Well, I said, he's deid!

It came out sounding so brutal, so *Scottish*, that I was shocked into laughing out loud. I couldn't help it. Shouldn't I at least have said 'dead'? Out of respect for the?

By now they were all in hysterics because they saw me laughing and what I'd said was so shocking, so impossible, what else could it be but a joke?

Oh aye? Jean said. As if to say, On ye go, then. Whit's the punchline?

She was still laughing. But I could sense something else behind her eyes now: a wariness, a hint of fear.

Naw but – it's true, I said, fighting to control myself. He's deid . . . Honest, Jean, Ah mean it. Ah don't know whit Ah'm laughin' for, Ah cannae help it, but it's true whit Ah'm tellin' ye. Ah mean . . . aboot Laff.

Laff. Laugh. Very funny. Which set us off again, all of us giggling hysterically until at long last, through her laughter, struggling to catch her breath, she managed to say out loud what her eyes had already given away.

It's a' right, she said. Ah believe ye. Ah know it must be true. It's a' right . . .

We stood there, the tears streaming down our faces, giggling desperately at each other across the gulf that yawns between teenage boys and girls, a gulf that was widening with every moment that passed. We were like small boats being borne apart on divergent currents and the only lifeline between us, our friendship with Laff, was already fraying and splitting.

I stood there for as long as I could bear it, dying with embarrassment, hoping I might summon enough composure to talk sense to her. But it was no good. It was no good. And so at last, my message delivered, my duty done, a foolish grin still numbing my face, I turned from her and swaggered away through the scheme.

A canal. Early morning. A milky fog sagging over still water. A rowing boat moves slowly over the surface, one man at the oars, another one crouched in the stern, looking over the side. The slow, deliberate strokes, first one oar, then the other, make barely a ripple in the oily surface, barely a sound but the creak of the rowlocks.

A single rower comes along in another boat, moving much faster, with long rhythmic strokes. It's Laff, in his school uniform, and as he sprints past he's laughing at them.

Come on, he calls. Ye'll never catch me at this rate!

And he's gone. The men in the first boat don't react. It's as if they haven't seen him. The man crouched in the back straightens up. He's holding a bunched, coiled rope with a grappling iron on the end of it. He leans over the side and drops the bundle into the water with a dull splash.

TWENTY-THREE

Life goes on, or so they keep telling me. I'm in Sixth Year at the Academy retaking my French Higher and trying for Higher History as well, because the Boss says French on its own is not enough to fill the day. He's right enough there; one day just drifts endlessly into another. Nothing happens, and just keeps on happening for months on end . . .

Everybody in Paisley is talking about a picture called *Room at the Top* that's on at the Regal so I go to see it. It's about this young workingclass guy, Joe Lampton, from a rough Yorkshire town. He's very ambitious and moves to the big city to an office job, where he starts going out with the boss's pretty daughter until he gets her in the family way and ends up having to marry her. The actor playing Joe is quite good, though to my mind he talks very posh himself and he looks far too sure of himself among all these snobs: you can tell he's not real working class, not like us. The best bit is when he takes up amateur dramatics and meets this beautiful Frenchwoman, Simone Signoret, and after a while she becomes his mistress, even though she's married to some bigshot and she's much older than Joe. Simone Signoret is gorgeous: blonde, foreign-looking somehow, not so much in her features as in her expression, and she speaks with a husky French accent. She smokes as well, and the cool, casual way she holds the lit cigarette drooping at an angle in the corner of her mouth, the way her beautiful eyes narrow to screen out the smoke when she looks at you, and the soft round pout her lips make when she breathes out the smokestream, as if she's blowing you a kiss; she looks so calm and mysterious and worldlywise that you just know she would understand you and soothe away all your troubles and pain if only it could be you instead of Joe Lampton, if it could be you alone with her in that upstairs room. All I know is – and I know this as sure as anything I've ever known in my life – I could never abandon her as he does. Sitting there in the dark gazing up at her, at that beautiful, luminous face in giant closeup on the screen, I know for sure that if it was me with her, just the two of us alone in that room, nothing outside would ever matter.

But I'm pretty depressed on Monday at the Academy when it turns out that every boy in our class who's seen the picture fancies Simone Signoret as well. Then I realize there's a good chance that every man in Paisley, maybe even every man in Scotland, feels the same. Still, none of this stops me fantasizing about meeting her somehow, maybe getting to know her. It reminds me of a newspaper competition I entered one time, in the *Sunday Mail*, I think it was. It was some promotion for a film starring Natalie Wood, and the first prize was a week's holiday in Paris – *The Week of your Dreams in the City of Light!* – culminating in dinner for two at a luxury restaurant with Natalie Wood herself. All you had to do was write a letter in French (*A French letter!* Cantwell scoffed when I was daft enough to tell him about it one day at the Academy) saying why you thought you were the one that should be chosen.

Determined that my entry would stand out and be different I composed a wee poem and sent it off:

> *J'aime Paris*
> *Les vacances aussi*
> *Mais plus*
> *J'aime Natalie*

I was so proud of this masterpiece I kept checking the post at our house for weeks after the competition closed, long after the date for the week of your dreams in the city of light had come and gone, so convinced was I that I must win. I could not believe that something I'd composed with such pride, this wee poem full of longing, could go out into the world and just disappear without trace. Eventually I gave up hope and decided that Natalie Wood could not be half as nice a person in real life as she was cracked up to be.

But something tells me that Simone Signoret is not like that. For a while I fantasize about working like mad on my French in Big Wullie's class, maybe even taking extra lessons, so I can write and tell her in perfect French how beautiful she is, how *magnifique* her performance in *Room at the Top*, and she is so touched and impressed at getting a letter in her own language from an unknown Scottish schoolboy that, impossibly, she replies, inviting me to visit her in Paris . . . But I suppose I always know in my heart that I have no chance, I'd never be good enough; Simone Signoret is out of my league. I also know I'll never find anyone like her in Paisley, though for weeks after the picture I scan the faces of likely-looking older women I pass in the High Street and at Paisley Cross. I'm searching for signs of tragedy, beauty, mystery, but all I get for my trouble is some funny looks. Then I remember Kathy Lavelle, a young Irish woman we know, a second cousin of my mother's she goes to visit sometimes when she's up the High Street shopping. Kathy lives by herself in an upstairs flat (a room at the top!) in Wellmeadow. I've been up there once or twice with my mother, on days when she's dragged me along with her to help carry the shopping bags.

She's a good woman, Kathleen, my mother says afterwards, when we're back out in the street. Pity she smokes, God help her. And her a lovelylooking woman, too, apart from that dirty habit she has.

My mother's dead against women smoking, especially outside in the street. She doesn't say, but I know it's because she thinks women look sinful with a cigarette hanging from their lips, especially with lipstick on. I know she's thinking of an advertisement she's seen in the *News of the World*, a woman in a skimpy swimming costume, smoking; she's always complaining about that. I don't say anything, but the idea of Kathy having dirty habits is quite exciting.

Kathy is mysterious as well, at least to me, because she keeps herself to herself and nobody in the family seems to know much about her except that she's not married and works at the mill. And that's exciting as well, because the mill girls have a bad reputation in Paisley. Wee Hairies, they call them; I don't know what they mean by it, not really, but it's got a kind of dirty, sexy sound to it. And though Kathy seems like a nice Irish woman, you never

289

know, maybe working alongside all the wee Hairies every day might have put dirty ideas in her head. She already talks like them: her accent is more Scottish than Irish. She doesn't look anything like Simone Signoret, I have to admit, but she's got a strong, tragic, gypsy-looking face and long black hair: she reminds me a bit of Silvana Mangano, the Italian filmstar Laff and I both fell for after seeing her bustin' out all over on the posters for a foreign picture called *Bitter Rice*. We went to see the picture on the strength of that poster and never understood a word of the story – it was all in Italian, with subtitles – but it didn't matter, we just sat there in the dark, watching Silvana Mangano smouldering in the ricefields.

That's another thing I notice about Kathy, in her mill overall dress that she always wears about the house – a kind of olivegreen wrap that she folds snug across her chest and belts tight round her waist. She's got a lovely bust, from what I can see in the deep V of her neckline (the way it gapes open when she leans forward . . . !). Even sitting there with my mother and listening to their homely, boring chat about families and weans, just the sight of her is enough to get me excited.

Two young guys stand arguing on a deserted wharf. Night. In the harsh sodium glare from a security light overhead, they're lurching this way and that. Their long shadows merge and separate, merge and separate. They're drunk, and they're wrestling, but it's nothing serious because they're laughing as well. The light glints on the dark water beyond them. One breaks free from the other, waving him away. He sits down on the wharf, takes off his shoes, ties the laces together, hangs them round his neck. The other guy stands apart, watching, shaking his head. Then he sits down, starts tugging his shoes off.

The guy sitting down is Laff. The other one is me.

Hurry up, I say to him. We haven't got all night.

A'right, Laff says. He's struggling with a knot in his laces. As long as Ah don't get ma blazer wet, he says. Ah don't wantae get in trouble wi' the Boss.

I'm up in Wellmeadow one day, looking at the horror comics and detective comics on display in Yankee Mags' window, especially the True Detective ones that always have a gangster with a gun and his pouting moll on the cover. There's one cover with a half-naked woman on it who looks a bit like Silvana Mangano and this makes me sad all over again because it makes me think of Laff, and how we both used to fancy her like mad. And suddenly the idea comes into my head to go up and see Kathy. She's related to my mother, after all, I keep telling myself all the way up the stairs; I must be her half-nephew or something; it's only natural I would drop in and see her. Isn't it? I have to keep telling myself that because I'm scared I'll lose my nerve at the last minute. I press her bell as soon as I get to the door, in case I change my mind: I can't possibly turn back now. Then I stand there waiting, in the humming silence after the bell buzzes, praying she won't be in, praying she will.

When she opens the door it's every bit as awkward as I feared it would be. She looks really surprised to see me, even looking over my shoulder as if she's expecting to see my mother on the stairs behind me.

Oh. John . . . Hello, she says. What is it?

Oh God, she must think there's some problem or else I wouldn't be coming up to her door on my own.

Eh . . . ? Oh, nothin'. Ah wis jist . . . passin' the door

and Ah thought . . . Ah just thought Ah'd come up and see ye.

Oh. Right, she says, still looking bewildered. Aye, well, ye better come in.

I walk in, and I'm like the condemned man walking into the room where they're going to strap him down in the electric chair. What the hell am I doing here? What am I going to say to her?

Sit yerself down, she says. Were ye up the street shoppin'?

Thank God for that, I'm thinking: something to talk about.

Aye, that's it. Ah wis up there at Cunningham's. Buyin' a record. Ye know?

Oh aye? What record?

Eh . . . 'Runaway', by Del Shannon, I say, relieved at thinking of something so fast.

Oh, she says, I like that yin as well.

Great. She's smiling now. But still looking puzzled.

Where is it? she asks, and now I realize how much trouble I'm in. I can't believe how daft I've been, talking about buying a record, and me emptyhanded.

How d'ye mean? I say, playing for time, trying to smile. But my mouth's gone dry and funny.

The record, she says. 'Runaway' . . . did ye no manage taze get it, then?

Eh? Oh . . . naw. They were sold oot. Ah jist – had tae order it for next week.

Saved. Again. But I'm still in a panic. I can't tell her I came up here specially to see her. What would she think?

She busies herself then making us a cup of tea, thank God, and while she's doing it she's asking me questions, making conversation.

How's yer mammy? And yer daddy? Family all well?

And before I know it, I'm telling her about Laff, I don't know why, it just comes out. I tell her that my best pal went away to join the Merchant Navy and now he's dead. The way I tell it, it's as if he had to go, had to run away from home, because his father was that cruel to him and everything. Kathy stops what she's doing and turns round to listen, and I can see from the look on her face she's very touched and this only makes me want to tell the story better, to make it worthy of the attention she's giving it. I'm angry with myself in a way for exaggerating, making it sound like something out of *Grimm's Fairy Tales*, the misunderstood youth running away to sea to escape his tyrannical father, but at the same time I'm proud of myself, showing Kathy that even though my best pal is dead I'm taking it like a man – and then the next thing I know I nearly burst out in tears right there in front of her. One minute I'm talking away quite the thing and the next my eyes are swimming and my breath starts failing me and I know that any second now I won't be able to speak, and the only way I can cover it is by pretending to cough and choke a bit, so I have to wipe my eyes. And it seems to work all right, though I get the feeling that Kathy knows what's happening and she doesn't think any the worse of me for it, far from it, and suddenly we're more at ease together than at any time since I walked into the room.

Ah know, Kathy says. Ah know. It'll be all right, John. Ye'll be all right. But what a terrible thing tae happen, eh?

She sighs and stoops to give me my cup and saucer, then hesitates there beside me, awkwardly, as if she's going to pat me on the shoulder or something, and for a minute I'm in a panic, wondering what I'll do if she does, if she puts her hand on me – and then she goes to the armchair by the fireplace and sits down there, and I don't know whether to be relieved or sorry.

We get back to the smalltalk about the family for a while, then we run out of things to say, and the funny thing is, it doesn't matter. She sits there in front of me with her cup in her lap and her slim fingers holding a lit fag at rest on her knee. She sits there in her tight workdress with her bare, shapely legs crossed and her front foot swaying dreamily, with the slipper hanging half-off but never quite falling, and I'm still awkward for a while, fiddling with my cup, trying hard not to stare at her.

She sits smiling at me and I smile back at her, and the only noise we make is the odd sip (hers) or slurp (mine) as we drink our tea, and the rattle of my cup and spoon in the saucer as I try to hold it as steady in my lap as she keeps hers. On a discreet clock somewhere, that I can hear but can't see, the minutes go by on tiptoe, tiptoe, tiptoe . . . Outside in Wellmeadow a bus goes rumbling past occasionally, or a car noisily changes gear, and then we both look towards the window and back at each other and smile. At these times she looks as sheepish as I feel, and it gives me confidence. By now I'm starting to wonder if she's wearing anything at all under that dress, because it sags open at the bust whenever she leans forward to tap her ash into the ashtray and I can see the upper slopes of pale, soft hills in there and a soft valley in between, and no sign at all of straps for a brassiere or even a slip. Tiptoe, tiptoe. I can see she's not wearing nylons, and the thought that she might be stark naked under that thin overall is making me tremble; I have to push my saucer down hard to cover the swelling in my lap and keep holding the cup in place by the handle in case it starts to rattle.

The heat spreading through me is not just coming from the tea. At the same time I'm desperately trying not to think about these things because we're not saying anything at all now so there are no other distractions and the images in my mind are getting so vivid and intense that I'm feart Kathy must be picking them up as well.

I definitely get the feeling by now that she knows what's really going on: that I came up just to see her, to have these few moments here with her, just the two of us. She knows, but doesn't have to do anything about it; she's the grownup (she must be, what? About twenty-seven?) and she's in her own house and she seems happy just to sit there and let me look at her, and wonder. Tiptoe, tiptoe. And I know nothing can come of it unless . . . I have a sudden vision of me putting my cup down, rushing over to her and sinking to my knees in front of her like some distracted lover out of a romantic novel, maybe laying my cheek against the soft swell in her thigh, the top one, just there, where her legs are crossed . . . and this vision is so intense, so powerful, that I'm afraid it must be creating a force field around me, surely Kathy must see it as well, and for a moment I'm past caring, I'm ready to take the risk, just see what happens . . . and then I panic at the very thought of it and my grand gesture, my all-or-nothing declaration of lust, fizzles out in a splutter and a coughing fit, a real one this time, as a gulp of tea goes down the wrong way.

Bless you, Kathy says. Mind ye don't choke yourself!

In the confusion I manage to recross my legs, and stir my spoon noisily in my cup.

I sit there watching her for God knows how much longer, as the light starts fading outside and the time tiptoes past on the unseen clock. I watch her as she sips now and again at her tea, then puts her cup neatly back in its saucer, or as she draws deep on her dwindling cigarette, causing the tip to burn bright red, then takes it from her mouth – her lips part with a tiny, moist *click* – and breathes out a thin stream of smoke, taking her time, taking all the time in the world. Tip. Toe. Her head angled back, her strong face a mask, her eyes cast down to follow the smoke streaming from her pouting mouth, as if intent on getting the line absolutely straight. And then the line scatters, the smoke drifts up in front of her, hazing her features, and for a few dreamlike seconds she *is* Simone Signoret, then Silvana Mangano, then a blurred composite of both, and her gaze suddenly levels so she's looking through the smokehaze directly at me, with that same intensity, a hint of speculation maybe, even encouragement . . . and then the smoke clears and she's Kathy again, and she's only smiling and nodding at me as if to say: It's OK, son, don't worry, I understand.

Like an auntie, or a mother.

TWENTY-FOUR

The last months in Sixth Year went by in something of a blur because we spent most of the time thinking – dreaming, in my case – about what we were going to do when we left. Some of the boys, the ones from what my mother liked to call 'good homes' – meaning the respectable families, the better-off ones who lived in the posh areas – had always assumed they'd go on to 'Uni', as they comfortably called it, meaning University. And as it turned out, that was more or less what happened. But for the rest of us it was a different story. And not because we were stupid, for the rest of us included Duffy, who had already left at the end of Fifth. He had been by far the brightest boy in our year. We knew that because Big Chic had been ranting on at us one day in 4A about the gulf as he saw it between our supposed intelligence and our behaviour and in the heat of the moment he let slip what was supposed to be confidential information, Duffy's IQ score of 153, which it seems was so spectacular it placed him in genius class.

But that's only according tae Big Chic, Grib said when we were teasing Duffy about it afterwards. So ye have tae allow for a modicum of exaggeration.

Grib, Duffy said. Ye're a master of understatement.

For me, it was never 'Uni': it was always University. Just the thought of it was as mysterious and threatening to me as Mathematics had been on my first day at the Academy – and as my Latin and French homework still was to my mother. Still, I managed to scrape enough Highers to be able to dream plausibly for a while about taking a BA in English Literature or Foreign Languages. To be fair to her, my mother never said a word to discourage me. She seemed ready to face another three years without any financial contribution from her eldest son with the same stoic acceptance that had got her this far, and her family along with her. My old man was a different story. With his own horizons confined to the rough barriers around a building site, or sometimes for days on end to the rim of a mucky trench, it was hardly surprising. He could no more have grasped the implications of University than he could imagine life on another planet.

He overheard my mother and me talking about it one day. She was saying something about having to get me a new blazer. (As usual my aspirations towards the higher learning were being yanked back to earth by my mother's concern for practical matters.)

What does he need a new blazer for? said the old man.

It's for when he goes to the University, said my mother, and there was a reverence and pride in the way she said it that touched me.

The old man looked at us and gave that upward toss of the head, his eyes fluttering up so you could only see the whites.

Is that where he's going next? he said. An' how long will that be for?

Three years, I said.

At least, I was going to add, but didn't, because I could swear I saw his shoulders slump. He just shook his head and walked away, but in that small gesture I had seen a lifetime of bafflement and hopelessness in the face of things that were beyond his power to influence. I had seen something else there too: not resentment – he was too sweet-natured for that – but a glimpse of how desperately unfair life must have seemed to him. In the harsh world he and his workmates lived in, boys left school at fifteen and got a job and made their contribution to the household. Yet here was his eldest son, already two years older than the usual school leaving age, blithely looking forward to three more years. The way he saw it – and who could blame him? – it meant three more cushy years of higher education for me, the life o' Riley, as he'd have put it, and three more years for him of backbreaking work on building sites, shovelling muck and laying concrete, come rain or come shine.

That moment was a kind of watershed. Up to that day I had vaguely imagined going to University as a possibility, a fantasy that might one day come true; very soon after it I started to put it out of my mind. There were other reasons: I still had the urge to get away from Paisley, and however glamorous the University of Glasgow – the logical next step for bright Academy boys – might sound as an intellectual destination, it was still only seven miles up the road. Not exactly what I'd had in mind when Laff and I used to share our dreams, fuelled by the fiction of John Buchan and Robert Louis Stevenson, of faraway lands, whole new worlds out there for us to explore. I had a sense that I'd be letting Laff down in some way: he'd made it to the other side of the world in pursuit of his dream, it was up to me now to do the same. I even thought seriously for a while about joining the Army, maybe trying for a posting to Cyprus or Hong Kong. I learned I had the entrance qualifications for officer training at Sandhurst and sent away for the brochures. Then they arrived, and that was another dream shattered. The physical challenges, training, assault courses and so on, looked daunting but I knew from my ATC days that with practice I could do them, might even enjoy them, and I was reasonably confident about the academic work. What scared me was the social life. From the moment I saw the photographs of clean-cut young officer cadets in their dress uniforms, sitting down to formal dinner at long tables laid out with gleaming candelabra and elaborate place settings, being waited on by uniformed lower ranks, I knew I could never be at ease in that company. Someone like Cantwell could have carried it off, even McArdle might have brayed and bluffed his way through, but not Laff, and not me. For the first time I found myself mentally repeating one of my old man's sayings, which I'd always rejected, instinctively and utterly, as defeatist: *That kinda thing's not for the likes of us.* I knew it would be a rerun of my tortured early years at the Academy, crippled all over again with complexes about my social shortcomings (not to mention my old man's Army service during the war, as a reluctant recruit in the lower ranks of the Pioneer Corps). I kept the brochures on the chest of drawers in my room for a while, gathering dust, until one day my mother, who believed even less than I did in this fantasy of me as an officer in the British Army, threw them in the bin. I tried to protest, but my heart wasn't in it.

The Civil Service was the fallback position, the easy option for the likes of me, as the Boss had made clear the day he stormed into the class to give us some impromptu careers advice. His top lip practically curled in distaste as he pronounced the words, and I noticed that he wasted little time talking to those of us who dared to admit that we were even considering it as a career option. The sense of complicity between equals that I'd felt from him on the day of the Donnelly incident was gone.

I was stung by his disdain, but by then my mind was practically made up. I knew it would make my parents happy; a cushy collarandtie job, the old man would say: inside work, regular wages, a job for life! To him it must have seemed the stuff of dreams. I felt I owed him that much; it was high time I made some contribution to the household. But I had my own reasons too. I envisaged a job in London, a jumping-off point maybe for my dreams of getting into journalism one day. If I could make a go of life in the biggest city in Britain, I thought, a place at the hub of everything, then everything else could follow. With my French, I could work in Paris. With my Spanish, Barcelona or Madrid. The world was my oyster – in my dreams. In my talks with Laff, I'd even gone so far as to consider the ultimate romantic cliché, the French Foreign Legion. I longed to do something as bold and impulsive as Laff had done, disappearing overnight to join the Merchant Navy, then sailing off round the world. Yet in the end I made a craven compromise, not even risking the move to London but applying first to the Ministry of Labour in Paisley.

Underwater. The big, blurred figure of a drowning man, threshing helplessly in slow motion, then sinking in the green depths, down and down and down. At the last minute the body turns, leisurely, like somebody turning in a deep sleep and I see the pale face. It's Laff. He's in his Academy uniform, his tie drifting, and his eyes are wide open but they're empty eyes now, just holes in his face; I can see right through them to the seawater behind. Yet he seems to be looking straight at me. His mouth moves slackly and a slow stream of bubbles comes out.

D'ye still live in Feegie? he says.

TWENTY-FIVE

To my surprise, after the nervous first weeks of initiation into the real world, I came to enjoy the experience of working at Paisley Labour Exchange, or the Buroo as its regulars called it. I grew to like the feeling of responsibility, sitting there in my cubicle interviewing applicants for jobs, with a big black telephone at my elbow like some hotline to the Powers That Be. But all that came later. We'd never had a phone at home so I had no experience at all of handling calls and the ones I took in those first weeks were incomprehensible to me. Employers with names I'd never heard of would ring up to talk about matters I hadn't a clue about. At first I didn't even have the presence of mind to field the calls by taking a number and promising to call back. Instead I'd have to ask the callers several times to repeat or spell out their names, then get into such a sweat of panic at their audibly mounting impatience that I could only drop the phone and go running in search of someone who could talk some sense to them.

The someone was an older clerk, Bill Durrant, an ex-Grammar school boy who'd been working at the

Exchange for several years. He was Paisley born and bred, but you'd never have guessed it to listen to him. He had the most surprising accent I'd ever heard, such a caricature of upperclass English that the first time I heard it I thought he must be doing a Goon voice or a Kenneth Williams impression. I swear I was about to respond in kind when I realized, just in time, that he was not joking. He was also a most unusual-looking fellow in those surroundings, at that time. Even for the Fifties, he managed to look old-fashioned. With the quiff of fair hair flopping over his forehead and his dapper moustache he looked more like a young World War II RAF officer than a clerk at the Buroo. I actually said that to him one day and though he waved it away with a dismissive laugh I sensed he rather liked the comparison.

He was another man of literary aspirations thwarted, or at least temporarily on hold – he was writing a novel, he told me one day, with that air he had of effortless superiority, 'in the Galsworthian manner'. To this announcement I could only respond with the wise, under-standing nod of the truly baffled. After that a certain literary rivalry began to develop between us in the casenotes we wrote about job applicants. Other clerks might limit their comments to the bare facts of the man's work experience: Bill and I would indulge ourselves in page-long character sketches of quite elaborate pretension.

One morning a petite blonde girl I'd noticed around the office appeared at the back of my cubicle, leaning casually against the curved panel. We'd been introduced on my first day but never had occasion to speak since. Her name, I remembered, was Janet Irving.

Mister Boyle, she said, with a slight ironic stress on the

'Mister' that I wasn't sure how to take. Mr Divertie would like to see you in his office.

Charlie Divertie was the department supervisor.

What about? I said, trying to look and sound casual.

I think you're about to find out, she said, smiling. Don't you? She had a posh accent, and flirty eyes, and there was a fresh, lemony scent from her hair as she showed me into the supervisor's office.

Charlie Divertie sat at his desk with a claim form open in front of him at the casenotes page. Even upside down, I recognized my handwriting.

Ah, he said, looking up over hornrimmed halfmoons. Walter Scott, I presume.

I heard Janet giggle as she closed the door on us.

Sit yourself down, then, Mr Divertie said.

He managed to sound sarcastic and friendly at the same time. He was an elderly man with a mane of white hair and a cheery, slightly flushed face. Although he was the supervisor everybody called him Charlie. The word in the office was that he'd been called back from retirement because of a staff shortage, and he certainly seemed more relaxed than the other supervisors in his approach to his work and in his dress sense. Today he was wearing a wine-coloured shirt with a skyblue knitted tie, loosely knotted, and a dark brown jacket with a polkadot hanky flowering in the breast pocket.

'A lively, rather garrulous man,' he read aloud from the casenotes. 'Perhaps prone to a certain ambiguity, not to say confusion, about his chosen path in life.'

He looked up at me.

Very good, John, he said. That's yer name, isn't it? Aye, no' bad at all. The sad fact is, though, nobody in the Employment Department gives a tinker's fart about any of that. What we need to know is: where did he work last? Why did he leave? Did he jump or was he pushed? And whit kinda work's he lookin' for now?

He glanced down at the notes again.

Odd, he said. Very odd. These vital statistics appear nowhere in your casenotes.

I could feel my ears burning.

Ah just thought a bit o' background information would be . . . erm . . .

He held up a hand.

There's a whole page o' background information, as ye call it, son. But none of it's any use to us. And if Mr McCann here – he tapped the claim document with his fingernails – is, quote, prone to a certain ambiguity, not to say confusion, about his chosen path, unquote, it's hardly surprising, is it? The man's registered here as a cook and so far we've sent him for jobs as a packer, a postman, and a bookkeeper's assistant!

To my surprise he started heaving with suppressed laughter.

Ah, Paddy, Paddy, he said. You're a case, all right. A case an' a half.

It took me a few seconds to twig that he was referring to the subject of the claim form. I could feel myself grinning. His laugh was infectious.

Och, Ah don't really blame ye, son. That Paddy McCann could talk the hindlegs off a donkey. He led *me* up the garden path for a while. The man's that full o' blarney he could launch a hot air balloon. He signed on here as a cook because he knows fine there's not a cat in hell's chance we'll ever get him a job like that in Paisley. Might as well sign on in the Gorbals as a shepherd!

By this time I was laughing as hard as he was.

But we're wise to him, ye see, he said, wiping his eyes with the big polkadot hanky. Why d'ye think we keep sendin' him to a' these other jobs? Aye, he might be drawin' unemployment benefit and a national assistance supplement for himself and a family of dependents back in Ireland – whose existence I seriously doubt, by the way – but by God we'll make damn sure he works for it!

That was the first of many encounters I had with Charlie Divertie. He seemed to take a liking to me, and called me into his office every so often for 'a wee chat about your progress': I was still officially a trainee. I enjoyed these sessions with Charlie, and not only because it was nearly always Janet who came to get me – she seemed to act as some kind of unofficial assistant or messenger for him – and we'd swap repartee sometimes at her desk outside his office. Charlie took me under his wing, put up with my growing cockiness and the numerous gaffes that it led to: one quick glance over those hornrims could do more to put me in my place than a telling-off from anybody else. He became my mentor, and in ways that were to extend far beyond the confines of the Labour Exchange.

What are ye doin' here, John? he said to me one day, out of the blue, after one of our review sessions in his office.

What d'ye mean, Mr Divertie?

Listen, he said. Ye know Mr McKinnon?

Ye mean, at the Academy?

The same. Well, Ah've known Neil McKinnon for years. He's not a bad man, ye know. His bark is a lot worse than his bite. Anyway, he calls me up every year and tells me what trainees we'll be getting from the Academy. He's never very flattering about them.

Aye. He doesnae think much o' the Civil Service . . .

Ye're gettin' all the dead wood, are his exact words. He says the same thing every year.

I looked closely at Charlie. He didn't appear to be joking. I tried to laugh it off anyway.

Oh aye. That's the Boss all over. He—

The thing is, Charlie said. He's right, most of the time.

I could feel my face reddening. I had no idea what to say.

But not always, he said, smiling now. You, for example, are not dead wood.

How d'ye know? I asked, still trying to keep it flip, cover up my relief.

Because I know, Charlie said, suddenly very serious. Listen, John. I've seen your IQ mark. D'you know it?

No, I said. We're not supposed to—

Aye, and we're not supposed to tell ye. But I'm going to – in complete confidence, ye understand – because it's in a good cause.

He told me what it was. It was higher than I expected, though it fell well short of Duffy's stellar score.

Now that doesnae mean ye're Einstein, or anything close. But it means ye shouldnae be wastin' yer time as a clerk in the Civil Service. A boy like you should be at University, studying to be a lawyer or something. Ye're not dead wood. Not yet, anyway. But you could easily turn into it if ye stay stuck here.

Ah always wanted to be a journalist, I told him.

Well then, he said, spreading his hands. Away and be a journalist! He smiled. Mind you, Ah pity the editor that has tae curb yer literary flights o' fancy. Oh, and by the way, ye want to watch that Janet.

What d'ye mean? I ask him. She seems nice enough. Very friendly.

Oh, she's friendly all right. But nice is not the word. She's a wee delinquent is what she is. Trouble on wheels. She's a good worker as far as that goes, and Ah like her fine. But take ma word for it, son. Ye don't want tae be getting mixed up with the likes of her.

Charlie's warning only heightened my interest in Janet. I overheard her talking one day in the staffroom about a jazz club she went to at weekends, the Sheiling. It was run by some former pupils at the Grammar, and it turned out Bill Durrant was on the committee, though he'd never mentioned it to me.

A jazz club, eh? I said, breaking into the conversation. Ah like the sound o' that.

Pretending an interest in jazz, I self-consciously dropped a few names I'd heard: Chris Barber, Monty Sunshine, Johnny Dankworth.

Oh well, she said, with that mischievous smile she had. In that case, you better come along then, hadn't you?

By then there were only a few of us left in the staffroom. I knew that smile was just for me. I could hardly wait.

The Sheiling was a revelation to me. It was little more than a hut on the braes above Glenburn, and a real trek to get to by bus, but the atmosphere inside was dark and smoky and unlike anything I'd experienced. The music was not rock 'n' roll, but it was certainly an improvement on Big Bland, by the sound of it, and as I walked in I saw Bill Durrant, who seemed to be doubling as MC, up on the stage introducing the band.

The only band in Scotland, he was saying, to master this Afro-Cuban style of jazz.

Afro-Cuban jazz. I had no idea what it meant but both the name and the music sounded promisingly exotic and when Janet came over to greet me and introduced me to some of her friends, I felt curiously at home. They all called her Jinty, I noticed, and during a dance I had with her – on a floor so crowded, mercifully, that we could only shuffle round in an embrace more intimate than I would otherwise have dared – she invited me to call her Jinty, too. Jinty Two? I quipped. Ah like the sound of that, and lame joke though it was I was rewarded with a quick bonus squeeze and a dazzling smile. Later, standing at a corner of the bar – shouting over the music, squinting through the smoke – I was trying to amuse her with an exaggerated account of my overland trek to get there on the bus, and to my astonishment she said she'd run me home.

Have ye got a car? I asked, in disbelief. I didn't know anybody who had a car. As Grib would have said, this was undreamt of in our philosophy, Horatio.

Well, she said. In a manner of speaking. It actually belongs to my dad. It's only an old Hillman Minx.

A Minx, eh? Sounds pretty good to me. Suits you, somehow.

D'you think so? she said. That mocking smile again. And the eyes. Narrowed against the smoke, gleaming with devilment.

And that's how it started with Jinty. We'd meet in the Sheiling, or I'd go with her to a party with her posh friends, ex-Grammar school like herself, or to a dance at the Uni – places I'd never otherwise have dreamed of going to – and always she'd drive me home in the Hillman Minx. Not home, exactly, because I didn't want her to see the dump I lived in on Blackstoun Road, and though I never spelled that out she seemed to understand. Anyway we had to stop somewhere we could park in peace and kiss and hug and claw at each other, and we found a place she seemed to know, up on the Red Road at the far end of Feegie, a dark, secluded place well away from street lighting, under big railway arches. For all her enthusiasm, Jinty seemed at first almost as reluctant as Rosemary had been to go all the way, as we said then. Yet there was no guilt about her, no shame. She would caress my exposed lust with no more embarrassment, it seemed, than she would handle the gearstick, but still stopped me short of what the *News of the World* in those days called full intimacy. We would lie there sometimes in the dark, in the awkward semi-recumbent position the car allowed, her underclothes dishevelled but still doing their job – like a flimsy No Entry barrier – and we'd talk. Taking a breather, she called it. She liked Catholic men, she told me. Preferred them. Found them more sensitive, gentler somehow. They're lovely, she whispered. Like you, Mr Boyle. It amused her to call me by the name she used in the office. I liked that too.

Makes me feel we're cocking a snook at all the old fogeys there, I told her. Except Charlie, of course. And Bill.

Cocking a snook, she repeated, smiling, sly, her eyes slanting down to watch herself stroking me. It became our shorthand for the sessions in the Hillman.

D'you think we'll have time to cock a snook tonight? she would say to me sometimes, brazenly, in front of her friends, and they'd just laugh. They didn't care. I liked that about Jinty and her crowd. The freedom of it. The daring.

D'you know what they used to call me at the Grammar? she asked me one night, when we were having one of our breathers. She'd seemed unusually thoughtful and serious as she drove me to the arches.

I shrugged; how would I know?

The Mersey Tunnel, she said.

Can you believe that I honestly did not know what she was talking about? Somehow I intuited enough through my shock to realize that I didn't want to know. My mind was just not ready for the implications. I knew that if I let that thought in and the flood of images that would follow it, I could not have stayed with her. How could I, with my upbringing, my conditioning, ever accept something like that? I liked her, I was a little bit in love with her, and I wanted to stay with her, at least for a while yet. I wasn't ready to leave.

Not very nice, is it? she prompted.

So what? I said, and shrugged. It was the kind of casual, non-committal response I'd learned to fake for survival purposes among Jinty's crowd.

Maybe Bill's said something already? she said, warily.

No, I said. We never talk about you.

It was true. Although they were both ex-Grammar and roughly the same age, Bill never talked to me about Jinty. He'd crooked one ambiguous eyebrow when he first learned that we were going out, but that was as close as he ever came to making any comment. I started to wonder how he was supposed to know, but shut that thought out, too. Don't ask. Don't even think about it.

You don't mind? she said.

Nothing to do wi' me, I said, in my best worldly, nonchalant manner. To change the subject, I moved in to kiss her again. She responded with a passion unusual even for her. It had palpable relief in it, and gratitude. Gratitude for what? I wondered as we lay there, wrestling inconclusively. And then something happened that stopped me wondering. In my inept attempts to couple with her in that front seat, with the gearstick everpresent as barrier, hazard, mocking rival, I had always tried to push her pants to one side. In that cramped position, the two of us side-by-side, penetration would have challenged an adept of the *Kama Sutra*, let alone a fumbling adolescent. I never dared to try to take them off, far less ask her to do it. But this time when we arrived at our usual impasse – our anticlimax as I called it, much to her amusement – always the cue for a breather and a gradual return to the real world, she placed her hand flat on my chest as if to push me away, but with no pressure behind it. She lay there gazing intently into my eyes.

Mr Boyle, she said, this is just too frustrating for words, isn't it?

Miss Irving, I said, with a nonchalance I did not feel, you are a mistress of understatement.

A giggle, a pause, and then the miracle. She pushes me gently away, brings her legs together and swings her feet down to the floor in front of her, usually a sign that she's rearranging her clothes, getting ready to go. But not this time. Instead, unbelievably, she arches back against the seat to hitch her skirt up behind her. Sits down again, sighing as she does so, and hooks her thumbs into her panties. Holds that pose for a second, her eyes and teeth gleaming as she smiles at me sidelong, brimming with mischief, like a little girl caught doing something naughty. I can just see her thighs above the darker stockingtops, palely glowing in the halflight. Pale as unlit candles in a dark church. Then another little hitch of her hips, matter-of-fact, almost jaunty, and the swish as she slides something down over her stockings. And off. And then the move that nearly finishes my sex life before it begins, a move at once so shocking and so beautiful it actually stops my breath.

The way she leans away from me, graceful, almost balletic, to incline her head on the windowledge, and in the same languid movement brings her left leg back up towards me, loosely flexed, so I see first the stockinged sheen of her knee and, below and beyond, the pale underside of her bare haunch. She pauses there for a moment, gazing at me, smiling, her foot still poised coquettishly on the seat edge, masking her. And then she raises that foot and threads her leg oh so delicately, so deliberately, between me and my seatback, her thighs frankly open now before me in a pale inverted V, and I can't look, I don't dare, it seems that all the mystery of the world lurks there in that vague shadow at its crux, and in the musk with faint seaweedy connotations that wafts up from it, and so moved am I by the completeness of this surrender, its frankness, its generosity, that I feel I'm going to faint.

Please be careful, I hear Jinty whisper from a long way away, from a nether world, from another world entire. Oh you will, won't you? Please? she says. Sounding helpless and not like her.

It brings me back to my senses. I remember to breathe.

Don't worry, I mumble, still trying to sound gallus and knowing as I manoeuvre clumsily above her, straining to keep my tone level, controlled, keep from her the knowledge of how immense, how sacramental, this moment is for me.

Don't worry, I say again. Ah always am.

And I fumble, and find.

Falling into her. The fear of falling, the thrill of it. That time in Achill as a boy when Fat Annie with the red beefy legs dared me to get up on the old pony from her father's field, that day I saw her exercising him down on the strand, and she whistled to make him run, just for a laugh she told me afterwards. I never thought he'd bolt like that, she said, didn't think the oul' fella still had it in him. And me clinging in panic to his coarse mane, hauling him back, back, making him rear up like a real horse in a cowboy picture. Like Roy Rogers and Trigger ye were, the two of ye, she said, laughing. The memory of it. Hanging on, nearly sliding off when he starts to gallop, then the thrill of realizing I'm not going to fall, not caring now if I do, my knees high on his shoulders, flexing to the rocking-horse rhythm of his pounding hooves, the undulation of his bony back, and me still clinging to his mane but with one hand now, because the other is slapping his bare flank and I'm like a jockey gone mad, wild with excitement, the fear and the joy of it. And Jerry Lee pounding the keys. Whole lotta shakin', gotta take the bull by the horn. The piano rumbling like low thunder, the hooves drumming along, the waves rolling in. And me astride my mount, a charging bull now, my fists closed tight on the horns, racing out along the water's edge, splashing through the spray in the bright shallows and on out to sea and we're skimming the surface, striding high there, not sinking, impossible but true, we ain't fakin', whole lotta shakin', we're surf-dancer and bull-rider, and then we're underwater and plunging down, down, and it's dark here and terrifying. I can't breathe, can't breathe, and a big shadowy figure is plunging and threshing alongside me in this underwater tunnel, not the bull anymore but the big boy we called Billy Bunter diving in to save me that time in Paisley Baths, and I'm greetin' like a wean and shouting, Never mind me, Ah'm OK, whit aboot Laff? It's Laff that's drownin', no' me. That shadowy shape, the one behind Rosemary in the dark at the back of the close, moving, breathing, was that Laff? Or is it me? Rosemary's white face turning back to me, turning up to me, under me, saying Stop please stop but I'm not stopping, no fear, don't care now if I fall and she doesn't care either, doesn't care at all, she's smiling up at me and she's Mademoiselle O with that pouting mouth of hers and she's whispering You're lovely, lovely, it means inspiring love, did you know that? except she's saying it in a Scottish accent, with Jinty's voice, and it sounds so soft and kind and comforting I feel a surge of tenderness that makes me want to cry. And someone is calling Land ahoy, Land ahoy, far and wee, and I think it must be Poor Pat, my mammy's long-lost brother away on the ships to England and never heard of again, poor soul, but no it's Laff, it's Laff, and he's not drowned at all but high up in the crow's nest shouting into the wind, it must be him, I hear the canvas sighing and snapping about him and the wind's warm breath in my ear and the seasounds heaving and then it's the rocking, rocking of this old Hillman Minx under us and Jinty under me a bit of a minx herself as I told her that first time and the rocking's stopped now, yes, subsided, and I'm exhausted, exultant, beached flat on my face arms outflung on the wet strand at Sraheens among the brackish seawrack smells and Fat Annie's long gone but Jinty is here, oh yes she's still here, all around me, enfolding me, and she's stroking my neck and whispering, Well now, Mr Boyle, there now, better now?

TWENTY-SIX

A few weeks later, I stood at the counter of the Labour Exchange like an actor preparing for a performance, all my senses heightened. My turn had come round again to man the cash desk for the Friday morning payout session. I was nervous, though nowhere near as bad as I'd been the first time. But I was still wincing at the memory of my ineptitude that day the Finance Officer had called me into his office.

I'd been worried, wondering what trouble I was in: Old Gault was a big, stout man with a permanently bad-tempered expression. He gestured towards a table on which were arranged stacks of banknotes and neat columns of coins, more money than I'd ever seen.

There ye are, he said. It's all yours.

I smiled to show I had a sense of humour.

Oh aye, very funny, I said.

He looked at me sharply.

Ah'm no' jokin', sonny, he said. Very far from it.

He told me I was to run the cash desk at the payout the following morning.

There's two thousand four hundred and thirty-five

pounds on that table, he said. First ye count it, then ye sign for it, and tomorrow, ye'll be paying it out.

This was the kind of sum I'd only heard of in fiction or arithmetic problems at school. I stood gawping at him. He looked at his watch.

We close at half past five, he said. So ye better get crackin'.

But . . . Ah can't do that, I said. Ah've got no experience of handlin' cash.

He looked at me dourly, riffled through a buff folder on his desk – I glimpsed my name on the cover, in stencilled block letters – and slid a document across to me. It was the Conditions of Service I'd had to sign on my first day at the office. He jabbed a huge finger at one of the clauses.

Are they your initials by any chance?

I recognized my rather flash squiggle in the margin.

I was actually shaking as I counted the first stacks of banknotes – I was acutely conscious of Old Gault's dubious eye on me – but eventually I managed a show of composure. In the meantime another traineee, Toner, had come in and started counting a similar amount on the other table, which at least divided Old Gault's attention. When at last I finished I had to sign for the total, and did so with huge relief: at least I'd got past this hurdle.

What's this? Old Gault said, staring at the paper. Is that Toner's name you've signed there?

It was true. In my panic I'd signed the other clerk's name. Old Gault looked at me suspiciously at first, as if he thought I was trying to be funny, then he seemed to realize how much worse than that it was. He gazed up at the ceiling as if for support, shaking his head in disbelief. As if that wasn't bad enough, Toner – who already had two payout sessions behind him – stood there smirking.

And since the pay clerks had to witness the Finance Officer placing the money into leather bags and locking them, I had to endure long minutes more of silent mortification before I could escape.

To my surprise and relief the payout the next day went well. Nervous during the handover of cash at the start of the session, I fumbled through the first few transactions, then gradually settled into a rhythm that suited me. The sums were not that difficult and I found I was actually enjoying the sensation of riffling the notes and making the coins ring on the shiny wood surface. By the end of the morning I was doing this with an ease bordering on panache. Afterwards, in the Finance Office, I won grudging approval from Old Gault when my balance squared first time. By contrast, Toner's was an untidy one pound three and sixpence short, which would call for some painstaking detective work, and Old Gault was well into one of his notorious moods, frowning over the figures, his mouth an inverted U between heavy, flushed jowls. Deflated and apprehensive, Toner sat watching him across the broad desk. I strode jauntily from the office, leaving the condemned man to his fate.

Smiling now at the recollection of Toner's comeuppance, I looked on with interest as the big public area in front of me began to fill up. My audience was arriving. It was cold outside, and groups of men clustered for warmth by the radiators and around the public benches. Some called out hoarse greetings as they came in, their breath fogging on the chill air, stamping their feet on the grey lino. A grey pall of cigarette smoke was already drifting over the rows of benches, turning piss-yellow in the shaft of daylight that filtered through a meshed window high on the back wall. The ragged morning chorus of smokers' coughs had started up. One man, huddled on the front bench in a drab overcoat, was providing the solo part, a rasping, hawking cough that soared above the others.

Small queues had started to form at the counter. The four box clerks were already sliding the heavy boxes of claim documents onto the wood counter, riffling through them to check for names out of place. The big room was loud with these noises, with coughing, shouted greetings, the constant shuffling of feet. The air of expectancy was making me apprehensive again. I felt exposed and vulnerable under the harsh neon lighting. I could feel sweat on my palms, and my collar rasping against my throat – shaving still gave me a rash. The persistent, gargling cough of the man on the bench was starting to grate on my nerves.

Today my fellow pay clerk was Maisie Higgins, spinster of this parish, as Jinty and I privately called her. Round rimless glasses perched halfway down her long, thin nose. Her lank hair was cut short and clung about her face as she fussed with her paysheets. Her small head and narrow shoulders sat incongruously atop a huge pendulous bosom that pulled her body forward in a permanent stoop. This stupendous feature was normally camouflaged and contained by a high-buttoned jacket of stout tweed, but today she wore a soft wool jumper of eye-catching purple that was visibly not up to the job. I was seeing all this through the eyes of a recently qualified man of the world, my flesh still tingling with the recollection of my latest session with Jinty in the Hillman. The short-comings of Maisie's jumper had already drawn ribald comments from the box clerks, causing Maisie to flush and giggle in an oddly girlish way. Well, she's not giggling now, I thought, with a spurt of malice that surprised me. She stood drooped over her empty cash tray, checking and rechecking her papers, her moist lips moving as if in prayer. Pathetic, I thought: like an old woman in church, saying her penance.

The queues lined up in front of the four boxes were starting to get unruly. At Box Three someone near the back started singing in an undertone to the tune of *Adeste Fideles*:

> *Why are we wai-tin'*
> *Wha-aye are we wai-tin'?*

The big clock over the entrance showed nearly five past ten. Sedition started to spread. Open the box! shouted a wee man in a check bunnet. This was the catchphrase from *Take Your Pick*, a TV show popular at the time, and brought a ripple of laughter from the crowd.

Naw, take the money! came the riposte, rewarded with more laughter.

The four box clerks looked at one another, smiling self-consciously. Big George Robb on Box One checked his pocket watch, then looked over his shoulder towards the frosted glass doors. For a few seconds there was a lull, broken only by another machine-gun burst of coughing from the man on the benches. Big George turned back to the counter, shrugged and gave a slight nod to his colleagues. Almost simultaneously, like chefs revealing a banquet, the four clerks removed the plastic dust covers from their boxes. The first man in the queue handed his card across the counter and the clerk pulled out the claim file, slid out the pale blue coupon, rammed his rubber stamp down on the inkpad, then vigorously stamped the card. An uneven salvo of rapid percussions went off, like guns on a firing range. The sign-on was under way.

Where are they with that money? Maisie fretted as the first claimants arrived in front of her station and stood waiting expectantly. I gave a casual shrug but glanced over my shoulder none the less. It would do nothing for my own peace of mind if a restless queue formed before the cash arrived. The wee man in the check bunnet had now taken up position opposite me and was watching me appraisingly.

Whit's the matter, son? the man said. Some bugger absconded wi' the funds, or what?

I smiled and spread my hands, as if to say: Sorry, mate, but what can I do?

The wee man was cheery enough, but I didn't relish the thought of swapping repartee with some of the dossers from the Model lodging house on Well Street; they'd be champing at the bit to get away to the bookies in good time for the day's racing. I'd already spotted some notorious hardcases in the queues. As two other men stepped into line behind Check Bunnet, I glanced sideways at Maisie, who was fussing and fidgeting more than ever.

Where were they?

Just at that moment, the frosted doors swung open and Old Gault made his entrance, followed by Wee Wullie, the ancient messenger. Each carried a heavy leather bag. Plainly enjoying the effect of their entrance, the two men marched along in stately procession behind the counter.

Christ, said Check Bunnet, in a stage whisper. It's Mutt an' Jeff!

This set up a ripple of appreciative laughter in the crowd which continued during the transfer of bundles of banknotes and bags of coins to the pay clerks. I was grateful: it distracted the attention of the men in my queue while I nervously checked the sums.

All set now, Maisie? Old Gault said cheerily when the handover was done.

Eh? Oh yes, well, I hope so, Mr Gault, Maisie said, all of a fluster.

Old Gault turned to me with a smile and a conspiratorial wink that said: She's a case, isn't she?

I felt a stirring of pride, as if I was being admitted to some privileged inner circle of old hands from which the likes of Maisie were forever excluded.

All right, Young Boyle? said Old Gault, his tone almost matey.

Oh aye, Mr Gault. No problem, I said, and when he and the messenger had gone I turned to my duties with something like joy.

I exchanged easy banter with Check Bunnet as I made up my first cash amount of the day. This set the tone for the next fifteen minutes while I worked through the queue that had formed. I soon settled into the easy rhythm I'd found on the first occasion: making the coins ring on the polished wood, then sliding the pile briskly across; licking my finger to count out the notes, snapping them between finger and thumb then skimming them across the counter. Sometimes they skimmed across so fast that the claimant had to slap his hand down to stop them flying to the floor. In case they thought I was being flash (which of course I was) I took care to follow through with a smile and a shrug that said: Sorry, mate. Ah just don't want tae keep ye waitin'. And the man would move away with that characteristic sideways jerk of the chin, the Glasgow nod, a familiar gesture of acknowledgement here tinged, I was sure of it, with admiration. So intent was I on my performance during this spell that I was oblivious to anything else: I saw only the cash tray before me, my own fluent fingers, the succession of faces across the counter. Gradually the queue diminished and now there were lulls when I could relax and look around. With a surge of glee that I was careful to hide I saw that Maisie's queue was moving very slowly. The men at the back of it were muttering in mock-complaint.

Christ. Whit'd we dae tae deserve her?

Och, leave the lassie alane, can ye no' see she's got a heavy burden tae bear?

Aye, she's double-breested a' right, that yin!

Fussing over her work, glancing up in her birdlike way, Maisie seemed oblivious to all this. I gave the men a nod and a smile, to let them know that I appreciated the humour but had to be loyal to my colleague. One of them caught my eye.

Any fear o' a transfer tae your queue, son? he said in a stage whisper, behind his hand. This got laughs and murmurs of approval and I hunched my shoulders, spread my hands and gave them the rueful grin that said: I know, fellas, I know – but what can I do? I remembered O'Hanlon's unruffled cool in the Academy yard, and thought, This is what it must feel like to be him.

The man on the bench behind the queues was still coughing intermittently, sometimes with such force that heads were turning to look at him. I could barely make him out in the blur of grey smoke and drab clothing back there: a man in late middle age, slumped in the same place he'd been at the start of the session. Probably from the Well Street Model, I thought, judging by the unkempt grey hair and that scruffy old coat. But that noise he was making – it was embarrassing. Worse, it was annoying.

What did he think he was playing at anyway, coming to a public place with a cough like that?

Sounds like somebody had a rough night last night, I quipped, my confidence now in full flow, jerking my head in the direction of the racket. Facing me was a man in his forties. He smiled back as he pushed his coupon across.

Aye, he said. Poor bloke.

I read out the amount on the coupon and started counting aloud in my slick, efficient way. But my flow was interrupted by another burst of coughing, even louder and more violent than before.

Oh, that poor man, I heard Maisie say. He sounds in a very bad way.

I looked up, shaking my head in mock-exasperation, and grinned at the man in front of me.

Och, can he no' just die and get it over with? I said, cheerfully.

As soon as the words were out, I knew I'd gone too far. Maisie looked appalled. The man across the counter actually flinched; then pursed his mouth in a silent intake of breath, shaking his head slowly from side to side. Mercifully there was a distraction now in the crowd, some commotion as Big George Robb raised the flap at the end of the counter and shoved his way through, trying to clear a space around the man. The men in the queues shuffled back, exchanging glances, unsure how to react.

A fan-shaped avenue had opened up between my queue and Maisie's, giving me a clear view. The man on the bench gave a loud, despairing whoop, then retched and gasped as if he were being choked to death. These horrible noises echoed in the sudden stillness. Everything else had stopped. Everybody was watching Big George as he stooped over the dark figure, which was now slumped sideways on the bench. We watched as he sat down beside the man, fumbled under his sleeve and held him by the wrist for a few seconds, staring down at his face. Then he put his hand inside the dark coat, high on the chest, and held it there. He held it there a long time. Then he looked up, shook his head gravely and waved his free hand, palm down, from side to side.

Ah think he's away, he said. Better phone for the ambulance.

I stood staring at the scene as if in a trance. And saw a canal wharf in a misty dawn. A body covered in a tarpaulin, lying in a puddle on the ground. A rowboat in the water. On the wharf a police car and an ambulance. Two uniformed men heaving the dripping body onto a stretcher, sliding it into the ambulance.

A sudden sense of my own mortality passed over me like the shadow of a bird, leaving me fearful and ashamed.

I was still staring as somebody helped Big George to lift the dead man's feet onto the bench. They rearranged the bulky coat over the body. Big George stayed beside it, waving back the curious. For a few moments nobody moved, nobody spoke; then slowly the spectators began to shuffle back to their queues, back to the business of the day. A low buzz of speculative chatter started up.

Oh, that poor man, I heard Maisie say. Poor soul. What a terrible way to die!

She was talking to the men in her queue. And they, all their earlier mockery forgotten, were talking to her and amongst themselves, with relief almost, like friends who'd come through a crisis together. I felt totally isolated. I was convinced that people all around me were avoiding my eyes, but I was afraid to find out: I couldn't bring myself to face the man across the counter. Desperate to recover my composure, I pretended I'd lost count and kept my eyes down, repeating my calculations mechanically, over and over.

Eventually I had to look up.

The man stood there watching me. In his eyes I saw reproach softened by pity.

Don't worry aboot it, son, he said. Ye werenae tae know.

When he'd gone, a deep depression settled over my spirit. I felt I'd been exposed as a buffoon, so obsessed with showing off that I'd been blind to the suffering of another human being. It was as if by my stupid remark I'd condemned the man to death. How could I have done that, so soon after the loss of my best mate? I felt I had betrayed Laff's memory. What had become of the promise we'd tacitly made to each other? To get away from here? He'd acted on it, and it had cost him his life. And what had I done? I'd settled for less – for what I had. For this menial job that seconds before I'd actually been proud of. For Jinty and the joys of the Hillman Minx. Jesus. Old Charlie Divertie was right. It had to end. I had to go.

From some corner of my troubled mind a favourite refrain of Mother Agnes, a brisk wee nun at my primary school, came back to me. *Offer it up, children!* That was always her recipe for dealing with troubles – a knee gashed at football or a loathed dish, like rice or sago, served at school dinners. *Offer it up!* I now found myself clutching for solace at a notion I'd been scoffing at for years.

The men who shuffled up to the counter for the rest of the session probably noticed nothing unusual in the demeanour of the clerk who made up their payments, but in my heart I was a penitent, bowed over my work, counting out the sums in a rhythmic undertone, the low chant of a sinner seeking absolution.

A tall woman in a dark overcoat stands with her back to a big frosted-glass window, her silhouette blurred in the glare, her face in shadow. A wee man in a white overall is standing by a bank of large steel cabinets lining one wall. They go up and up, to infinity, reflecting the windowlight, dazzling. The man grips a handle placed about knee high and slides out a long steel drawer. It makes a smooth, heavy sound and as it rolls out a wave of water overflows at the sides and splashes onto the floor, making a dark, spreading puddle. The drawer contains a man's body: it's Laff, and he's not wet at all, just lying there quite the thing in his Academy uniform, his school tie hanging askew. The man motions to the woman and she steps forward. It's Mrs Lafferty, I can tell from the dark rings under her eyes. She stoops to look down at Laff. Shakes her head, straightens his tie and tucks it under the button on his blazer.

My, my, she says. We'll have to get you a new blazer.

What for? says Laff.

For when ye go down to London, she says.

The man steps forward and takes her elbow.

Time for your X-ray now, Mrs McKendrick.

It's true, it's not Laff's mother anymore. It's Mrs McKendrick. She stands there in blazing light, stripped to the waist, her beautiful breasts bared.

I'm sorry, she says to me, and vanishes into the brightness at the window.

The man slowly slides the drawer back into the cabinet. Laff gives a cheery wee wave as he disappears. The loud clunk! of the drawer closing resonates and echoes . . . The room whites out in the glare.

TWENTY-SEVEN

The very next day I spoke to Charlie Divertie about my transfer to London and he said he'd speak to the Office Manager and set things in motion. He looked pleased for me, and I was so proud of myself for finally acting on my instincts that I mentioned it to several people in the office, including my colleague in the Employment Department, Bill Durrant.

Bill's reaction took me completely by surprise.

London, eh? he said. What a splendid idea. Why not? Why not indeed?

He stared at me for a while, but it was as if he wasn't seeing me. He looked distracted. Then he said: Look. Tell you what. How about if I came with you?

I looked at him warily.

I'm not kidding, you know, he said.

He wasn't. He told me that he himself had put in for a transfer to London when he'd first started, about five years earlier, and then withdrawn it after a few months. He'd never mentioned this before.

Nothing much seemed to be happening, you see, he said. And I got cold feet, if I'm honest about it. I suppose things were getting too comfortable up here, too cosy, and I just thought, Well, this'll do.

He looked around, at the neon strip lights, the beige walls, the battered old steel desks and filing cabinets, the grey lino. He shook his head.

But it won't, will it? It won't do at all . . .

He crooked one eyebrow that quizzical way he had, and I had to laugh. So, what d'you think? he said.

I couldn't admit it to him, but I was actually very relieved. I hadn't thought, hadn't dared to think, beyond the joyous vision of me leaving on the train to London, to my new life, the stepping stone to my glorious future. Beyond that lay all the uncertainty of what I'd do when I got there. I wouldn't know anybody in London; even the people in the office would be strangers to me. And where would I live? This way, at least there would be two of us: we could share a flat. It would be a start.

And so it proved. Old Charlie Divertie told me that the Ministry would be more likely to grant a transfer to a young lad from the provinces – it took me a few seconds to twig that he meant me – if they were reassured that he had suitable living accommodation in London. There was no guarantee that Bill Durrant and I would be sent to the same Exchange, but there was no shortage of vacancies in central London so the transfers should go through without difficulty. The chances were that Bill's request would be actioned first because he'd applied before, and he was older. That way he could do the groundwork, find us a place to live, and ideally I'd move down not too long afterwards.

The news came as no real surprise to Jinty, who must long ago have drawn her own conclusions from our conversations in the Hillman Minx. She'd be devastated to see me go, she told me, but she'd been expecting something of the sort. She was fatalistic and wistful, but there had always been an element of playacting in our dealings with each other, a sense of sending ourselves up which helped to keep the implications of our impending split at a safe distance. Without ever really discussing it we decided to carry on as before until my big day came. And when it did, she promised, she would drive me to Glasgow Central and make sure I got a proper send-off.

At home, my old man's reaction was predictable enough. For the first few days after he'd heard the news, he moped about the house, in a huff, not speaking to me. He wouldn't even meet my eyes.

I was sitting at the kitchen table one day with the *Daily Record* crossword and a cup of tea when he came in. He looked away as usual, and opened the door of the press. Then he started rooting in there for something, muttering away irritably to himself the way he did sometimes. Annoyed at the distraction, I tried to concentrate on my crossword. After a while I became aware that the rummaging noises and the mutterings had stopped. I looked up. He was just standing there, one hand on the press door, watching me with a woeful expression. He dropped his gaze immediately, inclining his head as if he'd been caught doing something shameful.

What is it? I asked.

Ah, nothin', he said. Nothin' at all. Sure, what's the use?

Whit d'ye mean?

He looked at me.

What d'ye mean, what do I mean? he said. Isn't it as plain as day?

What?

Well, ye'll be away down to London in a few days' time, will ye not?

Aye. So what?

Ah'll tell ye somethin' now that might do ye a bit o' good, he said, suddenly angry. Smart an' all as ye are. Ah hate that sayin': 'So what?' Ah hate it when people say things like that. Sure it's oney them that couldn't give a damn about anythin' at all would come out wi' the like o' that.

Oh, I said, sarcastically. Sorry. Whit am Ah supposed to say?

He shook his head in exasperation.

What d'ye have to go all the way down to London for? he said. Haven't ye a grand job here in Paisley? An' a job for life, into the bargain. What's the matter wi' ye at all?

Well, you came over to Scotland from Donegal when you were young, did ye no'?

He looked hard at me, shaking his head.

Ah, God Almighty, he said. Ye have no idea. Ye have no idea at all. Sure there was nothin' left for us over there. We had to leave.

I knew in my heart that he was right: there was no possible comparison. But I wasn't going to admit that. A tone of pleading had crept into his voice, and I could see his eyes misting. These were the danger signs. Any minute now, I knew, he could start crying. His eldest son was leaving, and there was nothing he could do about it. It was just one more thing he was powerless to change, a feeling he must have been used to after a lifetime navvying on building sites at the whim of gangermen who were no better than himself, but had a harder edge. He took things to heart, and he couldn't help showing it. That was his way. This weakness of his, as I saw it, had always embarrassed me and, though I had to struggle now to suppress a surge of pity for him, it was embarrassing me again.

Aye, well, I said, pointedly folding my paper to let him know the conversation was over. It's the same for me: Ah've got tae go away. That's just . . . the way it is.

I got up and moved to the door.

Och, listen, I added awkwardly, straining to sound cheery. Ah'll be back up for visits 'n' that. Ye'll no' be gettin' rid o' me that easy!

He raised his downcast eyes in a long, moist look of reproach that saw right through this evasion. Then he stepped back, jerking his head up and back in that hopeless gesture of his, as if to say: What's the use?

I brushed past him and walked away down the lobby to the sanctuary of my room. I felt bad for him, but what else was I supposed to do?

My mother was very different. When she was sure I was serious about leaving she said nothing one way or the other but went out and bought me a secondhand suitcase, a good one, brown, a bit scuffed but roomy and with brass locks slightly rusted that jammed a bit but worked all right. I never knew how she felt; she said nothing, gave nothing away. The day she helped me pack she talked only of practical matters – how many shirts I'd need, how in the name of God would I ever manage to keep them clean or get them ironed, was I sure about the address I was going to, would somebody be meeting me at Euston?

Are ye OK aboot this? I asked her tentatively at one point. Ye know, aboot me goin' tae London an' that?

Oh well, she said. When ye've got to go, I suppose, ye've got to go.

Sounding almost cheery, making light of it. She carried on folding socks, one inside the other, matter of fact, saying nothing. Then she sighed.

Sure isn't that the way o' the world, *ahashki*?

She stopped then for a few seconds, looking down into the suitcase, her gaze unfocused, as if she was thinking of something else altogether. Then shook her head and started shoving the folded socks down into the spaces at the sides.

I remembered a day in Galloway Street, years ago, the day the telegram came to say her father had died in Ireland. She hadn't even shed a tear, just sat quietly for a while then put the telegram in her apron pocket and got on with her washing at the sink. I could see something of that same fatalism in her now, a sense that this was how it had to be, how it had always been. Hadn't she herself grown up on an island off the west coast of Ireland, a place that had been seeing off its native sons for generations? Hadn't she told me as a boy the old tales of the Achill fishermen, the riders to the sea, setting out in their frail curraghs into the mountainous Atlantic, like so many human sacrifices to the implacable ocean gods? And hadn't later generations of Ireland's young embarked on much bigger ships, as emigrants to the promised land on the far side of that ocean: the girls to domestic service in grand houses in America, with dreams maybe of advantageous marriage to a decent man – a Catholic with God's help, but a good, Godfearing man anyway, even a Jewman – and a comfortable home of their own in a Boston suburb; the boys to jobs in public houses and the dream of someday running one, or to join the teeming construction gangs that were raising the skyscrapers of the New World along its Eastern shore? All of them convinced they'd be making fortunes to send back to the oul' ones and the young ones at home, confident they'd be going back there themselves one day. Her own father had spent years in America and he was one of the few, the very few, who ever did come home to settle in Ireland. And when her own time came she had chosen the other route, like her sisters before her and their brother Pat before them (Poor Pat as they called him, their only brother, who was carried off in the flood of young Irishmen to the building sites of England and never heard from again), crossing the Irish mainland by slow train, west to east, discovering their homeland for the first time the day they left it forever, then sailing on the packed ferryboats to Scotland to work on the potato harvests. And there she'd met my father, who'd made a similar journey from his own father's tiny croft in the wilds of Donegal. Why should she now question or mourn the departure of her eldest son to London, the new Promised Land for young Scots whose dreams had outgrown their reality?

The trip to Glasgow Central on the Saturday I left home was surreal, as if Fate had determined that day to bring together compartments of my life that until then I'd kept carefully apart. Wullie Logan from the close was coming to see me off. I had the feeling he was more excited than I was about my departure – he was genuinely sorry to see me go, I never doubted that, but I could also see that he was relishing the drama of the occasion, and his small part in it. And Jinty had insisted on coming to Blackstoun Road to pick me up. I had wanted to take my case on the bus to Paisley Cross with Wullie, and have her meet us there, but she wouldn't hear of it.

What? Drag a big heavy suitcase all the way in on the bus?

A few months earlier, I'd have enjoyed reminding her that that's what most people had to do, because they had no choice, but if she hadn't actually removed the chip from my shoulder, her teasing had long ago cured me of that kind of remark. So I resisted the temptation, and nervously agreed to let her have her way.

When the old Hillman Minx pulled up and parked just outside our house – how well I knew the creak of that handbrake! – I had my suitcase all packed and Wullie briefed well in advance to leave at once, but my mother wouldn't hear of it.

God forgive ye, she said to me. Surely ye wouldn't expect the girl to bring you up to Glasgow in the car, and not even ask her into the house for a cup of tea? Sure ye have loads of time yet.

My old man was working that morning: he couldn't get the time off. To my shame, I was more relieved than disappointed. So there we sat, the four of us, unbelievably, in the livingroom with cups of tea in my mother's best china balanced on our knees: Wullie awkwardly jiggling his saucer and teaspoon – I don't think the McNairs went in much for saucers (though in fairness I didn't know: it occurred to me that in all those years I'd never set foot in their house; nor had Wullie, until today, in mine) – and Jinty looking perfectly at home, almost demure in a sensible suit and much lower heels than usual, her 'meeting the parents' outfit, I guessed sarcastically, but with a tug of tenderness that surprised me. And facing her, chatting with her usual strained politeness, my mother. In her shrewd way she had surely guessed that this was rather more than just 'this lassie from the office who's offered tae run me up tae the station'. Why else would she have been so insistent on inviting her in? I sat there watching her anxiously, as if by some wily Irish second sight she might see through Jinty's respectable outfit to the wanton delinquent that I knew and lusted for, or as if the blameless old Hillman, which was directly in her line of vision outside our window, the scene of all the carnal romps that were even now replaying in my mind, might somehow retain some ghostly, some ghastly impression of them, projected there by a perverse and vengeful conscience.

TWENTY-EIGHT

At Glasgow Central we're hurrying along the platform looking for an empty compartment and when I see one with just one man in it I scramble in at the next carriage door. To my amazement I recognize Big Eamon, of all people. I'd heard word he was leaving for London, but I'd thought he was already gone. And now here we are, the two of us, leaving on the same train.

Hey, John, he says, when he sees me. Jaisus, is it you! Here, let me get your case up here for ye and let ye concentrate on that elegant-lookin' woman out there. Is she wit' you? Begod, no flies on you, eh? It's true what they say, it's the quiet ones ye have to watch . . .

I have to admit I'm secretly pleased that the Ladykiller himself is here to witness a woman like Jinty seeing me off. At the same time I'm relieved there isn't much time left, in case he starts chatting her up. He keeps me talking for a while as we struggle to get my heavy suitcase into the overhead rack, and when I slide down the window to talk to Jinty, the whistle blows almost immediately and the train starts moving.

I see Jinty and Wullie standing there on the platform,

together but oddly apart, from the same town but different worlds, and it occurs to me that I am probably the only thing they have in common – a thought that makes me suddenly proud for some reason. And now they're waving, drifting away behind me and already I'm aware of the separation between us. I can feel the windowrim pressing into my chest, cutting me off from them, and the tug and roll of heavy traction under my feet contrasting with their still figures on the platform. Alongside Wullie with his comicbook apple cheeks, Jinty seems even paler than usual, her urchin face under the pale blonde hair looking wistful and lost – though I know her, she'll be putting that on a bit, playing it up, and she'll know I know. It's something we've got used to, this conscious playacting, and I reflect that though we weren't together that long, and there was never a chance that we'd last, we still knew each other well enough to play these games, and I feel a genuine pang as I watch her face receding along the platform, sad and wee. I see Wullie making a self-conscious salute of farewell, raising a finger to his forehead and flicking it after me, dead gallus, like a US cavalry officer at the pictures. He turns to go, then realizes that Jinty hasn't moved and comes back in his awkward, polite way to join her. And though I'm very conscious of Big Eamon in the compartment behind me and I don't want to look like a softie, I think, If she's watching me out of sight, I can do the same for her. And so I do, and I'm glad that I do.

We're well clear of Glasgow now and Big Eamon's been asking me about my plans, where I'll be living, the job I'll be doing. And I've told him the whole story, about my transfer, and the flat Bill's found for us in Bayswater. I'm

339

talking it up a bit, to be honest, making it sound better than it is, but Big Eamon's such a good-natured soul I know he'll like to think of me doing well, in my collarandtie job in London. At the same time I'm still feeling the undertow of sadness about leaving; I'm still seeing Jinty, that lost look she had standing there on the platform, and Wullie awkward beside her, and I'm remembering my life in Paisley, and Nocky and Grib and Duffy, and how sad it is that we all lost touch after the Academy. They're still in the town, I know that much, but I don't even know where they're working. Except Duffy. Poor Duffy, the brightest of us all by a mile, his girlfriend pregnant at eighteen and him standing by her, honour-bound, tied down for years probably to some meaningless office job in a warehouse, the money more important to him now than building a career. Dead wood, McKinnon would say. Dead wood. But he'd be wrong. Timber felled before its time, more like it. And Laff. For some reason I start talking to Big Eamon about Laff. And before I know it I'm making up all kinds of sentimental stuff about him, how he was supposed to be coming with me to London, and the plans we had, sharing a flat down there, maybe even working together if I could swing something in the Labour Exchange at Paddington, get him in as a temporary clerk maybe, and how tragic it is the way things turned out that now I'm going down there without him.

Ah, right ... poor James, God rest him, says Big Eamon. He always called Laff James. He looks at me, puzzled. But I thought he was stayin' in the Merchant Navy? Didn't he sign up for a couple o' years at least?

I just shrug, as if to say, Who knows?

But I'm thinking, What the hell's the matter with me?

Why am I telling him all this stuff? He's bound to know it's not true and now he'll know it's just me being melodramatic. Which it is, of course, though it's also me wishing that things could have worked out that way, and sad as hell that they didn't.

Ah, sure, what do I know about it? Big Eamon says, after a while. You were his pal, you knew his mind. I suppose he'd'a got fed up o' life on the ships soon enough, all right.

I feel like a boxer who's been trapped in a corner and then let out. I sit there, grateful to him, not daring to say any more.

Jaisus, though, says Big Eamon. Wasn't he a lovely fella?

Hmm, I say, nodding. I don't trust myself to speak, to tell you the truth. I don't know why, maybe it's the force of all the things I'm remembering, my feelings about leaving, but I know that if we keep talking about Laff I'm going to start greetin'.

But Big Eamon changes the subject, thank God, and starts asking me about Jinty so we're back on safer ground. I do my best to keep my answers ambiguous, not give the game away altogether, but saying just enough for him to read between the lines. The truth of it is, I'm dead chuffed that I managed to lose my virginity before leaving for London, and who better to appreciate a milestone like that than the Ladykiller?

Ah, he grins when he gets the message. Good on ya. And a fine, elegant woman, too, by the look of her. A convent girl, was she?

Went to the Grammar, I tell him proudly.

Jaisus! he says. Posh *and* a Protestant into the bargain! Put it there, boy!

He sticks out his hand, pumps mine vigorously, then sits back, thinking about it.

Would she be a bit older than ye, by any chance?

Aye, I tell him. She's twenty-three.

Is she now? he says. No flies on you, eh? Ah, he says, nodding, Ye can't beat the older woman when ye're a learner driver. Ye'll be well set up now, I'd say.

Och, I say, modestly; meaning it. Ah don't know about that.

Ah now, says Big Eamon. Ye don't know where ye're goin', man! Ye've never been to London, have ye?

I shake my head: No.

This is the metropolis, man! Ye wouldn't believe the women is walkin' the streets down there. The talent is unbelievable, I'm tellin' ye.

The totty, I say under my breath.

Big Eamon looks at me.

The wha'?

Totty. That's what Bill calls it. Ye know, the guy I'll be sharing the flat with? He calls it totty. The women, I mean.

Totty? Ye mean like spuds . . . ?

I have to laugh: my own initial reaction had been the same.

Naw. No' totties. No' spuds. It's just a daft word Bill uses. He puts on this posh English accent, and that's his word for goodlookin' women. Totty.

Totty, eh? Well, I tell ye this, whatever ye want to call it, talent or totty, there's plenty of it where we're goin'.

He chuckles, delighted with this new word.

Totty! Isn't it comical when you think of it, he says. Me auntie Mary and uncle Seamus, and your folks and James's folks, God rest him, all yon renegade Irish, comin'

342

over to Scotland for the totties, ye know, the totty harvest. And here's us now, away down to London and begod, we're chasin' the totty as well. Doesn't that beat the band altogether?

He looks out the window at Scotland slipping away behind us, and he's beaming and nodding, well pleased with this thought. Big Eamon, philosopher.

Jaisus, he sighs, almost to himself. Isn't this grand? Away down to the Smoke, the pair of us. Eh?

Listen, he says, turning to me. Here's a good one. There's this fella from back home in Ireland is leavin' for London and an oul' wan, Missis Dunn, asks him to look up her son for her, Paddy Dunn.

He left home about a year ago, says Missis Dunn, and the divil the word we've had from him, only the wan letter after he arrived.

Whereabouts is he? asks yer man.

Oh, London, WC1, says the oul' wan. That's all the address he gave us.

Well, says yer man, I'll do me best.

So he arrives at King's Cross and he's caught short, ye know, has to go the toilet at the station. So he sees a big sign, WC, and down he goes and there's three cubicles there, one, two and three, and they're all engaged.

So he knocks on the door of the first one, WC1.

Hey in there, he shouts, are you done?

An' a voice behind the door says: I am, but there's no bliddy paper in here!

Ah now, says yer man. That's no excuse for not writin' to yer mother!

Big Eamon's laughing before he's even finished the joke. I have to laugh as well, I can't help it. It's daft, but it's pretty funny.

It reminds me of something that's been on my mind.

As a matter o' fact, I say to him, Ah've been worryin' aboot that . . .

What? he says. Moving to WC1? I think it might be a bit crowded! And away he goes into another big horse laugh.

Naw, I say. Writin' letters home. Ah mean, what're ye going to call them?

Who?

Yer ma . . . Ma mammy and daddy. Ye see what Ah mean? Ah cannae put that in a letter: Dear Mammy 'n' Daddy. It sounds . . . babyish.

Not like a young man going down South to make his way in the big world, I'm thinking.

Ah, right, says Big Eamon. I see what ye mean . . . Well, then, eh . . . what about Dear Ma and Pa? Dear Mum and Dad?

It doesnae sound right, does it? Dear Mum and Dad. Ah've never called them that in ma life.

Dear Mother and Father?

That's as bad. Sounds like some guy in public school, ye know? Greyfriars College? Billy Bunter?

Oh aye, the wee tubby fella there . . .

It widnae work. Ye might as well go the whole hog and put Dear Mater and Pater. Can ye imagine? Writin' to somebody in Feegie: Dear Mater and Pater!

Ah, Jaisus, says Big Eamon, grinning. That's a good one. If the neighbours got ahold o' that one, they'd make their lives a misery altogether.

Aye, well, they do that anyway.

Ah, sure I know, but ye don't want to be givin' the bastards ammunition.

We fall silent for a while. I'm feeling a bit guilty at the

thought of the rest of the family still stuck in that dump in Feegie. Especially my mother. God help her.

Ah did think o' somethin', mind, I say after a while.

Oh aye? an' what was that?

Ah thought maybe Ah'd just put M and D. Ye know? Short for Mammy and Daddy? Dear M and D. Solves the problem. What d'ye think?

He looks at me.

M an' D? he says. Isn't that a brand o' biscuits? And he bursts out laughing again. BeGod, that's a good one! Ye'll have the wee ones in stitches! M and D biscuits. Jaisus, they'll have a good oul' laugh at that, I'd say. Ye'll have them fightin' to open yer letters. They'll be queuin' up waitin' in ambush for the postman.

He goes into another of his laughing jags, then shakes his head, chuckling away to himself. M an' D biscuits, he says under his breath. That's the best yet . . .

I'm really disappointed. I've been thinking a lot about the kind of letters I'll be sending home – character sketches of people I'd meet, maybe, descriptions of places – trying to keep it natural, of course, not too literary, not like my casenotes at the Labour Exchange: Margaret and Frankie and the rest would only jeer at that. And now, with this M and D business, it seems they'd have been laughing at me anyway.

Big Eamon's asleep, his head nodding forward, his *Daily Record* slipping off his lap.

I've been watching the telegraph wires beside the track, the way they keep pace with the racing train, that slow, hypnotic way they climb up the windowframe till they disappear above it, so you think they've broken free and soared to the sky, then *slam!* they're stunned by the next telegraph pole and start falling back to earth. Poleaxed, I think, the very word! I'm pleased with myself for thinking of the word, but at the same time there's something sad about the thought of it. Like Joe Duffy, and felled timber. Soar, stun, fall. Soar again, fall again, soar again, fall again ... the phrase echoes in my mind, putting words to the rolling rhythm of the train, and making me drowsy ...

I turn my eyes to the darkening fields unspooling behind us and see the ghostly reflection of our compartment sailing through the landscape, a space capsule, brightly lit, self-contained, impossibly intact. I try to focus on my reflection to see how I look, check if my hair's in place, but the image blurs and shifts, comes and goes with the changing landscape, and then it's no longer me who's out there looking in, but Laff: Laff as we last saw him that day in Feegie before he went back to sea, with the brilliant red silky jerkin and the Tony Curtis and the tan, and that lovely shy smile of his, like a young god. It's Laff sitting out there, gliding over field and fence, ghosting through isolated farmhouses and outbuildings, through thick woods, past railway junctions and stationhouses, over and under the fleeting visions of urban blight along the tracks, the factories, the dumps, the back ends of poor tenements and council houses of small towns like ours, the people in them preparing now for sleep, for tomorrow, for lifetimes of tomorrows spent in that place. Not like us, eh, Laff? And Laff glides on, soaring not falling, untouched by any of it, immune, in that final godlike image of himself, that image I know will live on in my mind, and I think I realize even then that early death has given him the gift of eternal youth: he will stay that way forever; he will stay with me forever.

And then the shock and the blackness and the roar of a

sudden tunnel jolts me back to wakefulness and I see our whole compartment bright and clear again in the window, Big Eamon sprawled on the seat opposite, deep in sleep now, already dreaming maybe of the talent and the totty and the good times awaiting him in the Metropolis, his mouth sagging open, the wreckage of his *Daily Record* scattered in his lap and on the floor.

But when I turn to find my own reflection beside me in the corner, for a last fleeting moment before my pale, apprehensive face comes fully back into focus, it's not me I see out there, it's still Laff: Laff looking in at me, Laff smiling.

GALLOWAY STREET
John Boyle

'FULL OF HUMOUR IN THE MIDST OF GRINDING
POVERTY'
Lesley McDowell, *Scotsman*

John Boyle was born and raised in Paisley, son of poor
immigrants from the West of Ireland. In this acclaimed
memoir, he tells the story of his childhood, beautifully
capturing the poverty and the rough humour of the streets
he grew up in, and the poignancy of growing up Irish in
Scotland, never quite sure where you belong.

'COMPELS COMPLETE ATTENTION BECAUSE
EVERYTHING HERE, DOWN TO THE LAST FULL STOP,
HAS BEEN CAREFULLY CONSIDERED . . . A PRECISE
AND DEEPLY MOVING EVOCATION OF THE VANISHED
IRISH IMMIGRANT WORLD THAT ONCE FLOURISHED
IN SCOTLAND. IT IS SO GOOD, INDEED, IT
ESTABLISHES A BENCHMARK OTHER MEMOIRISTS
WILL HAVE TO STRIVE VERY HARD TO REACH. AND
OF ITS MANY ACHIEVEMENTS, SURELY THE MOST
IMPORTANT OF ALL IS THAT *GALLOWAY STREET*
DESCRIBES A MISERABLE CHILDHOOD WITHOUT A
SHRED OF SELF-PITY'
Carlo Gébler, *Irish Times*

'*GALLOWAY STREET* MAY NOT BE MOMENTOUSLY
DRAMATIC, BUT IT IS GENTLY EVENTFUL,
ILLUSTRATING HOW IT'S REALLY THE LITTLE THINGS
THAT ULTIMATELY CHANGE OUR LIVES'
Mark Robertson, *The List*

'SHARPLY OBSERVED . . . POWERFUL AND, OFTEN,
FUNNY'
Albert Smith, *Irish Independent*

0 552 99914 8

BLACK SWAN

DANCING SHOES IS DEAD
A tale of fighting men in South Africa
Gavin Evans

'A GIDDY COCKTAIL OF SPORT AND SUBVERSION'
Independent

Gavin Evan's childhood dreams of becoming the heavyweight
champion of the world ended when he realised he would never
grow taller than 5 foot 2. He settled for becoming a journalist with
a ringside seat.

But growing up in South Africa under apartheid, Gavin found a
different corner to fight. Recruited into the ANC underground, his
active role in the struggle led him into a clandestine world of
detentions, assaults, 5am meetings, spy-catching and attempts on
his life.

A memoir of twin passions, boxing and politics, *Dancing Shoes
is Dead* is a vivid portrait of two strangely connected worlds, and
of the characters, brave, brutal and often bizarre, who inhabit
them both.

'POWERFUL . . . A SEARING INSIGHT INTO TWO BRUTAL
WORLDS, WEIRDLY LINKED TO EACH OTHER, RECOUNTED
BY SOMEONE WITH A UNIQUE INSIGHT INTO BOTH'
Giles Foden, *Conde Nast Traveller*

'BOASTS SOME OF THE MOST GRIPPING AND INTELLIGENT
WRITING ON THE SPORT I'VE EVER READ . . . EVANS PAINTS
A VIVID PICTURE OF A DEEPLY DISTRESSED BUT SOMEHOW
RESILIENT SPORTING SUB-CULTURE . . . HE EMPATHISES
WITH BOXERS BUT DOES NOT ROMANTICISE THEM'
Mike Marqusee, *Guardian*

PROVOCATIVE . . . IN ONE BOOK, THE READER CAN ENJOY
BOTH A WANDER THROUGH SOUTH AFRICAN BOXING AND
THROUGH THE TURBULENT YEARS OF THE 1980s . . . IT IS
WORTH THE SWITCH-BACK RIDE'
Robert Hands, *The Times*

0 552 99932 6

BLACK SWAN

BEFORE THE KNIFE
Memories of an African Childhood
Carolyn Slaughter

'WRITTEN WITH SUCH BEAUTY, COURAGE AND
TRUTHFULNESS THAT IT WILL RANK WITH OTHER
MASTERPIECES ABOUT LIFE IN AFRICA'
Amanda Craig, *The Times*

*What happened to me affected all of us – my mother, my father,
my sisters and me: we all fell apart under the horror of it, and we
all tried to pretend that there was no horror.*

Growing up in a remote British protectorate (now Botswana) in
the heart of the Kalahari Desert, Carolyn Slaughter was inspired
by the stark beauty of her childhood home. All too soon, this
magnificent and isolated landscape would become a refuge for a
six-year-old girl with nowhere to turn. Neither her mother,
doomed by depression and guilt, nor her sister could shield her
from the most terrible of violations. In the end she would learn
not only how to survive but how to save her soul.

In prose unforgettable for its lyric beauty and subtle irony, prize-
winning novelist Carolyn Slaughter tells the story of a family that
destroyed itself from within, offering us powerful lessons about
survival and about the triumph of love over hate.

'HER LANGUAGE IS POWERFUL, VISCERAL . . . SHE
FORCEFULLY CONVEYS THAT JITTERY, POWERFUL
INTOXICATING THING – THAT THING OF AFRICA, THAT
THING THAT, ONCE YOU LOVE IT, YOU DON'T ESCAPE'
Louisa Young, *Independent*

'SHOWS THE TRAGIC AND LASTING CONSEQUENCES OF A
CHILDHOOD BLIGHTED BY FEAR AND HATE . . . WRITES
WITH LYRICAL IMPRECISION ABOUT THE PRIMAL
INNOCENCE AND BEAUTY OF THE AFRICAN WAY OF LIFE'
Anne Chisolm, *Sunday Telegraph*

'PAINFUL, TRAGIC FAMILY SAGA . . . A BRAVE BOOK,
BEAUTIFULLY WRITTEN AND FULL OF VIVID IMAGERY . . .
I READ IT AT A BREATHLESS SITTING'
Tenniel Evans, *Daily Mail*

'HYPNOTIC . . . DEEPLY MOVING AND DISTURBING . . . FOR
THOSE WILLING TO BRAVE THE DARK WITHOUT A CANDLE,
ILLUMINATION LIES AHEAD'
Margarette Driscoll, *Sunday Times*

0 552 99988 1

BLACK SWAN

IN THE SHADOW OF A SAINT
A son's journey to understand his father's legacy
Ken Wiwa

'COMPELLING AND SURPRISINGLY MOVING . . . WIWA
WRITES WITH CLARITY AND LUCIDITY'
William Boyd

*'My father. That's what this is all about. Where does he end and
where do I begin?'*

Ken Saro-Wiwa was executed in November 1995. One of Nigeria's
best loved writers and an outspoken critic of military rule, he was
a prime mover in bringing the human rights abuses of Shell Oil
and the Nigerian Military to the attention of the world. His death
was headline news internationally. The Ken Saro-Wiwa name
became a potent symbol of the clash between a traditional way of
life and the juggernaut of globalization.

In the Shadow of a Saint is Ken Wiwa's frank and moving
depiction of his turbulent relationship with his father. Written
against the foreground of Ken Saro-Wiwa's political fight on
behalf of his people, it is a tale of a struggle within a struggle, an
account of how Ken Wiwa went searching for his father and
ended up finding himself.

'ALL THE INGREDIENTS OF A SHAKESPEAREAN DRAMA . . .
YOU FEEL FOR HIM. YOU FEEL FOR HIS FATHER. HIS
ELEGANTLY WRITTEN BOOK IS A WEAVE OF NIGERIAN AND
FAMILY HISTORY, BOTH TURBULENT, BOTH TRAGIC, NEITHER
WITHOUT HOPE. IT IS, MOREOVER, A STORY OF BEING
TRAPPED IN HISTORY; THE CHILDREN OF HEROES WHO FIND
THEIR LIVES SHAPED BY THEIR PARENTS . . . POIGNANT'
Sandra Jordan, *Observer*

'POWERFUL AND THOUGHT-PROVOKING . . . AN EXTREMELY
HONEST BOOK, WITH NO ATTEMPT TO CONCEAL THE WARTS'
Tariq Ali, *Financial Times*

'PAINFULLY HONEST . . . ALL THE MORE MOVING BECAUSE
IT DOES NOT SHY AWAY FROM THE DIFFICULTIES OF THE
SON'S RELATIONSHIP WITH THE FATHER'
Anthony Daniels, *Sunday Telegraph*

0 552 99891 5

BLACK SWAN

A SELECTED LIST OF FINE WRITING
AVAILABLE FROM BLACK SWAN

THE PRICES SHOWN BELOW WERE CORRECT AT THE TIME OF GOING TO PRESS. HOWEVER
TRANSWORLD PUBLISHERS RESERVE THE RIGHT TO SHOW NEW RETAIL PRICES ON COVERS WHICH
MAY DIFFER FROM THOSE PREVIOUSLY ADVERTISED IN THE TEXT OR ELSEWHERE.

99927 X	THE STATELY HOMO: A CELEBRATION OF		
	THE LIFE OF QUENTIN CRISP	ed. Paul Bailey	£7.99
99914 8	GALLOWAY STREET	John Boyle	£6.99
99600 9	NOTES FROM A SMALL ISLAND	Bill Bryson	£7.99
77161 9	HOLD THE ENLIGHTENMENT	Tim Cahill	£7.99
99926 1	DEAR TOM	Tom Courtenay	£7.99
77076 0	NICE JUMPER	Tom Cox	£6.99
99923 7	THE MYSTERY OF CAPITAL	Hernando de Soto	£8.99
99932 6	DANCING SHOES IS DEAD	Gavin Evans	£6.99
99802 8	DON'T WALK IN THE LONG GRASS	Tenniel Evans	£6.99
99858 3	PERFUME FROM PROVENCE	Lady Fortescue	£7.99
99983 0	OVER THE HILLS AND FAR AWAY	Candida Lycett Green	£7.99
99680 7	THE IMAGINARY GIRLFRIEND	John Irving	£6.99
99958 X	ALMOST LIKE A WHALE	Steve Jones	£9.99
14595 5	BETWEEN EXTREMES	Brian Keenan and John McCarthy	£7.99
77133 3	MY WAR GONE BY, I MISS IT SO	Anthony Loyd	£7.99
99841 9	NOTES FROM AN ITALIAN GARDEN	Joan Marble	£7.99
99803 6	THINGS CAN ONLY GET BETTER	John O'Farrell	£7.99
99852 4	THE ELUSIVE TRUFFLE	Mirabel Osler	£6.99
	Travels in Search of the Legendary Food of France		
99908 3	STAR DUST FALLING	Jay Rayner	£6.99
99913 X	THE JADU HOUSE:		
	Intimate Histories of Anglo-India	Laura Roychowdhury	£7.99
99988 1	BEFORE THE KNIFE: MEMORIES		
	OF AN AFRICAN CHILDHOOD	Carolyn Slaughter	£6.99
99750 1	SPEAKING FOR THEMSELVES: The Personal		
	Letters of Winston and Clementine Churchill	Mary Soames ed.	£15.00
99929 6	DOWN THE HIGHWAY:		
	THE LIFE OF BOB DYLAN	Howard Sounes	£8.99
99928 8	INSTRUCTIONS FOR VISITORS	Helen Stevenson	£6.99
99638 6	BETTER THAN SEX	Hunter S. Thompson	£6.99
99891 5	IN THE SHADOW OF A SAINT	Ken Wiwa	£7.99
99366 2	THE ELECTRIC KOOL AID ACID TEST	Tom Wolfe	£8.99
77000 0	A SCIENTIFIC ROMANCE	Ronald Wright	£6.99

All Transworld titles are available by post from:
Bookpost, PO Box 29, Douglas, Isle of Man, IM99 1BQ
Credit cards accepted. Please telephone 01624 836000,
fax 01624 837033, Internet http://www.bookpost.co.uk
or e-mail: bookshop@enterprise.net for details.
Free postage and packing in the UK. Overseas customers: allow
£2 per book (paperbacks) and £3 per book (hardbacks).